1001
INDOOR PLANTS

Copyright original edition © Losange 2005

Created by Losange with the collaboration of Paul Collen
Editorial management: Hervé Chaumeton, Jean Arbeille
CAP: Nathalie Lachaud, Francis Rossignol, Isabelle Véret
Photo-engraving: Stéphanie Henry, Chantal Mialon, Hélène Peycheraud

Copyright © 2007 for the US edition

Parragon Books Ltd
Queen Street House
4 Queen Street
Bath BA1 1HE
UK

US edition produced by Cambridge Publishing Management Ltd
Translation: Alayne Pullen
Copyediting: Juliet Mozley
Proofreading: Alison Rasch

ISBN 978-1-4054-9548-6

Printed in China

1001
INDOOR PLANTS

ODILE KOENIG
Horticultural agronomist

with the collaboration of PAUL COLLEN
Honorary professor
of the French National Institute of Horticulture

Bath · New York · Singapore · Hong Kong · Cologne · Delhi · Melbourne

Contents

How to use this book

This book has been designed to provide the maximum amount of information in the most accessible form possible. It includes an introduction containing general information and advice on caring for houseplants, an at-a-glance chart to help you choose the right plant, plant profiles arranged in alphabetical order by the botanical name of the genus (see example below), and two indices: one listing the common and scientific names of the plants and the other a thematic index to the topics dealt with in the introduction.

Arranged in alphabetical order.

Botanical name of the genus (in Latin).

Scientific name of the most common species available.

General information on the plant.

Photo of the species in question.

Photos of associated species and varieties.

Name by which the plant is commonly known.

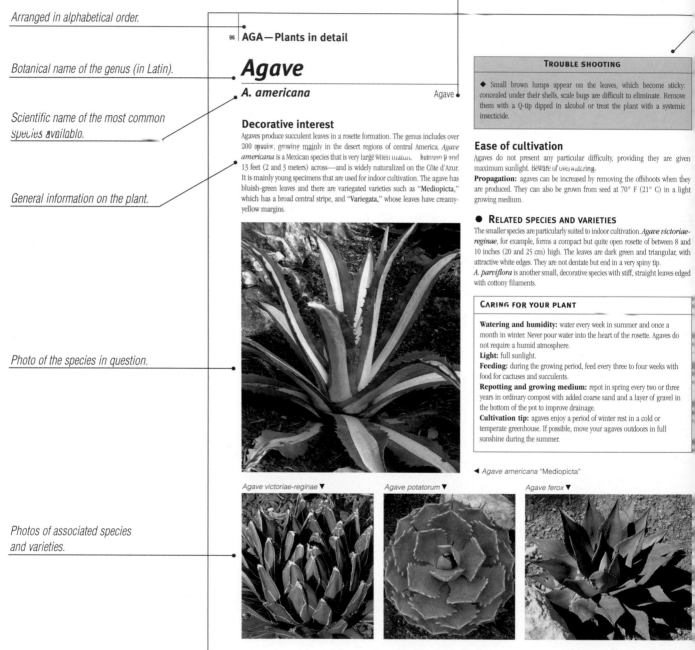

96 AGA—Plants in detail

Agave

A. americana
Agave

Decorative interest
Agaves produce succulent leaves in a rosette formation. The genus includes over 200 species, growing mainly in the desert regions of central America. *Agave americana* is a Mexican species that is very large when mature—between 9 and 13 feet (2 and 3 meters) across—and is widely naturalized on the Côte d'Azur. It is mainly young specimens that are used for indoor cultivation. The agave has bluish-green leaves and there are variegated varieties such as "**Mediopicta**," which has a broad central stripe, and "**Variegata**," whose leaves have creamy-yellow margins.

TROUBLE SHOOTING

◆ Small brown lumps appear on the leaves, which become sticky; concealed under their shells, scale bugs are difficult to eliminate. Remove them with a Q-tip dipped in alcohol or treat the plant with a systemic insecticide.

Ease of cultivation
Agaves do not present any particular difficulty, providing they are given maximum sunlight. Beware of overwatering.
Propagation: agaves can be increased by removing the offshoots when they are produced. They can also be grown from seed at 70° F (21° C) in a light growing medium.

● RELATED SPECIES AND VARIETIES
The smaller species are particularly suited to indoor cultivation. *Agave victoriae-reginae*, for example, forms a compact but quite open rosette of between 8 and 10 inches (20 and 25 cm) high. The leaves are dark green and triangular, with attractive white edges. They are not dentate but end in a very spiny tip.
A. parviflora is another small, decorative species with stiff, straight leaves edged with cottony filaments.

CARING FOR YOUR PLANT

Watering and humidity: water every week in summer and once a month in winter. Never pour water into the heart of the rosette. Agaves do not require a humid atmosphere.
Light: full sunlight.
Feeding: during the growing period, feed every three to four weeks with food for cactuses and succulents.
Repotting and growing medium: repot in spring every two or three years in ordinary compost with added coarse sand and a layer of gravel in the bottom of the pot to improve drainage.
Cultivation tip: agaves enjoy a period of winter rest in a cold or temperate greenhouse. If possible, move your agaves outdoors in full sunshine during the summer.

◄ Agave americana "Mediopicta"

Agave victoriae-reginae ▼

Agave potatorum ▼

Agave ferox ▼

Description of other species, varieties and/or cultivars.

Aglaonema

A. commutatum   Aglaonema

Decorative interest

Native to tropical Asia, aglaonemas have attractive variegated foliage. *Aglaonema commutatum* forms a clump of large, oblong, dark green leaves with silvery-gray or very pale green variegation, 12 to 16 inches (30 to 40 cm) tall. Mature plants sometimes flower, producing a rather dull inflorescence similar to that of arums.

Associates well with... other plants with decorative foliage such as philodendrons, crotons, and cordylines.

Ease of cultivation

Aglaonemas can be a little tricky to cultivate. They need good humidity and must be kept out of cold drafts. Use tepid water when watering.

Propagation: divide the clump in spring when repotting.

Worth remembering

The sap and berries of aglaonemas are toxic.

Aglaonema commutatum ▶

● RELATED SPECIES AND VARIETIES

Aglaonema commutatum "Silver Queen" has gray-green leaves with silvery-gray variegation. "Silver King" is a closely related cultivar with more marked variegation and a more upright habit.

Aglaonema crispum has thick, broader, gray-green leaves, with dark green margins. After a few years the plant forms a thick stem marked by foliar scarring.

Aglaonema "Pattaya Beauty" ▶

CARING FOR YOUR PLANT

Watering and humidity: water moderately in spring and summer, using tepid water. Water sparingly in winter and keep at a lower temperature: 59° to 61° F (15° to 16° C).

Light: enjoys filtered light; keep out of direct sunlight.

Feeding: from spring to the end of summer, feed every two weeks with food for foliage plants.

Repotting and growing medium: if necessary, repot in spring in ordinary compost enriched with a little fibrous peat.

Cultivation tip: avoid moving your plant. Remove dust from the leaves regularly by wiping with a damp sponge. Aglaonemas do not tolerate cigarette smoke.

Aglaonema "Silver Queen" ▼   *Aglaonema "Compact Maria"* ▼

TROUBLE SHOOTING

◆ Small brown lumps appear on the leaves, which become sticky: under their protective shells, scale bugs can be difficult to eradicate. Remove them using a Q-tip dipped in alcohol, or treat your plant with a systemic insecticide.

◆ The leaves become pale and covered in small, whitish dots: red spider mites thrive in hot, dry conditions. Increase the ambient humidity and spray the foliage more often. If necessary, treat the plant with an appropriate acaricide.

➤ **Ajania** see *Chrysanthemum*

INTRODUCTION

The foliage and flowering plants that adorn our homes are far more than simple decoration. For those of us who live in apartments, they serve as a reminder of nature—which can sometimes seem so remote to city dwellers. In a house with a yard, they provide continuity with the plant life outdoors and come into their own in winter, giving us the pleasure of gardening indoors when the yard outside becomes impracticable.

But it is important to remember that to begin with these were outdoor plants. The great majority of houseplants are native to the tropical and subtropical regions of the world and are not frost tolerant. So, we have to grow them indoors, providing them, as best we can, with the conditions suited to their needs. Houseplant lovers must find the ideal spot for each individual plant—the situation that offers the environmental conditions closest to those of its natural habitat—or, better still, choose plants to match the conditions available and thus avoid repeated failures.

In this book you will find all the practical advice you will need in order to choose, care for, feed, protect, and make the most of your plants. The Plant Profiles section provides information on a very wide range of almost 1,000 species and varieties.

The aim of this book is to help you to get to know more about houseplants. After all, developing green fingers is first and foremost a matter of individual effort and experience.

▼ *Hedera helix* "Esther"

VERNACULAR AND LATIN PLANT NAMES

A vernacular plant name is the common name by which a particular plant is known in a particular country, for example, *Tradescantia fluminensis* is known as the wandering Jew or inch plant. The Latin name of a plant is its internationally recognized scientific name and corresponds to botanical nomenclature. It consists of the genus name, given in italics and beginning with a capital letter, followed by the species name, also in italics but beginning with a lower case letter, and finally the name of the variety in question. For example, *Ficus benjamina*, often known as the weeping fig, belongs to the genus *Ficus* and to the species *benjamina*.

As most of our houseplants are not native to where we live, it is less common for them to have precise vernacular names in the same way that our native wild flora do. Consequently, the common name is often simply a rendering of the genus name.

The main problem with houseplants is that many plant lovers do not know their names, either common or scientific. To avoid falling into this trap, buy plants that are carefully labeled (information labels are increasingly included with plants for sale), and, if a plant does not have a label, find out its name! You will discover that you quickly become familiar with the Latin names, and these have a certain appeal and can be informative in their own right.

For example, you will find that a poinsettia is simply a very attractive species of euphorbia, *Euphorbia pulcherrima* (pulcherrima means very beautiful), and that *Ficus pumila* is a small (*pumila*) species of the fig (*Ficus*) genus.

▲ Variegated *Ficus benjamina*

Euphorbia pulcherrima ▶

Keeping indoor plants

PURCHASING ADVICE

■ Where should I buy my plants?

Buying a plant gives us pleasure. The desire to do so is often a sudden fancy or the urge to bring a little nature into the home. When purchasing a plant, you can choose between your local florist, who can offer you personal service and advice on how to look after your plant, or a garden center, which is often farther away but has the advantage of offering a wider range of plants. At a garden center you will also be able to buy any compost, pots, plant food, and pesticides you may need.

■ What is the best time of year?

The best time of year is between early spring and early fall, when the plants are in their growing phase and the conditions in which they are being cultivated—at the nursery, florist's, or garden center—and those at your home are most similar. In very hot spells, be sure to check the growing medium: the compost should be sufficiently moist.

Plants purchased in winter usually come from greenhouses or from premises (such as a florist's) where the temperature is cool and the air is kept very humid. They are transferred from this environment to the home, where the air is dry and warm. It can be very difficult for them to acclimatize, particularly in the case of delicate plants! However, certain seasonal plants, such as poinsettias, are available only during the winter period; in this case special care should be taken transporting them home.

▲▼ When purchasing a plant, it is important to bear certain things in mind. The plant should have a healthy, vigorous appearance and lush foliage.

CHOOSING A WELL-BALANCED PLANT

—When buying climbing or trailing plants, check that the stems are well branched, with plenty of foliage, rather than leggy and devoid of leaves at the base.

—With bushy plants and rosette plants, make sure they are compact, with well-balanced stems and plentiful foliage.

—With large upright plants and small indoor "trees," pay particular attention to the overall balance of the plant and to the distribution of the foliage. Plants that are unsymmetrical when young generally become more so as time goes on, unless they are given a hard pruning!

Platycerium bifurcatum ▲

■ Buying wisely

Don't let yourself be seduced by a plant simply because it's in full flower or attractively presented. It is better to select a plant with a large number of small, semi-closed buds than one in full bloom—the latter may look more appealing, but will not last as long. Even when buying a plant as a gift, it is better to choose an attractive plant in bud than one covered in flowers as these will not last and are likely to suffer more during transport.

Have a close look at the leaves, young shoots, and flower buds of the plant you are thinking of buying. This will allow you to check for the presence of any parasites or disease.

Reject plants with leaves that are pale, damaged or have yellow tips, and that are sticky, black, or blemished. Also avoid plants that have obviously been under-watered (the compost will be dry) or overwatered (the compost will be very damp, with moss on the surface), and plants that are pot-bound (with roots emerging from the drainage holes in the bottom), or the reverse—plants "lost" in an oversized pot.

Good balance between the size of the root ball and the plant growth above the soil is also very important for the harmonious development of the plant. Be rigorous when checking the health of the plant, even if it is being sold very cheaply. You could run the risk of it contaminating other plants at home, particularly if it is sheltering parasites such as aphids, whitefly or scale bugs, which attack many species of plant.

To summarize, choose a plant with a healthy, vigorous appearance, abundant foliage, and, if it's a flowering plant, plenty of flower buds. Preferably choose one with a label detailing its cultivation requirements.

TAKING YOUR PLANT HOME

Plants purchased in winter or in cold weather need to be treated with care. As far as possible avoid exposing them to the cold. Ask for the plant to be well wrapped, and if possible put it in a high-sided cardboard box to provide some protection—and take it straight home! It is very important not to leave plants for long periods in a cold vehicle.

Conversely, in summer make sure your car is well ventilated in hot weather and never leave a plant in a car parked in full sunlight.

Flowering plants are particularly sensitive to sudden changes of temperature which can cause the flower buds to drop.

■ At home

Plants sometimes take a while to acclimatize to their new environment, which is only natural. Be careful to avoid sudden harsh changes of temperature. If you move a plant too quickly into a room heated to over 68° F (20° C), don't be surprised if it drops a few leaves or flower buds.

Syngonium podophyllum "White Butterfly" ▶

Begonia "Lucernae" ▼

When you get home, choose a spot for your plant with filtered light and a temperature of between 61° and 64° F (16° and 18° C).

Even with a plant that requires plenty of light, wait at least a week before exposing it to full sunlight. Only water if the compost seems dry. If the plant is pot-bound, wait for a few weeks before potting it on to avoid it having to cope with too many changes at once.

Hypoestes ▼

CHOOSING THE RIGHT SPOT

Choosing where to put your plant is fundamental to its successful cultivation. Even if you treat it with care, a plant placed in the wrong spot will never thrive. Worse still, it may perish. Depending on their natural habitats, different plants need different amounts of light, different levels of humidity and specific temperatures, which may vary according to the season. To check your plant's requirements, consult the individual plant profiles later on in this book. Also be aware that of those species deemed to be "bomb-proof," some are a lot more tolerant than others!

■ Light

Light is essential to plants. Without light, or with insufficient light, the leaves become pale and the plant stops growing and perishes. Plants rely on photosynthesis—the complex chemical process that allows plants to produce the energy needed to grow— and photosynthesis depends on light.

For a plant to grow well indoors, try to find it a spot where it will enjoy a level of light similar to that in its natural habitat.

We all know that the light intensity indoors provided by natural light varies according to the season, the time of day and the amount of cloud cover. However, we tend to be less aware that light levels decrease rapidly the further away we are from the light source, because the human eye doesn't fully appreciate this. In fact, only 3 feet (1 meter) away from a window, a plant will receive only 50% to 70% of the light level available at the window itself; 6 feet (2 meters) away and the light level drops to only 25%. Furthermore, light levels drop even more sharply on either side of the light source. It's hardly surprising then that plants often suffer from lack of light, especially in winter!

To take account of seasonal variations, you can move your plants around during the course of the year. In winter, move plants that require only medium light levels during the rest of the year in front of a window. Conversely, in summer, move plants that might suffer from exposure to bright sunlight away from sunny windows, or install curtains or blinds to filter the light. Never make sudden, extreme changes. Move your plants gradually. The same applies to plants that you put outside in the yard or on a balcony during the summer: don't put them straight out into full sunlight, even if they need bright light. Allow them one or two weeks to acclimatize.

In winter you can provide additional light by using artificial lighting, particularly for flowering plants. "Daylight" light bulbs or tubes which produce light similar to natural daylight are available in garden centers.

Columnea hirta ▼

Brillantaisia subulugurica ▲

Generally speaking, it is worth remembering that the variegated forms of a species will often require more light than those with plain green leaves.

■ Aspect

The intensity of light provided by a window will, of course, depend on the aspect the window enjoys.

A north-facing window provides only low levels of light, particularly in winter, but the light will be relatively constant during the course of the day and through the seasons. Watch out for cold drafts during the winter months.

An east-facing window enjoys direct sunlight in the morning, a time of day when sunlight is not too strong during the summer months. It will provide good light in summer and medium light in winter.

A west-facing window enjoys direct sunlight in the afternoon and early evening in the summer. Afternoon sunlight can still be very hot in summer: it may be necessary to install some light shading. In winter, however, a west-facing window is an excellent spot for many plants.

A south-facing window provides the maximum amount of light. This is ideal in winter but in summer it can become excessively hot and cause leaf burn. Keep this spot for sun-loving plants such as cactuses and move more delicate species away from south-facing windows.

■ Temperature

Indoors, the temperature generally varies between 64° and 75° F (18° and 24° C) during the course of the year. This range suits most houseplants.

During hot spells in summer, the temperature can rise higher than this. Most of the time this does not affect houseplants, provided humidity levels are increased.

Some plants only thrive in cool temperatures: this applies to many flowering pot plants such as primulas, whose flowering period is cut short by being in a room that is too warm.

Plants are very sensitive to changes of temperature. Many cannot tolerate sudden, extreme variations and may drop their leaves and flower buds. On the other hand, some orchids need a marked change in temperature between day and night in order to flower. Other plants need a period of winter rest in a cool place. If all your rooms are heated in winter, these types of plant are not for you.

The temperature of a given room may not be as constant as we might imagine. In winter the temperature can drop significantly at night next to a poorly insulated window. A plant placed close to a radiator enjoys plenty of warmth but may suffer from exposure to very dry air: find a way of increasing

Anthurium andraeanum ▼

PLANTS FOR A COOL ROOM

A cool room is by no means a disadvantage when it comes to keeping plants! In fact, in winter many houseplants suffer because the temperature indoors is too warm and the air too dry. Providing it has plenty of light and the temperature remains constant, a room with poor heating can become your winter garden and provide a home for many species that require and benefit from a period of winter rest in the cool. These include many flowering plants such as clivias, camellias, small cactuses, cyclamens, etc.

If the room receives only limited light, you can use it for foliage plants that have low light requirements such as aspidistras, some small ferns, chlorophytums, and *Cissus rhombifolia*.

A poorly heated room with the low levels of natural light we receive in winter in our part of the world provides an environment that allows plants to enjoy a period of rest, that is to say a period when growth slows down or is even suspended.

Normal plant care routines must be adapted to suit these over wintering conditions: stop feeding the plants until the end of winter (except for certain flowering plants) and cut back on watering—once every ten to fifteen days is usually sufficient.

Plants that will enjoy these conditions:
—Almost all cactuses and succulents, with heavily reduced watering or no watering at all at low temperatures (from 41° to 50° F/5° to 10° C).
—Flowering plants, at least during their period of winter rest: aeschynanthus, zebra plants, beloperones, brunfelsias, bellflowers, clivias, cyclamens, dipladenias, geraniums, etc.
—Many foliage plants: asparagus, aspidistras, chlorophytums, cissus, aralia ivy, plectranthus, ferns, etc.

Clivia nobilis ▲

Mandevilla sanderi ▼

its ambient humidity. Temperatures rise quickly at a window exposed to full sunlight. In the kitchen, keep your plants away from direct sources of heat such as refrigerators and stoves.

■ Hygrometry

Hygrometry is the level of humidity relative to the air. Many houseplants native to the tropics require an air humidity level of approximately 60% to 70%, whereas during winter in a normal heated room, air humidity rarely exceeds 50%. With the exception of succulents, which are well adapted to cope with dry air, many of the species that we grow indoors suffer as a result of an over-dry atmosphere.

There are a number of ways of increasing air humidity around plants, both directly and indirectly.

—Stand pots close together, while allowing a certain amount of space. Each plant gives off water vapor through its leaves and this will benefit its neighbors.

—Spray the upper surfaces and undersides of leaves with fine droplets of water. This should be done frequently (every day for certain plants such as ferns and orchids). Use soft water at room temperature. However, spraying is unsuitable for downy plants and cactuses. Plants standing on polished or delicate surfaces should be moved before spraying: place them in a basin or bath, and allow the water to drain away after spraying before returning them to their usual spot. Don't spray water on to flowers as they are easily marked, and avoid spraying in sunlight (water droplets act like magnifying glasses).

—Sink the pot or pots in a larger container filled with peat, or clay balls, and keep this moist.

Some plants require regular spraying of the leaves. ▶

▼ *Vanda* x Rothschildiana

—Stand the pot or pots in a shallow tray with a bed of gravel, pebbles, or clay balls, soaking in water. Take care that each pot stands clear of the water; if not, the growing medium will become permanently waterlogged. To ensure the pot is raised clear of the water you can place a smaller, upturned saucer, or any other form of support on which the pot can stand, in the tray as if on an island, and fill the tray with water.

—There are other systems available to ensure a high level of humidity is maintained. The most practical of these is an evaporative humidifier. This is simply a receptacle hooked on to a radiator and regularly filled with water. Electric humidifiers, which are very efficient, maintain a perfectly controlled level of humidity. Water stored in a reservoir slowly evaporates on a warm plate, and a fan gradually diffuses this very moist air throughout the room.

Mandevilla sanderi ▼

▲ To increase air humidity, stand the pot on wet gravel or clay balls. The base of the pot should not be in the water as this can suffocate the roots.

PLANTS THAT TOLERATE DRY AIR

If you have trouble maintaining high levels of humidity, choose plants that tolerate dry air, particularly in winter when the heating is on.

    The majority of cactuses and succulents are well adapted to living in a dry air environment. However, some require a low winter temperature. The selection of plants listed below includes species that will tolerate heated indoor conditions with dry air in winter.

■ **Flowering plants**
- Calceolaria
- Clivia
- Echeveria
- Kalanchoe
- Saintpaulia

■ **Plants with decorative foliage**

—*Small plants*
- Agave
- Variegated aloe
- Small cactuses

—*Climbing and hanging plants*
- Chlorophytum
- Cissus
- Ivy
- Tradescantia
- Swiss cheese plant
- Climbing philodendron
- Plectranthus

■ **Upright plants**
- Aspidistra
- Rubber plant
- Crassula
- Dragon tree
- Elephant's foot
- Sansevieria
- Yucca

Notocactus claviceps ▼   *Calceolaria* ▲   *Clivia nobilis* ▼

Hedera helix "Ripple Green" ▼   *Philodendron bipinnatifidum* ▼

■ Ventilation

Like us, plants need oxygen to survive. It is important to ensure that rooms where there are houseplants are adequately ventilated. Ventilation is also important because stale air can encourage the occurrence of fungal diseases.

Controlled mechanical ventilation (CMV) systems installed in modern buildings provide gentle, continuous air circulation. But houses and apartments without this system need to be aired every day. Although ventilation rarely poses a problem in summer, the same is not true in winter. During the cold season, avoid having windows wide open, even if only briefly, as this is likely to cause a sudden drop in temperature. It is better to leave the window slightly ajar for a certain time, after moving nearby plants further away.

Generally speaking, it is better to open only one window at a time to avoid serious drafts.

Curcuma roscoeana ▼

PLANTS IN THE HOME

■ Positioning your houseplants

Different rooms in your home will provide different types of environment. It is important to get to know the advantages and disadvantages that each offers, so that you can choose the right location for each of your plants. If a plant is in a position that suits it, it will grow more vigorously and show greater resistance to attack from parasites and disease.

■ Plants in the living room

We naturally think of putting our plants in the room that is used the most. It is usually quite large, with good light and heat, and many plants will be happy in this environment. The air in the living room can sometimes become very dry during the winter period, so be careful to ensure that a good level of humidity is maintained.

One useful principle is not to scatter small plants around the whole room, but to use one, two, or three tall plants together to create a balanced arrangement. If you prefer small plants, try grouping them together on a low table or shelf to create a more orderly effect. You can combine a plant with an object—a picture, sculpture, or ornament—according to its shape and color.

Rossioglossum grande ▲

Think about the practical aspects too—avoid standing plants close to a fireplace or radiator as they are likely to suffer from the heat. Keep them out of transit areas and places where they are likely to be knocked and their leaves damaged. If you stand plants on a sunny windowsill, install a thin curtain or blind, if necessary, to filter the sun's rays during the hottest part of the day.

Take care with watering and use a saucer or dish that is large enough to prevent the water overflowing. Ceramic saucers are always porous but they can be made waterproof by being varnished or you can place a small support underneath to lift them free of the surface.

Cissus striata ▲

■ Plants in the kitchen

Kitchens do not generally provide a good environment for houseplants. There are significant variations in temperature and in the humidity of the air, as the stove makes the room hot, steam is released by cooking, and there is the issue of ventilation. On top of all this, there is often a lack of space as work surfaces need to remain uncluttered.

For the kitchen choose robust plants that enjoy high levels of humidity but which also tolerate variations in heat and humidity. Also bear in mind how much light is available. You can always opt for short-lived, decorative plants, which can be replaced when they are past their best.

A good option can be to use hanging plants at the windows as these offer swaths of greenery without occupying any precious space, or else sunny window ledges, which can accommodate some aromatic plants. If your kitchen receives plenty of light you could even consider training a climber (such as a pothos, climbing philodendron, or cissus) on a wall.

■ Plants in the bedroom

Bedrooms are often a little cooler than other rooms and sometimes receive less natural light. We are also less tempted to put plants in bedrooms as they tend to be less used than other rooms in the house. However, their relative coolness can be ideal for plants that need a period of rest or for plants that have finished flowering and are past their best. Remember to cut back on watering if the temperature is lower.

■ Plants in the bathroom

The bathroom is an ideal place for many foliage plants, providing it has plenty of natural light and is heated. The high humidity produced each time the room is used is highly beneficial to plants.

However, bathrooms can often suffer from a lack of light and this can be a limiting factor. Place your plants close to the window. If your bathroom has plenty of light, choose tropical foliage plants that enjoy warmth, light, and high humidity, such as pothos, philodendrons, and bird's nest ferns. Flowering plants can be trickier to keep in the bathroom as they often require good light and do not respond well to being splashed. In a bathroom with poor light choose small ferns or foliage plants that grow happily with a limited amount of light, such as maidenhair ferns, nephrolepis, and syngoniums.

Syngonium "Infra Red" ▼

■ Plants in the entrance, corridor, and hallway

Entrances and hallways can be rather dark and cool, so choose tough plants that can tolerate these conditions—aspidistras or sansevierias, for example. Always choose varieties with plain green foliage for dark areas, as the variegated forms, which contain less chlorophyll pigment, require brighter light than the plain forms.

Fatsia japonica ▲

However, if there is sufficient light, you can put a large, architectural plant in this area that will focus people's attention as soon as they enter. You can also use the entrance and hallway, providing they have some heating, as a winter store for those plants that enjoy resting in the cool during the winter months. But if you do decide to do this, remember that they still need as much attention as any other plant. Don't forget them and turn your hallway into a junkyard for abandoned plants!

■ Plants in the study or office

Creating a pleasant working environment by adding a few plants is bound to be beneficial! On the other hand, it's depressing to have an unhealthy, yellow, or etiolated plant on your desk. It is important to choose species that will become good work companions, plants that will be happy in the environment you can provide.

Studies and other workplaces are often well heated, but the air may be dry and the temperature often drops considerably during the night and at weekends. Choose sturdy plants that are easy to grow and capable of adapting to this type of situation. If there is plenty of light, choose small succulents such as aeoniums and kalanchoes. If your study is large enough, a tall, foliage plant can look very effective—a large-leaved ficus or schefflera, for example. If you like hanging plants you can choose from types such as asparagus fern, chlorophytum, pothos, plectranthus, and tradescantia.

Avoid mixed arrangements—that is to say, several plants grouped together in the same container—as these can be more difficult to take care of. Choose plants with decorative foliage as they will be easier to look after. But you can also enjoy seasonal flowering plants such as calceolarias or flowering begonias.

If you are often away, choose pots with a self-watering device or hydroculture. Generally speaking it is best to avoid species that require

Aeonium arboreum "Variegatum" ▲

Begonia x *rex-cultorum* ▲

frequent watering, especially during the summer. Before going away on holiday, ask a colleague to water the plants, or you can put them outside in your yard.

■ Plants as part of the decor

Once you have got to know many of the plants we grow indoors, you may feel like taking things a step further by choosing species that will match the style of your decor, trying different methods of cultivation, or creating more elaborate plant arrangements. Houseplants lend themselves to all sorts of experimentation, and providing you observe a few rules, you can achieve an effect that is both original and rewarding.

■ Plants to suit your style

While most houseplants can be incorporated into a range of decorative styles, some evoke a particular period, ambience, or style. The container or planter you choose can also be very important in suggesting different styles.

Here are a few suggestions for plants that will help to enhance the decorative style of your home. You can adapt them to suit your taste.

Deliberately retro: begonias with decorative foliage, cyclamens, clivias, gloxinias, gardenias, spathiphyllums, kentias, and nephrolepis.

◄ *Bambusa ventricosa*

Old-style planters, which are often very ornate, can be used for plants with decorative foliage. You could also try using old, white porcelain soup tureens, which will set off flowering plants very attractively.

Plain, minimal, modern: choose plants with strong, simple lines such as yuccas, palms, cordylines, spathiphyllums, lucky bamboo, papyri, ficus, scheffleras, African lindens, pachiras, succulents, and for flowers, amaryllis, phalaenopsis, or hibiscus,

Cane furniture and colorful fabrics: these combine well with foliage plants with luxuriant leaves to create an "exotic," warm ambience. Choose ferns, philodendrons, ficus, cheese plants, climbing and trailing plants, marantas, calatheas, palms, and for flowers, zebra plants, kalanchoes, saintpaulia, and Madagascar jasmine. Wickerwork planters and brightly-colored ceramic pots will set off the foliage.

Rustic style, wooden furniture: enhance the warmth of this style with colorful flowers such as primulas, cyclamens, poinsettias, Christmas

▼ *Sinningia speciosa*

cactuses, clivias, columneas, campanulas, hibiscus, and for foliage, try lush plants such as scheffleras and philodendrons.

Oriental or Japanese-style decor in black and white: choose plants with simple lines (elephant's foot, papyruses, indoor bamboo, lucky bamboo, or palms) combined with plants with vivid flowers, also originating in Asia, such as chrysanthemums and aeschynanthus. Be restrained in your choice of planter, choosing simple lines and plain colors.

South American decor: rugs with geometric designs, rustic pottery, for example—keep to the same style with cactuses (possibly arranged in groups), succulents such as euphorbias, agaves, crassulas and aeoniums, and yucca.

Mediterranean style: white walls and bright light call for plants to match: succulents, hibiscus, lemon trees, passion flowers, and jasmine. Choose subtle pots and planters in terracotta, for example, with splashes of strong color here and there.

Yucca elephantipes ▼

Aphelandra squarrosa ▶

■ Terrariums and indoor greenhouses

These are not the same as the mini-greenhouses or propagators used for germinating seeds and growing cuttings, which are plain, plastic containers. They are genuine miniature greenhouses, made of glass, and available in a variety of styles. Depending on the types of plants you want to grow, they can be left closed to provide a small, humid environment, similar to that of bottle gardens, or left open to give a dryer atmosphere, for a cactus garden, for example. Models with tinted glass are best avoided as these will reduce available light and this may affect the development of the plants.

A well-planted indoor greenhouse will provide a real point of interest, whatever room it is in.

Preliminary precautions: when selecting plants for an indoor greenhouse, choose plants with similar requirements in terms of heat, light, and water. Your greenhouse should be positioned to best meet the plants' requirements (light in particular) and not simply according to the decor of the room. Choose strong, young plants. Don't overfill the greenhouse—the plants will increase in size and need space to grow.

Echeveria ▼

Planting: before planting them, try arranging your plants while they are still in their pots to decide how they will look best. Experiment with contrasts in the size, shape, color, and texture of the leaves. Indoor greenhouses do not usually have drainage holes, so provide a 1 inch (2 to 3 cm) layer of fine gravel or small clay balls. Add a few pieces of wood charcoal to purify any water that may accumulate in the bottom of the container. Then spread the growing medium on top (using a special compost where necessary, for cactuses and bromeliads, for example) to a level deep enough to plant the root balls. For a more decorative effect, it is often a good idea to create a slope with the compost and plant up to the outer edge of the greenhouse. Moisten the compost, but avoid making it too wet, particularly if there is no drainage.

Gradually place the plants in the desired position, beginning at one side. Firm in with compost around the base of the plant to keep it in place. Finish by watering lightly with a spray as this will allow you to wash off the leaves at the same time (except in the case of succulents); if necessary, clean the inside glass walls of the greenhouse before closing it. If the glass becomes covered in condensation, the atmosphere in the greenhouse is too humid—open it a little. Always leave the greenhouse slightly open when growing an arrangement of succulents.

Plant care: water sparingly if there is no drainage and do not overfeed as young plants are often rooted cuttings, which require little in the way of nutrients. Be prepared to cut back or replace any plants that are growing much faster than the others.

Choosing the right plants: foliage plants are easier to grow in an indoor greenhouse than flowering plants. Plants that will enjoy this environment include small ferns (such as maidenhair fern, bird's nest fern, and blechnum), young dwarf palms, selaginellas, small plants (or dwarf varieties) with variegated foliage such as hypoestes, fittonias, pileas, and

◀ *Hypoestes phyllostachya* ▶

HOW TO MAKE A BOTTLE GARDEN

peperomias. You could also create a miniature garden devoted to cactuses and succulents (with special compost and minimal watering) or to bromeliad epiphytes such as tillandsias. Some orchids also enjoy the warm, humid atmosphere of a terrarium.

■ Bottle gardens

Bottle gardens are very decorative, particularly so if placed on their own, away from other houseplants. These enclosed gardens, with their sense of mystery and the unusual, capture the imagination, particularly of children. Use a demijohn or glass jar with an opening large enough to allow you room to plant and to care for your plants without too much difficulty (ideally large enough for your hand to fit in). Remember that tinted glass reduces the amount of light that can enter and makes it more difficult to see the plants. Also, it is not essential for the container to have a stopper. Never expose your bottle garden to direct sunlight. The temperature inside will rise very quickly causing a lot of condensation and there is a danger of the leaves being burned by the sun because of the magnifying effect of the water droplets.

Choosing the right plants: large, fast-growing plants are unsuitable if you want a bottle garden that will last for any length of time. Flowering plants can be difficult to grow in this environment as they usually need a period of rest, whereas growing conditions in a bottle garden remain more or

1. Spread a good drainage layer of gravel or clay balls in the bottom of the jar about 1 inch (2 to 3 cm) thick. Add a thin layer of wood charcoal then pour in the compost using a paper funnel. Spread the compost in a layer 2½ to 3½ inches (6 to 8 cm) thick. Create a slight dome in the center.

2. Remove the small plants from their pots and loosen their roots. Plant from the center to the sides. If the opening of the jar is too narrow, use some tools: a spoon and a fork with extra long handles, for example.

3. Bring the compost up around the base of each plant.

4. For a more decorative finish, cover the compost between the plants with fine gravel or moss. Water lightly down the inside of the glass. Close the bottle or leave it open depending on the plants used.

less constant throughout the year. Also avoid plants with downy foliage and plants that can't tolerate a humid atmosphere (cactuses, for example).

Choose small plants that enjoy a warm and humid atmosphere, and experiment with the shapes, colors, and textures of their foliage to bring some diversity into your arrangement. Dwarf varieties are particularly useful for this type of cultivation.

Planting: begin by checking the level of the growing medium (it should usually be slightly lower than the widest point of the jar) and decide the positions of the plants. Do not place them too close together; leave them room to grow or you will end up with a veritable jungle after two or three months!

In the bottom of the jar, spread a layer of drainage material (gravel or clay balls) about 1 inch (2 to 3 cm) deep, then add a little powdered wood charcoal and finally the compost, using a paper funnel to avoid making the inside of the glass dirty. Spread the compost 2½ to 3½ inches (6 to 8 cm) deep with a spoon attached to a stick. Create a slight dome in the center to make the plants here more visible.

Remove the small plants from their pots (after first watering them) and tease out the roots a little. Begin planting in the center. Slide the plant through the opening using a pair of wooden sticks to guide it. Bring the compost up around the base of the plant with a stopper fixed to the end of a stick.

Finish by covering the surface of the compost with moss or decorative gravel. Water lightly by dribbling water down the inside of the glass—this will both clean it and prevent water falling directly on the plants.

Close the bottle if appropriate, or leave it open. If condensation forms quickly on the inside of the glass, open it to reduce the level of humidity.

Selaginella apoda ▼

Plant care: this is minimal, particularly in the case of closed jars, once the desired balance has been achieved. For open bottle gardens, water as needed but avoid overwatering. Plants (such as ivy and hypoestes) which take up too much space as they grow should be cut back or eventually replaced. To prune back, use a fine pair of scissors or fix a razor blade to the end of a stick.

PLANTS FOR BOTTLE GARDENS

—**Small ferns:** maidenhair ferns, young bird's nest ferns, blechnums, pelleas, Cretan brakes.
—**Colored foliage:** fittonias, hypoestes, pileas, variegated ivy, cryptanthus.
—**Also try:** creeping figs, peperomias, and small ground cover plants such as helxines and selaginellas.

Blechnum "Fire Leaf" ▲

■ Foliage and flowering plant arrangements

Houseplant arrangements available from florists are plants grouped together in the same container. Unfortunately, these containers, except those with water reservoirs, often have no drainage holes (bowls, baskets lined with plastic, etc). Great care must therefore be taken with watering to avoid the compost around the roots becoming waterlogged.

These arrangements can remain in place for a few months but the different species should then be repotted separately, as they will grow at different rates.

You can also create your own arrangements. There are two ways of doing this:

—either plants can be planted directly into the same container, preferably a large tub or planter where they can grow at their own pace;

—or their pots can be grouped together with each plant remaining "independent." The pots are simply placed side by side or sunk in a large tub filled with peat and the tops of the pots hidden by moss, fine gravel, or decorative pebbles, depending on each plant's requirements.

The second option has the advantage of allowing greater flexibility. The arrangement can be adjusted over the course of the year as different plants become too large. It also allows for slight variations in the watering regime according to the different species.

Plant care: to ensure that your arrangement is long-lasting, you will need to establish a plant care regime to suit all the different species in the collection. Adjust watering and feeding to suit the requirements of the most delicate plants, which are the ones most likely to suffer from overwatering or overfeeding. The other plants should easily be able to cope with more limited watering. It is also important to find the correct location, the ideal spot being one with bright but filtered light and a coolish winter temperature of 61° to 64° F (16° to 18° C).

■ Hanging plants in the home

Putting plants in hanging containers is an excellent way of showing certain species at their best and filling a space with greenery. It is even possible to create a veritable curtain of plants at a window by hanging a collection of different species at different heights or a small collection of varieties of the same species—ivies, for example.

Where to place hanging plants: the spot must be chosen with care as it will be difficult to move the plant later. Hanging containers are usually placed close to windows. Be sure to provide your chosen plant with sufficient light or choose a plant that will accommodate itself to the position you have chosen.

The rosary vine, for example, will be happy hanging by a sunny window, whereas a Boston fern prefers a north-facing window. Also, make sure that the plant does not present a problem when opening the window and is not an obstruction to people passing by or underneath.

Choosing a container: the container you choose must, of course, be watertight, except perhaps in a bathroom. You can choose between planters with a chain system and those with a saucer incorporated beneath. It is perhaps easier to avoid water spillage with the pot/saucer combination, but water overflowing from the saucer could still cause damage.

Watering hanging plants: this depends on the species, but it is particularly important to avoid overwatering. Climb on to a stool or use steps to check how moist the compost is. Overwatering leads to waterlogging around the roots and this can go unnoticed until the plant suddenly collapses, when it will almost certainly be too late.

▼ *Hoya carnosa* "Variegata"

PLANTS FOR HANGING CONTAINERS

Foliage plants suitable for hanging containers
Asparagus "Sprengeri"
Begonia (certain types)
Boston fern
Chlorophytum
Cissus
Climbing philodendron
Creeping fig
Hypoestes
Ivy
Mother of thousands
Pellea
Plectranthus
Pothos
Rosary vine
Sempervivum
Staghorn fern
Syngonium
Tradescantia

Columnea ▶

Flowering plants suitable for hanging containers
Aeschynanthus
Campanula
Christmas cactus (or orchid cactus)
Columnea
Easter cactus
Hoya
Madagascar jasmine

Campanula isophylla "Napoli" ▼

■ Plant curtains or screens

Plants often benefit from being grouped together indoors. Such groupings can create a decorative effect, providing a focal point in a room, and for the plants themselves, grouping them together creates a beneficial microclimate.

You can create a plant screen composed of trailing plants (such as ivy, creeping fig, pothos, climbing philodendron, syngonium, etc). A plant curtain can in fact replace normal drapes at a window, providing privacy while at the same time bringing an original and natural note to the room. It is generally better to avoid placing plants in direct sunlight, so this option is best chosen for windows facing north, north-east, or north-west.

Ficus pumila ▼

The same hanging plant principle can be used to create a screen along the edge of a mezzanine area with plenty of natural light; the hanging vegetation will effectively "dress" the space.

Another idea, this time to conceal the view from a window, is to install some small shelves in the window recess and fill them with lots of small plants.

Depending on location and taste, you can opt for a collection of forms or varieties of the same species to create this "screen," for example, small-leaved, variegated, and plain ivies, or variegated and plain creeping figs, or you could combine different species that will grow happily together in the same spot.

Pellaea rotundifolia ▶

Syngonium "Pixie" ▶

Ficus pumila
"White Sunny" ▶

To create a plant screen you will need plants with flexible stems growing in a "climbing" position. In a large, well-lit room this can provide a divider, for example, between the living and dining areas, or the dining area and the kitchen.

The ideal method is to use a long container fitted with rot-proof trellising, and to plant on either side of the trellis. You can use a variety of species but take care to choose plants suitable for the light available (filtered light is ideal). For a permanent feature like this, you will need a majority of vigorous, foliage climbers to create an impact, such as cissus, pothos, monstera, and climbing philodendron.

◀ *Monstera deliciosa*

■ Forcing bulbs for winter flowering

Did you know that it's easy to bring traditional, spring-flowering bulbs such as crocuses, narcissi, and tulips into bloom indoors for Christmas and during the winter months?

You will need special bulbs, known as "prepared" or "forced" bulbs; these bulbs have been put through a treatment process at the producer's. They are specifically designed to be forced for indoor display and will flower more easily and earlier than bulbs that have not undergone this preparation process. The most common varieties are hyacinths, early tulips, crocuses, and narcissi, and also small muscari.

The secrets of forcing:
In the northern hemisphere, spring-flowering bulbs need a period of cold in order to bloom again. The same is true of prepared bulbs, which need to spend time in the cool and dark in order to form roots. When the roots are well developed and shoots are emerging, you can bring the bulbs indoors into the light and put them in the desired spot until they finish flowering.

Crocus vernus
"Remembrance" ▼

Hyacinthus ▼

Growing bulbs: plant your bulbs between September and November, depending on when you want them to bloom. Plant them close together, leaving the tips of the bulbs exposed, in bowls filled with a light growing medium with good drainage—for example, ordinary compost to which coarse sand has been added. If you use watertight containers, you will need to water sparingly to avoid the compost becoming too damp.

Use a single variety in each bowl to avoid staggered blooming. Plant an odd number of bulbs in small groups of 3, 5, 7, or 9, for example. An even number will produce too regular an effect.

Moisten the compost by watering with a fine spray so as not to disturb the bulbs, then put the bowls in a dark, cool place—41° to 50° F (5° to 10° C)—to form roots. You can keep them in a basement, a frost-free shed or even in the vegetable container in your refrigerator. To keep them in the dark, cover them with a black plastic bag. Check the compost regularly during this rooting phase to ensure it remains moist. You can bring the containers indoors once the roots are well developed and the bulbs have formed shoots about 2 inches (5 to 6 cm) long. You will need to allow seven to twelve weeks in darkness, depending on the species.

Hyacinthus ▲▶

Growing hyacinths in a jar: follow the same method to grow forced hyacinths in a jar. Fill the hyacinth jar with water to a level just below the base of the bulb, to prevent rotting. Put a piece of wood charcoal in the water to keep it clean and then move the bulb and jar to a cool, dark place. You can place the jar under a cardboard or aluminum foil cone to create a dark environment.

Indoors: place the bulbs in a bright, preferably cool position to ensure prolonged blooming, and water regularly. Then you can sit back and enjoy the flowers, which are so heartening in the depths of winter. By planting

Narcissus "Tête à Tête" ▼

bulbs at regular intervals, every two weeks for example, you can enjoy a staggered supply of blooms over a long period.

Growing narcissi among pebbles: for a refreshing, fragrant display of blooms, try growing tazetta narcissi among pebbles. These multi-bloomed narcissi produce small, highly perfumed flowers in white (Paper White) and yellow (Soleil d'Or). The prepared bulbs of these narcissi, which are not hardy in cold areas, do not need a period in the cold. Take a wide, fairly shallow container—a glass dish will allow you to see the roots as they grow—and spread a good layer of (previously washed) small pebbles, gravel, or clay balls. Plant the bulbs close together, holding them firmly in place by adding more pebbles or balls. Leave the growing tips of the bulbs exposed. Add water to a level just below the base of the bulbs. Place the container in a bright, ventilated spot, cool if possible. Add water as needed. The bulbs will come into bloom between one and one-and-a-half months after planting.

After indoor flowering: bulbs grown in compost that have flowered indoors can be transferred to the yard once the blooms have faded. They will build up their reserves for flowering the following year or the year after that. However, bulbs grown in water will have exhausted their nutritional reserves and are unlikely to survive.

Tulipa ▶

■ Indoor bonsais

These small trees make fascinating specimens for pot cultivation. If they are not to come to a sad end in a matter of weeks, it is important to establish their requirements and give them the care they need: this is quite specific as they are grown in very small containers.

When choosing a suitable specimen, you must first find out the species of tree or shrub that has been cultivated into a bonsai. It is important to distinguish between the hardy species which, while they may not be frost-resistant because they are pot-grown, will nevertheless not tolerate spending the winter in a room with dry air, heated to a temperature or 68° F (20° C), and the non-hardy species native to the tropics, which are suitable for indoor cultivation. Species that are well adapted to this type of

cultivation include ficus (*Ficus benjamina*, *Ficus retusa*), crassulas, scheffleras, young palms (such as *Rhapis excelsa*), and certain bamboos (such as *Bambusa ventricosa*).

Everyday care: because of the limited amount of soil they have available, bonsais require very regular watering—daily in summer for certain species—and two to three times a week in winter. With specimens placed in a warm room in winter, it is best to immerse the pot in warm, soft water to ensure the growing medium is fully soaked. Then leave the plant to drain before returning it to its spot. With the exception of crassulas, almost daily spraying of the foliage with soft water is essential.

▼ *Ficus benjamina* ▶

Stop all feeding in winter. From spring to fall, feed approximately every two weeks with heavily diluted ordinary plant food or, better still, with special bonsai plant food.

Pruning: it is essential to prune your bonsai regularly (with small pruning shears or special scissors), at least once a year, so that it keeps its attractive shape and to emphasize its venerable appearance (by removing basal shoots, for example).

Repotting: bonsais do not require repotting every year.

As a general rule, repotting in spring every two to three years is sufficient. Young specimens should be potted on into a slightly larger container, but older plants should be replaced in the same pot. It is basically a matter of renewing some of the growing medium and pruning the roots.

—Remove the bonsai from its pot, keep or replace the drainage layer in the bottom of the pot and remove any compost adhering to the inside of the pot.

—Untangle the roots as far as possible (special root rakes are available) and prune them back to about half their length.

—Repot the bonsai in fresh growing medium (special bonsai compost for preference), carefully spreading out the roots around the base of the trunk.

—Lightly firm the compost and then water with a fine spray.

Acer palmatum
(Japanese Maple) ▼   *Styrax japonicum* ▶

During the holidays: You cannot abandon your bonsai while you are away. Ask a friend or neighbor to step in. Some florists and specialist nurseries offer a "plant holiday" service. You could take this opportunity to ask them to prune and repot your plant if you are worried about doing it yourself.

■ Fragrance in the house

Any houseplant that is both fragrant and decorative is a winning combination! Some plants offer both these qualities and deserve to be cultivated, even though they may often be quite tricky. Fragrance is particularly welcome in winter as the yard has very little to offer in this regard during the winter months.

Fragrant blooms: plants to enjoy for their scent include: primulas, with their light fragrance in spring; exacums in the summer; Madagascar jasmine, with its more powerful fragrance and waxy, white flowers which are both beautiful and intoxicating; the celebrated gardenia, delicate to grow but highly perfumed; hoyas, whose porcelain flowers exude a heady fragrance; and indoor orange and lemon trees, particularly the calamondin.

Scented foliage: aromatic plants offer us another opportunity to enjoy fragrance through their foliage. Among the best for indoor cultivation in winter and outdoors in summer are scented geraniums, whose leaves give off a strong scent when rubbed. They can spend the winter indoors in a well-lit spot that is not too warm, and require moderate watering.

▲ x *Citrofortunella microcarpa*

◀▲ *Stephanotis floribunda*

Forcing bulbs for winter: forcing bulbs is easy and cheap to do and they will reward you with their soft, heady fragrance during the cold months of winter. A simple hyacinth in a pretty hyacinth jar will bloom and remain fragrant over a long period, while the small, fast-growing tazetta narcissi have a heady scent which will fill the whole room.

A real Christmas tree: when choosing a tree at Christmas, opt for the Norway spruce (*Picea abies*) over the Nordmann fir (*Abies nordmanniana*), even though the latter keeps better indoors once cut; you will be rewarded by the resinous fragrance of the spruce, so characteristic and reminiscent of that magical time in childhood.

Cut flowers: by using cut flowers you can broaden the palette of fragrant blooms in the home. Among the classics are freesias with their gentle perfume, the refreshing scent of sweet peas, the heady fragrance of lilies and roses, of course, but also try the peppery perfume of carnations, mimosa (with a perfume that quickly fills the room), wallflowers and lily of the valley.

A few precautions: make the most of fragrance but use it in moderation indoors. Strong, heady fragrances are not for the bedroom or the office as some people may find them unacceptable if exposed to the scents for long periods. It is also best to avoid mixing different fragrances. Do not put cut flowers and fragrant plants together in the same room. The result is rarely a winning one! It is better to put a single type of flower or plant in a room and vary the fragrance on a seasonal basis.

Plant arrangement ▲

Gardenia augusta ▼

Looking after your indoor plants

Once you have found the ideal spot for each of your plants, it will be up to you to keep them in good health by providing regular care. These little tasks will also allow you to keep a close eye on your plants and identify at an early stage any problems requiring immediate attention.

■ Indoor gardening tools

Looking after houseplants does not require any very sophisticated equipment! To start with, a small watering can and a bottle of liquid plant food may even be enough.

The following items will be of help when carrying out everyday plant maintenance.

A long-spouted watering can: this will allow you to water pots accurately, even those high up, without splashing water on the leaves. It's a lot better than a jug or plastic bottle! Choose a watering can with sufficient capacity, at least 3½ pints (2 liters), or more if you have large plant containers, as this will save you going back and forth to the faucet.

Liquid houseplant food: one type for foliage plants, one for flowering plants, if needed.

A combined houseplant treatment containing both insecticide and fungicide.

Pots and saucers of assorted diameters, and possibly planters. There are all sorts of plant holders available but you can also use your imagination and experiment with attractive bowls, soup tureens, small metal buckets, and different types of basket. If your plant holder is not watertight, place a saucer in the bottom.

Potting compost: use at least an ordinary houseplant compost for most plants and special composts for certain plants (such as cactuses, epiphytes, etc.).

A small fork and trowel or small shovel for use when repotting and top dressing. You could also use a large spoon and a kitchen fork (kept exclusively for this purpose).

Chamaedorea metallica ▶

Pruning tools: a good pair of kitchen scissors is sufficient for plants with thin stems; a budding knife or pruning shears will be needed for larger plants. These tools should always be kept clean and well sharpened.

Supports, hoops, trellising, ties: everything you need to provide your plants with support and encourage them to climb.

Spray: invaluable for increasing ambient humidity.

▼ At garden centers you can get not just pots but also compost and plant food… everything you need to take good care of your plants.

Onicidium boissiense ▶

WATERING

Water is of course essential for plants to grow. Pot-grown plants are always problematic where watering is concerned as they need just the right amount: it is a question of how much and how often. With a little experience it's easy to get it right.

■ Why water?

Water enables the nutrients present in the growing medium to be carried into the plant tissue. It also plays a part in all the major transformation processes that take place within the plant, such as photosynthesis and evaporation.

Plants grown in open soil rarely suffer from excess water as it drains away into the soil below. In a pot, however, excess water becomes stagnant, making the compost waterlogged and preventing essential gaseous exchange to take place at root level.

Lack of water will cause plants to wilt and will eventually lead to irreversible damage. It is therefore important to find the correct balance for each plant, as water requirements vary according to the species and growing conditions.

■ How to water

In most cases you can water your plants on the surface of the compost. There are, however, other ways of providing plants with water, some of which are better suited to specific types of plant:

▲ Water the surface of the compost, taking care not to wet the leaves.

▲ For succulents and tuberous plants (such as gynura, saintpaulia, etc.), pour water directly into the saucer—it will be absorbed by capillary action.

—rosette-forming succulents, small cactuses, plants with downy foliage, and tuberous plants: in these plants, the leaves and base of the stem are very susceptible to rotting and any water splashes can cause unsightly marks. It is better to water these plants by pouring water into the saucer or planter, from where it will be absorbed by capillary action. After ten or fifteen minutes, pour away any excess water from the saucer or planter;

—orchids and epiphytes: these plants take up water not only via their roots but also through their foliage. They can therefore be hydrated by frequent spraying of the leaves, accompanied by occasional immersion of the entire pot, basket, or host bark in a bucket of soft water so that the fibrous growing medium becomes fully soaked. You can also water hanging plants by immersing them.

WATERING

More watering is needed:
—during the growing period;
—when it is hot;
—in sunny situations;
—when the air is dry;
—when plants are in small pots;
—for large, soft-leaved plants which transpire a lot, and plants with thin foliage;
—for plants growing in terracotta pots;
—for peat-based composts which have low water retention.

Less watering is needed:
—during the period of vegetative rest;
—at low temperatures;
—in shady situations;
—when the air is humid;
—for plants in large pots and plants that have just been repotted;
—for cactuses and succulents;
—for plants growing in plastic pots;
—for soil-based composts.

■ Softening water

Generally speaking, houseplants respond badly to being watered with hard water. The toughest plants can tolerate it without a problem but others (such as gardenias, and many ferns) will soon begin to fade. In areas that are relatively free from atmospheric pollution, rainwater can be used, of course (although you will need a way of collecting it!). Here are a few ideas for softening tap water:

—always leave it to stand for several hours: the chlorine will evaporate and the chalk will settle;

—boiling also helps the chalk to settle;

—leave a sachet of peat moss to soak overnight in the watering can or bucket of water.

Avoid using chemically softened water, elements of which can sometimes be harmful to plants.

Tolmiea menziesii "Variegata" ▶

■ How to check soil humidity

With a little experience it is easy to check how moist the growing medium is:

— dry compost is paler than moist compost;

— feeling the surface also gives an indication;

— a terracotta pot sounds "hollow" when the compost is dry;

— the pot will of course be lighter when it is dry than when it has absorbed water;

— the presence of water in the saucer or planter is an indication that the compost is sufficiently wet.

To help you measure soil humidity, probes of varying levels of sophistication are available: from simple sticks which display different colors according to the level of humidity to battery-operated devices.

■ During the holidays

Ideally ask a neighbor or friend you can trust and who knows about your plants to take care of them while you are away.

If this isn't possible or if you are only away for a short time, there are various ways of making sure your houseplants don't go short of water.

Before you leave:

— check that your plants are healthy and free of parasites;

— cut them back if necessary and remove any faded blooms;

— move your plants away from windows, placing them in a less bright position to reduce water loss through evaporation. But don't forget that they do need some light, so don't close all the blinds;

— don't feed your plants just before going away; there's no point in stimulating plant growth while you're not there;

WATERING WHEN YOU'RE AWAY

You can check how moist the plant is by feeling the surface of the compost ▶

▲ Fill the sink with water and place a piece of absorbent fabric on the draining board with one end immersed in the water. Stand your plants on the fabric.

Cyclamen persicum ▶

—give your plants a generous final watering; fill up water reservoirs as these can often provide sufficient water for up to two weeks.

For an absence of just a few days
(not more than eight to ten days, depending on the time of year)
—Stand all your pot plants together in a large bowl filled with very moist peat.
—Better still, line the bottom of a large, watertight container (basin, bathtub, etc.) with expanded clay balls steeped in water; the water level should be just below the bottom of the pots. Water will be absorbed into the growing medium by capillary action.

WATERING WHEN YOU'RE ON HOLIDAY

▲ Push one end of a wick into the compost and the other into a bucket of water placed higher than the plant pots. Use as many wicks as there are pots.

For an absence of two or three weeks
—Use water wicks (special water wicks, porous terracotta water spikes, etc.) pushed down into the growing medium and connected to a water source higher than the level of the pots to be watered. The water will be carried down into the compost by capillary action when the compost dries out.
—If your kitchen sink receives enough light, put a piece of special absorbent felt matting on the draining board with one end in the bottom of the sink. Place your plants on the matting and fill the sink (check that the plug is watertight). This will ensure that the plants remain watered while you're away.

For a longer period away
You can sink your pots in the soil in a shady part of the yard, covering the surface with damp peat and watering generously before leaving. You will have to hope that it rains occasionally!

Another possible but more sophisticated solution is to use a programmable drip watering system.

Watering system consisting of "spikes" made of porous material. ▶

FEEDING YOUR PLANTS

In the wild or in the yard, plants find the nutrition they need in the soil. But when growing in pots they quickly exhaust their reserves, so it is important to provide them with some additional food.

■ How plant food works
There are three elements that are essential for plants to grow successfully. Nitrogen (which has the chemical symbol N) is essential for stem and leaf growth and to chlorophyll synthesis.

Phosphorus (chemical symbol P) promotes healthy root development.

Potassium (chemical symbol K) promotes the production of flowers and fruit, and improves disease resistance.

Plant food also contains other elements in smaller quantities: trace elements such as magnesium, copper, iron, zinc, manganese, etc., which play an important role in plant growth.

Plant food designed for houseplants contains all these elements but in different quantities to meet different plant requirements. Foliage plants need food with a higher level of nitrogen, while flowering plants, on the other hand, need food rich in potassium to ensure good flowering. So it is important to look at the packet for the "N-P-K" (nitrogen, phosphorus, potassium) formula. These letters will be followed by figures indicating the relative concentrations of these three elements. For example, "N-P-K 9-9-19" indicates a plant food rich in potassium—this is used for roses and flowerbeds. It can also be used for flowering houseplants. There are plant foods containing various concentrations and balanced to suit every kind of houseplant.

■ When to use plant food
In theory, when you buy a houseplant it should not have any immediate need for feeding as it has probably been recently repotted. You can leave it without feeding until the plant has exhausted a good part of the nutrients in the compost, either three months for a soil-based compost or six to eight weeks for a peat-based compost.

Most plants need to be fed throughout their growing period (generally from March to October). They will need a period of rest during the winter and so you should refrain from feeding them at this time so as not to stimulate growth, which in any case will be meager. The exceptions to this are certain plants that flower during this period.

Most plants can be fed once every two to three weeks. Don't worry if you sometimes forget to feed them: a few feeds of standard plant food during the growing season is generally enough to keep the plant in good health, providing you regularly renew the growing medium. Plants which grow more slowly, notably cactuses and succulents, should be fed less frequently (about once a month) with a special, heavily diluted plant food.

Refrain from feeding plants that are thirsty (plant food should be used after watering) or sick.

■ Types of plant food and their uses

Plant foods are available in different forms: liquid, granules, sticks, and powder.

The easiest to use are the liquid and powder forms as these can be diluted in the watering can and the lid often doubles as a measure. Plant food sticks have the advantage of providing two to three months' food, but they are quite costly and can cause root burn because of the high concentration of nutrients; they are best used in large pots rather than small ones, as in the latter it is more difficult to insert them away from the center of the root ball.

Foliar feeds are another option. These are specially formulated solutions designed to be sprayed on to the leaves. They have an immediate "perking up" effect and are well suited to certain plants such as bromeliads and other epiphytes which, in the wild, depend on their roots for food only to a very limited extent.

It is important to use the correct dose as indicated on the packet and better to over-dilute than under-dilute. There is no point in giving higher concentrations as this is liable to cause root burn and damage the roots. This will result in the plant turning yellow, followed by it wilting, as if it were

Calceolaria x herbeohybrida ▶

drying out. A plant lacking in nutrients or being fed with an inappropriate food will show this by producing smaller leaves, which are often deformed, and in the case of flowering plants, by a lack of flower buds.

REPOTTING AND TOP DRESSING

In pots, plants have a limited amount of soil available. Even with regular feeding, the growing medium becomes impoverished and, in particular, the roots gradually fill the inside of the pot. When this happens the plant needs to be potted on to allow it to continue to grow in favorable conditions.

It is essential to repot a plant when:

—the roots have completely filled the soil and are appearing on the surface or emerging from the drainage holes;

—the surface compost has become pale or covered in mould;

—you suspect the presence of disease or parasites at root level (rotting, scale bugs, etc.).

Apart from this, there is no exact rule about how frequently plants need repotting. Some species, such as saintpaulia and clivia, actually thrive when pot-bound and so are rarely repotted. Others have such a vigorous

Brunfelsia pauciflora ▲

▲ The roots of this dieffenbachia have filled the pot and compost. It's time to repot it.

growth habit that they need to be repotted twice a year. Often, young plants need to be potted on once a year, but as they get older, repotting every two or three years will suffice.

■ The best time for repotting

Generally speaking, the best time to repot your plants is in the spring, when they are coming back into growth. Plants will recover better from the shock of repotting and young roots will soon colonize the fresh compost you have provided. However, it is possible to repot in summer, up to September. Also, flowering plants are best repotted after blooming: if you repot them before they bloom, their flowering is likely to be affected.

On the other hand, houseplants should not be repotted during their period of rest (usually in fall and winter), or if they appear sickly: it could prove fatal. It is better to look after them and wait until they have recovered before attempting to repot them.

■ How to repot your plants

Make sure that you have plenty of room. Put down a plastic sheet to protect the floor because you are bound to make a bit of mess, no matter how careful you are.

Before beginning, check that you have everything you need to hand:

—the compost and possibly some peat, coarse sand, or ericaceous compost, if you need to make up your own mix;

—some terracotta crocks, large expanded clay balls, or pebbles for drainage;

—clean pots, disinfected with a very diluted solution of bleach (a few drops of bleach are sufficient) if they have already been used. The pots should be of a slightly larger diameter, about 1 inch (2 to 3 cm), than those they are replacing, or considerably larger when repotting a young plant in vigorous growth;

—clean, well-sharpened scissors or knife for any root pruning that may be needed.

Begin by giving the plant a good watering before repotting. This will make it easier to remove and replant.

Hold the base of the stems with one hand, turn the pot upside down, and tap it firmly against a hard surface (a table edge, for example) so that the root ball comes away from the pot. If it refuses to come out, do not persist: it is better to break the pot (if terracotta) or to cut it open (if plastic) to remove the root ball. Prepare the new pot by covering the drainage holes with clay crocks, then spread a layer of drainage material, 1 to 1½ inches (2 to 4 cm) thick, depending on the depth of the pot, followed by a layer of fresh compost that will leave the root ball slightly below the rim of the pot (to allow space for watering). If there are a lot of roots it is best to trim them back with a sharp knife. Also remove any dead or damaged roots. Remove a little of the old, hardened compost from the surface and place the root ball in the center of the new pot at the correct level. Fill in the gaps with fresh compost, firming it down carefully with your fingertips. To finish, water generously so that the compost is spread down around the roots.

1. Prepare the new pot by covering the drainage holes with crocks. Spread a small layer of gravel or clay balls for drainage, then a layer of compost to lift the root ball to just below the rim of the pot.

■ Top dressing

When a plant is old and large it is usually in a big pot or container, which can be difficult to handle. In this case it is better to top dress the plant rather than try to repot it. Top dressing is the process of renewing the compost on the surface and has the advantage of being less traumatic for the plant.

Begin by removing the surface layer of the compost to a depth of 1 to 2 inches (2 to 5 cm), depending on what is possible, by using a spoon or small trowel, and taking care not to damage the roots. Replace this impoverished compost with some fresh compost so that, after watering, the compost is at the same level as before.

Maranta leuconeura "Fascinator" ▼

2. Place the root ball in the center of the pot and fill the surrounding space with compost.

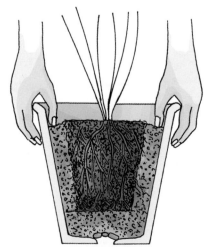

3. Tamp down the compost so that the root ball is held firmly in place. Water generously to settle the compost around the roots and to remove any air pockets.

■ Which compost to use

There are various standard composts available ("potting compost," "houseplant compost," etc.) which are suitable for the cultivation of most foliage or flowering houseplants. These compost mixes, whether peat-based, containing leaf mold, or made from topsoil, are enriched with nutrients. "Composts for flowering plants" are designed specifically for flowering plants.

There are also special compost mixes formulated to meet the needs of particular plants: "orchid compost"—which is very porous and fibrous for orchids; "compost for cactuses and succulents"—a mix with a high proportion of sand or vermiculite to ensure excellent drainage; and "ericaceous compost" (which is in fact a mixture because genuine heath peat, produced by the decomposition of the roots and shoots of heather, has become very scarce)—this is a light, acid compost designed for ericaceous plants, that is to say, plants that are unable to tolerate the presence of lime in their growing medium.

If appropriate you can also use blond peat, river sand, or vermiculite to lighten a compost that is too dense.

It is also possible to prepare your own "home-made" compost blend using good quality yard soil, for example, or well-rotted compost, peat, and

▲ Special compost blends are available to meet the specific requirements of different types of plant.

Terracotta pots are porous and generally provide good stability because of their weight. ▶

coarse sand, but the soil should be sterilized to avoid the risk of contamination (from disease, weed seeds, etc.).

■ Choosing a container

Pots, saucers, and plant holders are available in a wide range of shapes, sizes, colors, and materials.

Pots: standard pots have the same depth as their rim diameter and are described in terms of their diameter. They can be made of plastic or terracotta, each material having its own advantages and disadvantages.

—Plastic is increasingly used but does not suit all plants. It helps to retain water in the compost, hence the need for slightly less watering, but increases

the risk of waterlogging. Plastic does not break (though it can split) and is light to handle, but is less stable and not as attractive as terracotta.

—Terracotta is a porous material which allows moisture exchange to take place but which also absorbs some of the water in the compost. It should be soaked before being used for repotting. As it is heavy, it also provides greater stability than plastic and looks more natural. But beware, it breaks!

Terracotta pots are best suited to cactuses and succulents which cannot tolerate too much humidity, whereas ferns are less likely to dry out in plastic pots.

The essential saucer: With a few exceptions, pots have or should have drainage holes. So it is out of the question to stand them on a piece of furniture! You need to provide them with waterproof saucers (be careful, some terracotta saucers are not suitable for indoor use), with a diameter slightly larger than the base of the pot to avoid spillage when watering. Saucers are also needed in the bottom of containers that are not waterproof, for example, wickerwork or porous pottery. You can also reuse old kitchen saucers and plates.

Planters: the purpose of a planter is to hide the plant pot, which can often be unattractive, and thus enhance the decorative effect of the plant. Planters are available in different shapes, often round or square, either plain or decorated with patterns. For example, you could create a plant arrangement using different sizes of planter but all from the same range. For each plant choose a planter that is slightly larger than the pot itself.

▲ *Ficus benjamina* "Judi"

Fittonia verschaffeltii
var. *argyroneura* ▶

Do not "wedge" a pot into a planter that is too narrow or deep, as there is a risk of water accumulating in the bottom without you realizing. As a general rule, it is a good idea to lift the pot out from time to time to check that it is not sitting in water. For a more original approach you could use improvised plant holders such as an old soup tureen, a salad bowl, a large piece of decorative pottery, a wickerwork container with a dish in the bottom for large foliage plants, or an old copper pot.

Hanging plants: there are various types of containers that can be used for hanging plants. Plastic pots with an integral saucer are ideal for growing hanging plants indoors as, saving accidental spillage, there is no danger of water dripping on to the floor. Wire baskets lined with sphagnum moss are best kept for the greenhouse or balcony as water will drip freely from these. Some orchids are grown in openwork wooden or plastic baskets. At all events, make sure that the container is firmly attached and supported, as hanging containers are often very heavy, particularly after being well watered.

Containers with water reservoirs: these are ideal for people who are often away from home. The water reservoir consists of a watertight tank and an internal dividing grill with some woven fabric linking the two and acting as a water wick. The water is absorbed into the compost by capillary action as and when the plant needs it. A fill indicator will let you know at a glance when the water needs topping up.

PRUNING

Plants with a bushy habit and plants with long, soft stems need to be cut back regularly to maintain a balanced shape, or to trim them into the shape you want.

▼ *Pilea cadierei*

■ The principles of pruning

When you remove the end of a stem, it stimulates the buds on the stem just below the point where you cut to grow (as the terminal bud is no longer dominant). These buds then produce new shoots, giving the plant a more bushy and balanced appearance.

■ Different methods: pinching out and cutting back

Pinching out consists of removing the top of a softwood (not woody) stem by pinching it between the nails of your thumb and index finger. Pinching out stimulates branching and is used for small, thin-stemmed plants such as tradescantia, creeping fig, hypoestes, pilea, etc.

▲ Remove the end of the stem by pinching it off between your thumb and index finger.

Cutting back is a more severe form of pruning, is done lower down the stem and can be used on both woody and softwood stems. Depending on the diameter of the stems you will need to use scissors or a sharp knife, secateurs, or even a saw. Plants are cut back to alter their shape or to encourage new growth by the formation of new stems. It is therefore a procedure used mainly on well-developed plants such as hibiscus, large ficus, schefflera, etc.

■ How to cut

Always make a cut about ¼ inch (a few millimeters) above a leaf bud or pair of leaf buds (the point of leaf attachment also known as the bud eye). If you leave a length of stem above the bud eye this section is likely to dry out or rot, which would be unsightly to say the least.

Make a diagonal cut above the bud eye so that any sap that may emerge does not run on to the bud but on to the other side of the stem.

■ When to cut

Pinching out can be done at any time of year and several times over the course of the year with any plants that have a vigorous growing habit. More severe cutting back should be done between the end of winter and early summer so that the plant has time to develop strong, new shoots before the end of the growing season.

■ Two exceptions: palms and ferns

Ferns do not form aerial stems and so they should not be pruned. If necessary, remove any dry, yellow, or diseased fronds by pulling them off firmly or cutting them off at the base.

Palms usually have just one stem, the "trunk" or stipe, and all growth takes place from the top of the stem. As palms do not have any other leaf buds, the top must never be removed. As with ferns, simply remove dry or sickly leaves.

To maintain the balanced shape of this variegated ivy, remove the long stems. ▼

CLEANING THE LEAVES

Dust settles on plant leaves just as it does everywhere else in the house. If it is allowed to accumulate it will eventually block the pores of the leaves, which is where the gaseous exchange between the plant and the atmosphere takes place (respiration, transpiration), and will also impede the process of photosynthesis. It is therefore important to clean the foliage of your plants from time to time to keep them healthy, as well as for aesthetic reasons. The best way to remove dust will vary according to the type of plant.

■ Plants with fine, delicate, or serrated foliage

This applies to maidenhair ferns and numerous other types of fern, to helxines and to creeping figs. The best method is to expose them to fine, warm rain. If this is not possible, spray their foliage regularly with water. Very fine droplets will both clean the leaves and increase the humidity, which is beneficial to thin-leaved plants. Note that you should spray them with either rainwater or soft water, not hard water.

This plant, with its heavy inflorescences and weak stems, requires the support of a small trellis frame. ▼

Chamaedorea elegans ▲

STAKING AND TRAINING

Supports are essential for plants with climbing or trailing stems, but also for species which carry heavy inflorescences on thin stems and for plants with brittle stems. When a young plant is in the early stages of growth it is sufficient to support the stems with a thin stick or light trellis. But after a few months a more suitable form of support may be needed.

For plants with aerial roots, such as syngoniums, you can use a single, moss-covered pole. Regular spraying of the moss will encourage the aerial roots to anchor.

For plants with twining roots or with tendrils, choose hoops or trellising. Garden centers offer a wide range of wire trellises in different shapes: pyramids, spheres, spirals, etc. To prevent the plant becoming untidy, guide the stems carefully on to the supports at regular intervals or attach them with loose ties.

Some specialist stores now supply balls or animal shapes made of moss which can be a fun way of training small-leaved species like the creeping fig.

Soleirolia soleirolii ▲

■ Plants with downy or prickly foliage

This applies to plants such as cactuses, saintpaulias, and gynuras.

The foliage of these plants should not come into direct contact with water as it is likely to leave marks on them. To remove dust, use a soft paintbrush. Ideal is a puffer brush, like those used to clean camera lenses, as you can blow away the dust as you brush.

▼ Use a soft paintbrush to clean plants with hairy or spiny leaves.

■ Plants with large, smooth, glossy leaves

Plants like philodendrons, monsteras, and aspidistras can quickly become dusty. Regular cleaning is needed, preferably with a small sponge soaked in warm, soft water, while supporting the leaf from below with your other hand. Special cloths, which contain a kind of plant polish that leaves plants shiny, are also available for cleaning plants.

There are also leaf shine aerosols (some of which also combat scale bug infestation), but you should be aware that some plants, such as philodendrons and large-leaved ferns, will not respond well to use of these.

▲ Support large leaves with one hand while cleaning them with the other, using a damp sponge.

■ Multi-leaved plants with small or medium sized leaves

In the case of plants such as creeping figs, tradescantias, and hypoestes, cleaning the plant leaf by leaf is a daunting prospect. Here again, the best option is to expose them to warm, soft rain, or you can immerse the foliage in water (soft water for preference), or even give them a shower using a gentle shower spray.

■ What not to do

There are many home grown recipes for cleaning the leaves of your houseplants. Some recommend using beer, others milk, and even oil to make the leaves of an unfortunate rubber plant shine!

All these recipes should be forgotten and proscribed: they will all produce the same result, which is the very opposite of the one you are looking for—as they will only choke up the leaf pores still further. Sticky liquids such as these attract dust and literally block the pores of the leaves, gradually suffocating the plant.

After showering or spraying your plant, make sure that it is not left to stand in direct sunlight as the magnifying effect of the water droplets could cause leaf burn.

openwork inner basket containing expanded clay balls, with a water level gauge. You will need plant food or a nutrient solution specially formulated for use in hydroculture, which will provide your plant with all the nutrients essential for healthy growth.

When buying a plant cultivated by this method, be sure to find out what plant food it will need.

The roots of plants grown in water differ slightly both anatomically and physiologically from the roots of soil-grown plants. They need to be capable of absorbing the oxygen in the water. To avoid adaptation problems it is best to begin water cultivation at the propagation stage rather than repotting a plant previously grown in a soil medium into a water and clay ball environment. You can, for example, easily "start off" various cuttings in water (such as cissus, saintpaulia, tradescantia, plectranthus, etc.).

Although useful, special containers are not essential. You can use any watertight container, preferably a transparent one so that you can check the water level: a glass vase in a simple shape can make a very decorative container.

Ficus elastica ▶

Conversely, a plant that remains wet for a long time in a cool, humid room is liable eventually to rot.

HYDROCULTURE

As the name implies, hydroculture is a method of cultivating plants in water and is used, among other things, for growing houseplants. The plant is held in place by an inert material—generally expanded clay balls— while the roots are immersed in water.

■ The hydroculture technique

To grow plants in water you will need a special type of container, usually one consisting of an outer, watertight pot into which the water is poured, and an

▲ Hydroculture is a technique that allows you to combine the functional with the attractive.

■ The advantages of hydroculture

Although not commonly seen in our homes, hydroculture has its benefits:

—less frequent watering. Water and plant food are required less often than in traditional cultivation methods. There is no danger of overwatering or under-watering as the reservoir gauge makes it easy to maintain the correct level;

Plectranthus oertendahlii ▼

—mature plants almost never need repotting. Young plants of course require potting on a number of times to keep pace with their growth, but once they have reached their "adult" size they can remain in the same container for several years. Unlike traditional methods of cultivation, with hydroculture the nutrient reserves are never exhausted nor is there the loss of mass that occurs with traditional growing mediums;

—hydroculture is clean—there is no soil, no water spillage— which can be a great advantage in offices and entrance halls, for example.

■ Some words of advice

However, hydroculture may not be the ideal solution in all circumstances. It isn't suitable for plants that require a definite period of winter rest, for

▲ *Schefflera elegantissima*

◄ *Tradescantia fluminensis* "Variegata"

plants that require limited watering such as cactuses, nor for many flowering plants as it is not possible to vary the amount of water given.

Hydroculture is therefore best reserved for plants that require more or less constant growing conditions throughout the year, like many foliage plants that are native to the tropics—ficus, schefflera, philodendron, pothos, and many others—and certain flowering plants such as saintpaulia.

Don't confuse water reservoir tanks with hydroculture: water reservoirs may allow you to water less frequently but the plants growing in these containers are rooted in an ordinary growing medium.

PROPAGATION

How can you obtain several plants from a single plant? Sometimes it's child's play—for example, with water rooted cuttings—but it can also be more of a challenge. Whatever the case, it's always interesting to try your hand at propagation.

■ The different methods

There are several ways of propagating plants. With vegetative propagation you can reproduce a plant by using one of its parts: leaf, stem, offset, or plantlet. The principal techniques of vegetative propagation used for houseplants are cuttings, division, and layering.

Sexual propagation is done by sowing seeds. It is a process rarely attempted by amateurs as it requires a lot of time and patience to follow through the different phases from germination to maturity successfully. Furthermore, when using seed, it's not possible to reproduce an identical plant.

▼ *Vriesea* "Tiffany"

It is, however, interesting to attempt the seed propagation of certain flowering and foliage plants, and also to experiment with growing plants grown from exotic fruit you have bought to eat.

■ Cuttings

This is definitely the easiest method of propagation to try and is suitable for a large number of houseplants.

Cuttings are most often taken from the growing tips of the stem (terminal cuttings) but also from sections of fleshy stem (as with dracaenas), leaves, or pieces of leaf (as with saintpaulias and certain begonias).

Cyperus involucratus ▼

The best time of year to take cuttings is naturally in spring or early summer when the plants are in vigorous growth, as the cuttings will have time to root and develop before winter, which is a time of limited growth, even indoors. However, some vigorous species, such as impatiens, hypoestes, plectranthus, papyrus, and others, can be rooted from cuttings at any time of year.

ROOTING IN WATER

1. Remove young shoots with the aid of a sharp knife.

2. Fill a glass with water and put a few pieces of wood charcoal in the bottom. Cover the top of the glass with aluminum foil or cling film and then make some holes through which you will insert the cuttings.

3. Insert a number of cuttings. Check the water level regularly.

Taking cuttings

Take your cuttings from healthy, vigorous plants. Terminal cuttings are taken from the ends of the stem and are usually 3 to 4 inches (7 to 10 cm) long. Cut the shoot just above a bud eye (the point of attachment of a leaf or bud). Then prepare the cuttings for rooting. Cut the shoot again just below the point where a leaf or pair of leaves are attached (as this is where roots form most easily) and remove any lower leaves.

To encourage large-leaved species to root, it is advisable to remove half the leaves on your cutting, as this will prevent it losing so much water through evaporation.

Rooting in water

Many species can be rooted quite simply in water by putting the lower end of the cutting in a small vase or glass of water. Put a piece of wood charcoal in the bottom of the container to keep the water clean, and refresh the water regularly.

To put several cuttings in a single glass or jar without them dropping down into the water, cover the container with aluminum foil or cling film, make holes in this, and insert the cuttings through the holes.

Many species root easily in water, including: papyrus, saintpaulia (leaf cuttings), tradescantia, cissus, pothos, hypoestes, etc.

Rooting in compost

Houseplants that are easy to propagate can be planted in ordinary compost or, better still, in special rooting or cutting compost. A mixture made of equal parts of sand and peat is also suitable. Push the bottom end of the cutting 1 to 1½ inches (3 to 4 cm) down into the compost (in a small pot, tray, or propagator). Firm down around the base of the cutting and water just enough to make the compost moist.

To promote the rooting of woody stem cuttings—which can be more difficult—dip the bottom end of the cutting in hormone rooting powder. After a few weeks (usually one to four weeks), the roots will begin to form. When they are sufficiently developed, the cutting can be repotted into a larger pot, using a suitable compost.

▼ *Tradescantia zebrina*

Rooting cuttings under cover

Cuttings taken from soft-leaved tropical species are liable to lose a lot of water through evaporation before roots capable of absorbing water from the compost have formed. To prevent such cuttings drying out they should be placed under cover, for example, in a propagator where a warm, humid atmosphere can be maintained, or, more simply, by covering the pot with a transparent plastic bag. Small sticks or stakes can be used to lift the plastic away from the cutting and an elastic band placed around the pot will hold the plastic firmly closed and in place.

Place the pot or propagator in a warm position but out of direct sunlight.

Ventilate from time to time and remove the transparent cover as soon as the cuttings show signs of growth (i.e. new leaves begin to appear).

Leaf cuttings

Some plants can be rooted directly from their leaves (either whole leaves or cut into sections). This applies to saintpaulia, some begonias, streptocarpus, and sansevieria.

▲ *Saintpaulia ionantha*

Select a mature, healthy leaf, including the leaf stalk, and insert this into special cutting compost. After a few weeks the leaf will produce plantlets at the base of the leaf stalk. Once these have grown large enough roots, they can be removed from the mother plant and transplanted. Begonia leaves can also be slit or cut into sections and placed directly on the surface of the cutting compost. Use bobby pins to hold them against the surface. Plantlets will form at the point of incision.

You can also root leaves with long stalks, such as saintpaulia, in water: fill a container with water (glass, jam jar, glass yogurt pot, etc.) and cover it with aluminum foil. Make a small hole in the top and insert the leaf stalk through it. You will be able to see the roots as they develop.

■ Root division

Some plants form separate clumps of leaves: this is true of aspidistras, marantas, and many other plants. To propagate these, you simply need to remove them from the pot and then divide up the root ball, either by pulling apart gently at the point of division or by cutting through with a sharp knife,

ROOT DIVISION

1. Take the plant out of its pot and remove some of the compost.

2. With your fingers, separate the root ball into several pieces by pulling apart gently where the roots divide.

3. Pot up each piece individually.

making sure that each portion of leaves has a sufficient quantity of roots. Then repot each piece individually, taking care not to damage the roots.

■ Offset propagation

Some plants spontaneously produce offsets which can be removed with a sharp knife and transplanted into individual pots. Most bromeliads are propagated by this method, as well as certain succulents and cactuses. Offsets should not be removed until they are well developed and have reached a good size, which varies from 2 to 4 inches (5 to 10 cm) approximately, according to the species. There's no precise rule; it's really a matter of personal judgment.

■ Layering

Layering is a propagation method that is used relatively little with houseplants. But although it is a technique that takes time, it is easy to do and suitable for a certain number of creeping, climbing, and trailing plants. Air layering is a special technique used primarily for renewing plants with bare stems.

Taking a stem cutting from a small-leaved ivy ▲

Simple layering

This is just a matter of holding a piece of soft stem down against the surface of the compost until the stem begins to root on contact with the soil. The stem is then cut free from the mother plant and the young plant allowed to grow away.

PLANTS SUITABLE FOR SIMPLE LAYERING

Cissus
Ivy
Creeping fig
Columnea
Pothos
Climbing philodendron
Plectranthus

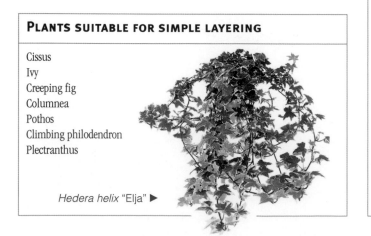

Hedera helix "Elja" ▶

To encourage root formation at a certain point along the stem, fold it back to slow down sap circulation or make a cut on the lower surface.

Choose young, vigorous stems and remember that the best time to try this is spring or early summer.

Fill one or more pots with ordinary compost and hold the stem against the surface, or slightly below it, with a piece of curved wire, then firm down. Water lightly until new leaves begin to appear, which is a sign that the layered stem has rooted. Then cut away the section of stem attached to the mother plant at the base.

Air layering

The aim here is to encourage a bare, leggy stem to put out roots higher up so that it can be cut at a point below the new roots and a "rejuvenated" plant with more abundant foliage produced.

Before beginning, check the state of the plant—it should be healthy and free from parasites.

—With a sharp knife, make a cut in the stem at the desired point at an upward angle (approximately 4 inches (10 cm) below the lower leaves of the bare stem) and about half the width of the stem. If necessary, wipe away any milky sap that emerges from the cut and apply hormone rooting powder to the wound with a small brush.

—Fix a transparent plastic sleeve (approximately 12 by 6–10 inches (30 by 15–20 cm) under the cut; hold this in place with a tie and fill it with peat or damp sphagnum moss.

—Close the upper part of the sleeve, above the cut, but not so tightly as to damage the stem. This will give the wound a damp environment that will promote root formation. Open the sleeve from time to time to moisten the peat or moss, which must not be allowed to dry out.

—After about two months, roots will appear inside the plastic sleeve. Wait until they are well developed and then cut away the leggy part of the stem just below the sleeve. Open up the plastic and carefully transplant the small root ball. Support the plant with a stake until it is firmly established in the pot.

PLANTS SUITABLE FOR AIR LAYERING

Rubber plant and other large-leaved ficus
Dragon tree
Monstera
Philodendron
Croton
Cordyline
Dieffenbachia
Schefflera

Codiaeum variegatum ▶

Plant health

Generally speaking, the parasites and diseases that affect houseplants are relatively few but capable of developing on many different plant species. If you learn to identify them you will often be able to make an accurate diagnosis of the problem. But remember that withered or yellow leaves and bud drop are not always a sign of attack by parasites or disease. Poor growing conditions can be the cause (overwatering, insufficient light, etc.).

PRINCIPAL PARASITES

Of the parasites that pose a threat to our plants, there are three that take the prize for determination and effort: aphids, scale bugs, and red spider mites.

■ Aphids·

Symptoms: green or black, and well known to gardeners. These prolific pests suck the sap from plants and weaken them. Leaves, shoots, and flower buds become deformed and are covered with a sticky honeydew, often followed by the fumagin fungus (sooty mold). They generally originate in the yard.

Remedy: remove the worst-affected shoots and spray the plant with a strong jet of water (if the plant is strong enough) to dislodge the aphids. If these measures are not enough, use an aphid-specific insecticide and repeat the treatment every eight to ten days.

Aphids ▲

■ Scale bugs

Symptoms: another common parasite, not always easy to spot. These are small, sap-sucking bugs concealed beneath a waxy, brown shell (hence the name "scale bug"). Scale bugs generally congregate on stems, on the underside of leaves, and along the veins. Leaves become sticky and then turn yellow.

Remedy: if they are small in number, scale bugs can be removed by scratching them off with your fingernail or a Q-tip dipped in 90% alcohol. In cases of bad infestation, treat the plant with an appropriate insecticide.

Scale bugs ▼

■ Mealy bugs

Symptoms: these small, sap-sucking bugs congregate at the base of leaves in small, whitish, downy clusters. They suck the sap and weaken the plant; the leaves become sticky.

Remedy: as for scale bugs.

■ Red spider mites

Symptoms: these tiny, sap-sucking acarines weave fine webs between and under the leaves. The leaves are covered in fine spots, become pale and yellow, and eventually drop.

Remedy: place the plant in a warm, dry atmosphere, particularly if it is winter, and one that is favorable to its development. Increase air humidity and spray regularly with water. Treat with an acaricide if necessary.

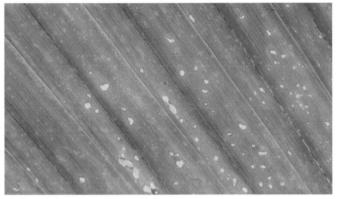

Red spider mites ▲

■ Whitefly

Symptoms: whitefly or aleurodes are tiny bugs that can be found on the underside of leaves and fly off in clouds when the foliage is disturbed. They lay numerous, greenish larvae on the underside of the leaves.

Remedy: a very common pest in greenhouses, whitefly are difficult to eliminate. Use repeated insecticide treatment, approximately every eight to ten days and, if necessary, change the product you use (i.e. the active ingredient) to prevent them becoming resistant.

Whitefly ▼

■ Thrips

Symptoms: these small, slender bugs are also commonly found on greenhouse plants. They are sap suckers. Leaves that have been attacked become covered in grayish marks, then become dry and eventually drop.

Remedy: shower the foliage to remove thrips, or treat with insecticide.

DISEASES

These are mainly caused by funguses, which tend to develop in a moist, cool atmosphere.

■ Oidium

Symptoms: oidium can be found in the form of a whitish or grayish powdery deposit on and under the leaves, and possibly also on the flowers. The conditions that encourage its development are humidity, irregular watering, and sudden drops in temperature.

Remedy: rectify the growing conditions and treat with an appropriate fungicide.

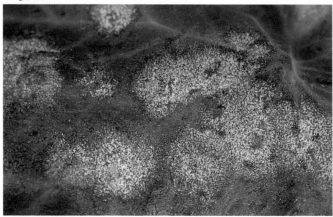

Powdery mildew on a begonia. ▲

■ Botrytis or gray mold

Symptoms: downy, gray marks on the flowers, leaves, and stems. This fungus is found mainly in a humid atmosphere lacking in ventilation.

Remedy: reduce the humidity in the air, avoid wetting the foliage, and increase light and ventilation. Cut off affected parts and treat with a fungicide.

■ Fumagin

Symptoms: the leaves become covered in a fine, blackish, powdery deposit, similar to soot. This fungus develops on the sticky honeydew secreted by sap-sucking parasites (aphids, scale bugs, etc.).

Remedy: clean the leaves with warm water, remove the most affected leaves, and hunt down the parasites that are responsible for the sticky secretions.

■ Neck rot

Symptoms: the base of the stems and then the roots rot and become viscous. The whole plant collapses.

Remedy: it is possible to save the plant if this disease is spotted quickly. Remove any rotten parts, treat with fungicide, and reduce watering. The plant can later be repotted in a healthy, well-drained compost.

PRODUCTS FOR TREATING HOUSEPLANTS

These are often multi-purpose, broad spectrum sprays, combining fungicide, acaricide, and insecticide. Insecticide (or insecticide + plant food) sticks are also available; these are pushed down into the growing medium. These products usually work on contact and are not very effective against scale bugs, which are protected by their shells. To combat these, a systemic product is needed as this is absorbed and diffused throughout the plant.

■ Treating your plants

If possible, take your plants outside into the yard or on to a balcony on a calm, wind-free day.

Follow the manufacturer's instructions carefully, in particular the spraying distance and frequency of treatment.

Wear gloves; do not stand "downwind" or you risk inhaling the products you are using; and of course, keep children, pets, and foodstuffs well away.

Be careful how you store plant treatment products: keep them out of the reach of children and animals, preferably in a locked closet, and make sure that the product labels remain legible.

CULTIVATION ERRORS

Leaves that are marked, yellow, or withering are not necessarily a sign that a plant has been attacked by parasites or disease. The cause could simply be a cultivation error—the plant has been placed in the wrong spot (too sunny, too dark, too drafty, etc.) or the regular care regime is wrong (overwatering or under-watering, overfeeding, etc.).

To diagnose the problem, examine the plant carefully to check for any parasites and to identify possible characteristic symptoms of plant disease. If you find nothing, turn to the appropriate plant profile, check the cultivation advice, and see whether the plant is in a suitable spot and if you are looking after it correctly.

■ Withering

This is generally due to a lack of water. To rehydrate the compost and the plant, stand the pot in water until the compost is soaked through. Then leave the plant to "recover" in a draft-free spot out of direct sunlight.

Always check how damp the compost is before watering, as withering can also be caused by an excess of water, for example, in the case of saintpaulias. If this is the problem, the saucer or planter should be emptied and the compost allowed to drain.

■ Bud drop and leaf drop

This can be due to overwatering, a sudden change in temperature, or drafts of cold air. With certain plants, such as Christmas cactuses, the buds will drop if the plants are moved after the flower buds have formed.

Globba winitii ▶

■ Dry, brown, or yellow leaf tips

This may be due to a lack of water at the roots, but is more often a sign of insufficient humidity. Increase the humidity around the plant.

■ Marks on the leaves

White or dull marks are the result of water splashing on the leaves, followed by exposure to sunlight. The magnifying effect of the water droplets can cause occasional burning. In the case of shade-loving plants, marks such as these could also be due to overexposure to light.

Yellow, dry, or corky stains are the result of a sudden drop in temperature, overwatering, or possibly a combination of the two.

Irregular brown marks along the edges of leaves can be caused by overfeeding and/or overwatering.

■ Discolored leaves

If the veins remain green but the limb of the leaf becomes yellow, this indicates that the plant is being watered with water that is too hard. This problem occurs among plants sensitive to hard water (such as gardenias). Use an anti-chlorosis solution enriched with chelated iron, and be sure to water only with soft water. If the whole leaf is yellow, it could be due to lack of light. With variegated plants, insufficient light leads to the formation of new shoots with plain, green leaves.

▲ Chlorosis

■ Leaf drop

If this happens suddenly, it is almost certainly because the plant has suffered a shock: a sudden fall in temperature or prolonged exposure to cold, for example. Try to maintain a gentle, constant temperature. If leaf drop is more gradual and continues, the plant could be suffering from too much water at root level, or from insufficient light.

Note: if your plants lose a few leaves in fall or winter, don't worry; it's quite natural. These plants remain in leaf throughout the year and this is how they renew their foliage.

A plant for every situation

The chart on page 66 takes account of the many different circumstances in which we live our daily lives and suggests a selection of plants suitable for each of these situations. By using the chart you can avoid making errors and quickly find one or more species of plant suited to your particular situation. You can then check the corresponding plant profile for more detailed information on the plant that interests you.

WHICH OF THESE DESCRIBES YOUR SITUATION?

■ You are a novice with plants

Plants are complex, living organisms with different needs: some are adaptable and undemanding, and can tolerate a few mistakes; others are more fussy, will not tolerate mistakes and require a specific care regime—so plant novices are well advised to choose with care and not take on just any species of plant!

To help you choose, plants have been classified according to their ease of cultivation: easy (E), quite easy (M), and more demanding (D). So, if you are inexperienced and have a limited amount of time available, choose "easy" plants. If later you find yourself with more time and have developed a genuine interest in plants, you could try some of the "quite easy" plants and then the "more demanding" ones. You may gradually discover that you have a real talent for growing plants—the famous "green fingers"—and then you will be faced with a new problem—lack of space!

▲ *Acalypha hispida*

This classification is of course relative and you may find that a plant described as "more demanding" is easy to grow, simply because you have found it exactly the right spot and established the correct watering regime.

Always remember that if a plant is not happy in your home, it doesn't necessarily mean that you don't have a gift for growing plants; it's probably just that certain factors (air, sun, heat) don't suit it.

Begonia eliator ▼

■ Lack of light

Light is essential for plants to survive as it allows them to synthesize the nutrients they need in order to grow. It is important to remember that light intensity decreases very quickly as soon as you move away from the light source. But not everyone is fortunate enough to have a large, brightly-lit picture window. So what can you do if your apartment only has small, poorly-lit windows? What plants should you choose for a darkish corner of the room?

Bear in mind that while certain accommodating plants tolerate low levels of light, no plant can survive in a spot that is too dark! When a plant lacks light it begins to lose its color, then puts out spindly shoots that grow long in search of the light they need.

Adiantum raddianum ▼

If this is the situation in which you find yourself, choose plants that are happy with a limited amount of light. Opt for green foliage plants rather than variegated forms which require a lot of light. Also consider using a few tricks that will help you make the most of the light you have available:

—place your plants as close to the window as possible; avoid using blinds or net curtains;

—remember to turn your plants around regularly so that they receive an even amount of light on all sides, as this will help them grow in a uniform manner;

x Fatshedera lizei ▶

—white walls give off more light than walls covered in wallpaper or light-absorbent colors;

—provide some extra lighting, especially in winter. You can use the "daylight" bulbs or tubes available in garden centers; the light these produce is similar to natural light.

■ Lack of space

Apartments and modern houses make maximum use of the available floor area and it is often difficult to find a place for your favorite plants in a living room where family, furniture, and pets are competing for space.

If this is your situation, don't despair! You can choose small species that will not grow inconsiderately large. There is a wide range of modestly sized plants whose attractions lie in the forms of their leaves, their colors, and their flowers.

Sageretia thea ▶

▲ *Kalanchoe blossfeldiana*

Some plants, such as schefflera, grow tall without growing wide. Other plants with a trailing habit can be grown as hanging plants. Small indoor greenhouses allow you to grow a large number of plants in a limited space.

If you are blessed with green fingers you could also try your hand at growing bonsais, obviously choosing species suitable for indoor cultivation.

Rather than scattering plants around the room, group them together: they will occupy less space and create their own beneficial microclimate.

If you really have no space, choose just one handsome, impressive specimen.

■ Heated conditions

In apartments that depend on a communal heating system, it is not always easy to regulate the temperature as you would like. In winter, temperatures in excess of 72° F (22° C) are considered too hot for plants. Such temperatures are often accompanied by very dry air because heating reduces air humidity considerably. Certain plants unsuitable for this situation include plants that dry out easily, such as ferns, and most flowering plants, as heat shortens their flowering period.

Some species that are native to hot countries enjoy heat, but it is almost always necessary to increase humidity levels by placing evaporation humidifiers on radiators or by installing an air humidifier.

Don't place pots directly on the ground if there are underfloor heating pipes. Place pots on wooden blocks or on inverted saucers to keep them out of contact with the floor.

Calathea makoyana ▶

Yucca rostrata ▶

Howea forsteriana ▲

Ananas comosus "Variegatus" ▼

Refrain from putting plants high up on shelves or in hanging baskets: the air will be even hotter nearer the ceiling.

■ Lack of time

There is no point in pretending—if you keep plants you must allow a certain amount of time for looking after them and maintaining them. But if you have very little time, don't let this stop you from enjoying the pleasures of gardening. Just choose your plants wisely and learn to organize yourself.

Of the various tasks associated with plant care, watering is the one that comes around most often. By choosing species that require less watering you will reduce the time you have to spend looking after your plants.

Group your plants together: they will be easier to look after, and will create their own, humid microclimate. Avoid small plants in small pots (except for cactuses!) as they require almost daily watering—try containers with water reservoirs. Use a large watering can to avoid repeat trips to the faucet.

■ Plants to avoid if you have young children or animals

Young children adore plants, but as their discovery of the world around them involves touching and tasting, certain plants are best avoided. This is also true of some pets, whose curiosity and greediness may result in them breaking the branches of your plants or chewing tender leaves.

Plants can be dangerous in different ways. There are some that can be harmful to young skin or eyes because of their shape and appearance; these include yuccas, certain palms, cactuses, and some euphorbias. And there are others that contain toxic substances or allergens, such as dieffenbachia and aglaonema.

◀ *Dieffenbachia* "Excellent"

◀ *Beaucarnea recurvata*

If a child ingests a dangerous plant, do not try to deal with this yourself. Telephone your regional or local poisons center immediately and tell them the name of the plant, or describe it as precisely as possible.

Some plants are particularly attractive to cats, who have a strong tendency to confuse the leaves of papyrus or elephant's foot with catmint. Cats also have the annoying habit of sharpening their claws on plants with trunks, such as yuccas and dragon trees.

■ Plants that children will find interesting

If you like plants and you have children, you will probably want to share your passion with them. Children are curious and often nature-loving, and will adore having their own plants.

Encourage them to plant fruit pips or stones and to watch them as they germinate. Avocados, mangos, lychees, lemons, and oranges offer plenty of potential and germinate quickly enough for children not to lose interest.

Solenostemon scutellarioides ▶

Some rather strange plants are also fascinating for children. These include the sensitive plant whose leaves close up when lightly touched; pebble plants—strange succulents that look like small, grayish pebbles; and carnivorous plants, such as the fly trap, which can be fed on bugs.

Lithops ▲

can achieve very effective decorative results that can be just as striking as a plant in bloom. This is true, for example, of caladiums and crotons.

You can also experiment with the texture of the leaves—some smooth and fine, some thick, crinkled, velvety, or waxy, some mat, some glossy—as well as with their shape.

Children will also enjoy watching the roots of hyacinths while they grow in transparent glass vases filled with water and the rapid growth of amaryllis flower-scapes.

You could also teach them how to root cuttings in water, which is very easy with certain plants such as tradescantia.

Codiaeum variegatum ▲

■ You like flowering plants

The advantage of flowering plants over a bunch of cut flowers is that they often last for several weeks and sometimes for much of the year. If properly cared for they will even flower again, year after year.

However, it is important to know that some plants are annuals and should be discarded after flowering. This is the case with *Begonia eliator* hybrids, primulas, calceolarias, hyacinths, and narcissi.

Many plants do not like heat and will flower for far longer in a cool room. The requirements of flowering plants in terms of light, watering, and feeding can be very different from those of ornamental foliage plants. It is advisable to cut back on watering for a while after flowering to encourage the plant to have a period of rest. To promote flowering, use a plant food low in nitrogen and high in potassium. Some plants need to overwinter in the cold to produce flower buds.

Hippeastrum "Wonderland" ▶

■ You like plants with colored foliage

Houseplants are cultivated for their foliage almost more often than for their flowers. Their leaves can be plain green, bringing a sense of calming greenness to a room, or strikingly colored, or even have multicolored variegation. By combining and blending these different possibilities, you

■ You want plants to grow in hanging containers

Foliage plants and flowering plants can also provide decorative shape. Species that are creepers or trailing in habit, and that can be grown as hanging plants, are excellent when space is at a premium (see pp. 28–29).

You can hang plants in a stairwell or a window recess, but always bear in mind what their light requirements are. You can bring life to an area of the room by hanging your plants at different heights. A wide range of containers suitable for hanging are available: plastic pots; wooden or wicker baskets; hanging baskets made of coated wire or macramé. Trailing plants can also simply be placed on a support (such as a shelf or column) at an elevated position.

Gibasis geniculata ▼

Don't forget that most plants require frequent watering, and make sure that your pots are securely supported as they can become very heavy after watering.

■ Plants for a cool conservatory

With its large, glass sides, a conservatory is paradise for many light-loving plants, especially in winter. But in our temperate climate it is essential to provide a heating system for the coldest months. It is the winter temperature that is used to describe the different types of conservatory.

If a conservatory is heated to the same temperature as the house, that is to say, to a temperature above 64° F (18° C), it is known as a warm conservatory. This is an ideal spot for tropical plants such as ficus, philodendrons, peperomias, bromeliads, etc. However, this requires considerable energy costs and your conservatory should be designed to limit this expense as far as possible.

It is almost better to have a cool or temperate conservatory where, in winter, the temperature remains at between 46° and 59° F (8° and 15° C). In addition to the savings on energy when compared with a warm conservatory, a cool conservatory also allows you to store a good number of plants that need a period of cool, winter rest.

A cold conservatory is only heated sufficiently to keep it frost-free. The temperature can drop as low as 33° or 37° F (1° or 2° C). It will provide

◄ *Peperomia obtusifolia* "Green Gold"

shelter for certain species that are borderline hardy and which grow outdoors in mediterranean regions, such as lemon trees.

Most of these plants enjoy spending the summer outside.

Generally speaking, you will need to pay attention to ventilation and provide a good shading system for the summer. In sunlight, the temperature in a conservatory can rise very quickly and may be damaging to plants.

■ Plants for your bathroom

Provided your bathroom has a window, it can often be an ideal place for plants as, with its warmth and humidity, it replicates greenhouse conditions. However, it is important to provide regular ventilation as an enclosed atmosphere is liable to give rise to disease.

Avoid large, cumbersome plants (unless your bathroom is very big, which is rarely the case in modern houses and apartments). Place your plants close to a window so that they enjoy maximum light.

Create focal points by grouping a small collection of delicate ferns in a pretty planter that matches the tiles, or in a wicker basket lined with plastic.

Keep flowering plants or plants with downy foliage away from the bath and the basin, to avoid them being splashed.

◄ *Citrus limon*

◄ *Syngonium* "Infra Red"

Latin Name	Page	Ease of Cultivation	Lack of light	Lack of space	Very heated conditions	Lack of time
Acalypha hispida	88	E				
Achimenes hybrids	89	●		●		
Acorus gramineus "Variegatus"	90	M		●		
Adenium obesum	91	M		●		●
Adiantum raddianum	92	●				
Aechmea fasciata	94	M				●
Aeonium	197	E		●	●	●
Aeschynanthus marmoratus	95	●				
Agave americana	96	E				●
Aglaonema commutatum	97	M	●			
Ajania	148	M				
Allamanda cathartica	98	●			●	
Alocasia macrorrhiza	99	●			●	
Aloe arborescens	101	E				●
Alpinia zerumbet "Variegata"	102	●				
Ampelopsis brevipedunculata "Variegata"	103	M				
Ananas comosus "Variegatus"	104	E			●	●
Anigozanthos	105	M				
Anthurium andraeanum	106	●				
Aphelandra squarrosa	108	●				
Araucaria heterophylla	109	M				
Ardisia crenata	110	M				
Aristolochia littoralis	111	●				
Ascocenda	362	●				
Asparagus densiflorus "Sprengeri"	112	E				

Unsuitable for young children or animals	Of interest to young children	Decorative flowers or fruit	Colorful or variegated foliage	Suitable for hanging	Suitable for a cool conservatory	Suitable for the bathroom
		●		●		●
		●		●		
			●			●
●		●			●	
						●
●		●	●			
			●		●	
		●	●	●		
●			●		●	
●			●			
		●			●	
		●				
●						●
		●			●	
		●	●			●
		●	●	●	●	
●		●	●			
		●			●	
●		●				
		●	●		●	
					●	
		●			●	
		●		●		●
		●		●		
●				●		

Latin Name	Page	Ease of Cultivation	Lack of Light	Lack of Space	Very Heated Conditions	Lack of Time
Aspidistra elatior	114	E	●			●
Asplenium nidus	115	M	●			
Bambusa vulgaris	116	M				
Beaucarnea recurvata	117	M				●
Begonia x hiemalis	118	E				
Begonia x rex-cultorum	120	M				
Billbergia x windii	122	M				
Blechnum gibbum	123	D				
Bouvardia	124	M				
Brachychiton rupestris	125	M				●
Brighamia insignis	126	M			●	
Browallia	127	M				
Brunfelsia pauciflora	128	M				
Caladium bicolor	129	D				
Calanthe	130	M				
Calathea crocata	133	M				
Calathea makoyana	134	D				
Calceolaria x herbeohybrida	134	M		●		
Callisia warszewicziana	135	M				
Callistemon citrinus	136	E				
Campanula isophylla	137	M		●		
Capsicum annuum	138	M				
Carex brunnea "Variegata"	139	E		●		
Caryota mitis	140	D				
Castanospermum australe	141	M				

Unsuitable for young children or animals	Of interest to young children	Decorative flowers or fruit	Colorful or variegated foliage	Suitable for hanging	Suitable for a cool conservatory	Suitable for the bathroom
			●			
				●		●
					●	
●						
		●			●	
			●			
		●		●		
						●
		●			●	
●		●			●	
		●			●	
●			●			
		●			●	
		●	●			●
			●			●
		●	●		●	
		●				
		●			●	
		●		●	●	
		●				
			●		●	
						●
					●	

Latin Name	Page	Ease of Cultivation	Lack of Light	Lack of Space	Very Heated Conditions	Lack of Time
Cattleya	142	D				
Ceropegia linearis ssp. woodii	143	M		●		●
Chamaedorea elegans	144	M				
Chlorophytum comosum "Vittatum"	145	E				●
Chrysalidocarpus lutescens	146	M			●	
Chrysanthemum hortorum	147	M				
Cissus rhombifolia	149	E	●			
Citrus limon	151	M				
Clerodendrum thomsoniae	154	D				
Clivia miniata	156	M				
Clusia rosea	157	D			●	
Cocos nucifera	158	D			●	
Codiaeum variegatum	159	D			●	
Codonanthe	161	M		●		
Coffea arabica "Nana"	162	M				
Columnea	163	D				
Cordyline terminalis	165	M				
Corynocarpus laevigatus	167	M				
Crassula	168	E				●
Crocus	170	M				
Crossandra infundibuliformis	171	M			●	
Cryptanthus zonatus	172	M			●	
Ctenanthe	173	D				
Curcuma alismatifolia	174	E				
Cycas revoluta	175	M				●

Unsuitable for young children or animals	Of interest to young children	Decorative flowers or fruit	Colorful or variegated foliage	Suitable for hanging	Suitable for a cool conservatory	Suitable for the bathroom
		●				
			●	●	●	
						●
	●		●	●	●	
		●			●	
				●	●	
		●			●	
		●			●	
		●			●	
						●
						●
●			●			●
		●		●		
						●
		●		●		
			●			
					●	
					●	
		●				
		●				●
			●			●
			●			●
		●			●	
					●	

Latin Name	Page	Ease of Cultivation	Lack of Light	Lack of Space	Very Heated Conditions	Lack of Time
Cyclamen persicum hybrids	176	M		●		
Cymbidium	177	D				
Cyperus involucratus	178	E				●
Dalechampia	180	M				
Davallia mariesii	181	M				
Dendrobium	182	D				
Dichorisandra thyrsiflora	184	D				
Dicksonia	185	D				
Didymochlaena truncatula	186	M	●			
Dieffenbachia	187	M	●		●	
Dionaea muscipula	189	D		●		
Dischidia pectenoides	190	D				
Dracaena	191	E				●
Drosera	194	D				
Duchesnea indica	195	M		●		
Echeveria	196	M		●		●
Echinocactus grusonii	198	E		●		●
Epidendrum	199	D				
Epipremnum aureum	200	M				
Episcia cupreata	202	D		●	●	
Erica x hiemalis	203	M				
Euanthe	362	D				
Eucharis	204	M				
Euphorbia milii	205	E				●
Euphorbia pulcherrima	207	D				

Unsuitable for young children or animals	Of interest to young children	Decorative flowers or fruit	Colorful or variegated foliage	Suitable for hanging	Suitable for a cool conservatory	Suitable for the bathroom
		●	●		●	
		●			●	
	●				●	●
		●				
				●		●
		●		●		
		●				●
					●	
						●
●			●			●
	●	●			●	
		●		●		●
			●			
	●	●	●		●	
	●	●		●		
		●			●	
●		●			●	
		●		●		
	●		●	●		●
		●	●	●		
		●			●	
		●		●		
		●			●	
●		●				
●		●				

Latin Name	Page	Ease of Cultivation	Lack of light	Lack of space	Very heated conditions	Lack of time
Eustoma	208	D		●		
Euterpe edulis	209	M	●			
Exacum affine	210	M		●		
x *Fatshedera lizei*	212	E	●			
Fatsia japonica	211	M				
Ficus benjamina	213	E				●
Ficus deltoidea	215	E				
Ficus elastica	216	E				●
Ficus lyrata	218	E				
Ficus pumila	219	M	●	●		
Fittonia	220	D	●	●		
Fortunella (and x *citrofortunella*)	153	M				
Gardenia augusta	221	D				
Gibasis	358	M				●
Globba winitii	222	D				
Gloriosa superba "Rothschildiana"	223	D				
Gloxinia sylvatica	224	D		●		
Grevillea robusta	225	M				
Guzmania	226	M			●	
Gymnocalycium	228	E		●		●
Gynura aurantiaca	229	M				
Hedera helix	230	E				
Heliconia	232	D				
Hemigraphis	233	M			●	
Hemionitis	234	D		●		

Unsuitable for young children or animals	Of interest to young children	Decorative flowers or fruit	Colorful or variegated foliage	Suitable for hanging	Suitable for a cool conservatory	Suitable for the bathroom
		●				
						●
		●				
			●			
			●		●	
			●			
●		●				●
						●
			●	●		●
			●			●
		●			●	
		●			●	
	●		●	●		
		●				●
●		●				
		●				
					●	
		●				
		●			●	
			●	●		
●			●	●	●	
		●				
			●			●
						●

Latin Name	Page	Ease of Cultivation	Lack of Light	Lack of Space	Very Heated Conditions	Lack of Time
Hibiscus	235	M				
Hippeastrum	237	M				
Howea forsteriana	238	E				
Hoya carnosa	239	M				
Hyacinthus orientalis hybrids	240	M		●		
Hydrangea macrophylla	242	D				
Hypoestes phyllostachya	243	M		●		
Impatiens x novae-guinea	244	E				
Ixora coccinea	246	D				
Jasminum polyanthum	247	M				
Jatropha podagrica	248	M				
Juncus effusus "Spiralis"	249	M				
Justicia brandegeana	250	M				
Kalanchoe	251	E				●
Kalanchoe blossfeldiana	253	E		●		●
Kohleria amabilis	254	D				
Lachenalia	255	D		●		
Leea guineensis "Burgundy"	256	M			●	
Licuala grandis	257	D				
Lithops	258	E		●		●
Livistona	259	M				
Ludisia	260	D	●			
Mandevilla	261	D				
Maranta	263	M				
Masdevallia	264	D		●		

Unsuitable for young children or animals	Of interest to young children	Decorative flowers or fruit	Colorful or variegated foliage	Suitable for hanging	Suitable for a cool conservatory	Suitable for the bathroom
		●			●	
●		●				
		●		●	●	
	●	●			●	
		●			●	
			●			●
	●	●		●		
		●				●
		●		●	●	
●		●				
	●				●	●
		●			●	
	●				●	
		●				
		●		●		
		●			●	
						●
						●
	●	●	●		●	
						●
		●	●			
●		●			●	
			●	●		●
		●				●

Latin Name	Page	Ease of Cultivation	Lack of light	Lack of space	Very heated conditions	Lack of time
Medinilla magnifica	265	D				
Megaskepasma	324	M				
Metrosideros	136	E				
Mikania	266	M				
Miltoniopsis	267	D				
Monstera deliciosa	300	M			●	
Muehlenbeckia	268	M				
Murraya	269	D				
Musa	270	D			●	
Muscari	170	M		●		
Narcissus	241	M		●		
Nematanthus gregarius	271	M				
Neoregelia carolinae "Tricolor"	272	M			●	
Nepenthes	273	D				
Nephrolepis exaltata	275	M	●			
Nertera granadensis	276	M		●		
Nidularium billbergioides	277	M			●	
Odontoglossum	278	D				
Oncidium	280	M				
Opuntia	281	E				●
Oxalis triangularis	282	M		●		
Pachira aquatica	283	M			●	
Pachypodium lamerei	284	M				●
Pachystachys lutea	285	M				
Palisota	286	D			●	

Unsuitable for young children or animals	Of interest to young children	Decorative flowers or fruit	Colorful or variegated foliage	Suitable for hanging	Suitable for a cool conservatory	Suitable for the bathroom
		●		●		
		●				
		●			●	
			●	●	●	
		●				
				●	●	
		●				
						●
	●	●			●	
	●	●			●	
		●		●	●	
		●	●			
	●		●	●		
				●		●
		●			●	
		●	●			
		●				
		●		●		
●					●	
		●	●			
					●	
		●				
		●	●			●

Latin Name	Page	Ease of Cultivation	Lack of Light	Lack of Space	Very Heated Conditions	Lack of Time
Pandanus veitchii	287	M				
Paphiopedilum	288	D				
Pavonia multiflora	290	D				
Pellaea	291	E	●	●		
Pellionia repens	292	D				
Pentas lanceolata	293	D				
Peperomia obtusifolia	294	M		●		●
Phalaenopsis	296	M				
Philodendron	298	E			●	
Phlebodium aureum	301	M				
Phoenix canariensis	302	M				
Pilea cadierei	303	E	●			
Pinguicula	305	D		●		
Platycerium	306	M				
Plectranthus	307	E				
Pogonatherum paniceum	308	D		●		
Polyscias	309	D			●	
Polystichum falcatum	310	E	●			
Portulacaria afra	311	E				●
Primula obconica	312	M		●		
Pseuderanthemum	314	D				
Pteris	315	M	●	●		
Radermachera sinica	317	E				
Rhapis	318	M				
Rhipsalidopsis gaertneri	319	M				

Unsuitable for young children or animals	Of interest to young children	Decorative flowers or fruit	Colorful or variegated foliage	Suitable for hanging	Suitable for a cool conservatory	Suitable for the bathroom
●			●			
		●				
		●				
				●		●
			●	●		●
		●			●	
		●	●			
		●				
			●			
			●			●
					●	
	●		●			
	●	●				
				●		●
	●		●	●	●	
						●
			●			●
					●	
					●	
●		●			●	
		●	●			●
						●
						●
			●		●	●
		●		●		

Latin Name	Page	Ease of Cultivation	Lack of Light	Lack of Space	Very Heated Conditions	Lack of Time
Rhipsalis	320	M				
Rhododendron	321	M				
Rosa	323	M				
Ruellia	324	M				
Saintpaulia	325	E		●		
Sanchezia	314	D				
Sansevieria	326	E			●	●
Sarracenia	328	D				
Saxifraga stolonifera	329	M				
Schefflera arboricola	330	E				
Schefflera elegantissima	332	M			●	
Schlumbergera hybrids	333	M				
Scindapsus	201	M				
Scirpus cernuus	334	M				
Scutellaria costaricana	335	D		●		
Sedum	336	M				●
Selaginella	337	D	●	●		
Senecio	338	M				●
Siderasis fuscata	339	D		●		
Sinningia	340	D				
Soleirolia soleirolii	342	M				
Sparmannia africana	343	M				
Spatiphyllum	344	M				
Stephanotis floribunda	345	D				
Streptocarpus	346	M				

Unsuitable for young children or animals	Of interest to young children	Decorative flowers or fruit	Colorful or variegated foliage	Suitable for hanging	Suitable for a cool conservatory	Suitable for the bathroom
		●		●		
		●			●	
		●			●	
		●				
	●	●				
		●	●			●
			●			
●			●		●	
	●		●	●	●	
			●			
			●			●
		●		●		
			●	●		●
				●		
		●				
				●	●	
			●			●
					●	
		●	●			●
		●				
			●	●	●	
					●	
●		●				
		●		●	●	
		●		●		

Latin Name	Page	Ease of Cultivation	Lack of Light	Lack of Space	Very Heated Conditions	Lack of Time
Strobilanthes	314	D				
Stromanthe sanguinea	348	D			●	
Syngonanthus chrysanthus "Mikado"	349	D		●		
Syngonium podophyllum	350	E			●	
Tacca chantrieri	351	D			●	
Tetrastigma	150	M				
Thunbergia alata	352	M				
Tillandsia cyanea	354	M		●	●	
Tolmiea menziesii	356	M		●		
Tradescantia fluminensis	357	E				●
Tradescantia spathacea	359	E				
Tulipa	241	M		●		
Utricularia	360	D				
Vanda	361	D				
Vriesea splendens	363	M			●	
Yucca elephantipes	365	E				●
Zamioculcas zamiifolia	366	E				●
Zantedeschia aethiopica	367	E				
Zebrina pendula	358	E				
Zygopetalum	369	D				

Unsuitable for young children or animals	Of interest to young children	Decorative flowers or fruit	Colorful or variegated foliage	Suitable for hanging	Suitable for a cool conservatory	Suitable for the bathroom
		●	●			●
			●			●
		●				●
			●	●		●
		●				●
			●	●		
		●		●	●	
		●				●
	●			●	●	●
	●		●	●		
			●			
	●	●			●	
		●				
		●		●		
		●	●			
●		●			●	
		●			●	
			●	●		
		●			●	

PLANT PROFILES

Acalypha

A. hispida — Chenille plant, red-hot cat's tail

Decorative interest

This shrub is particularly decorative when young. It has large, oval, pointed, dark green leaves. From summer to fall, long, soft, reddish-purple catkins appear in the leaf axils. As it matures, the chenille plant becomes less compact. It is best to cut it back in the spring or replace it each year by taking cuttings.

Ease of cultivation

This plant is quite easy to grow in a room with plenty of light, but does require a high level of ambient humidity.

Propagation: take 3½ to 4 inch (7 to 10 cm) long lateral cuttings in spring. Root them under cover in a pot containing a moist mixture of equal parts peat and sand at 70° to 75° F (21° to 24° C).

● RELATED SPECIES AND VARIETIES

Acalypha wilkesiana is another species that has given rise to numerous hybrids with insignificant flowers but foliage in a diverse range of variegation and color, most often in shades of red, bronze, or brown.

TROUBLE SHOOTING

◆ The leaves become pale and dry: red spider mites thrive in warm, dry conditions. Increase the ambient humidity and spray the foliage more frequently. If necessary, treat with an acaricide.

CARING FOR YOUR PLANT

Watering and humidity: during the growing period, water your plant generously. Keep the compost moist but don't allow it to get too wet. In fall and winter, water less frequently. Keep the atmosphere humid by standing the pot on a bed of wet gravel and spray the leaves regularly with water.

Light: bright conditions, but avoid direct sunlight in spring and summer.

Feeding. in spring and summer, feed every two weeks with food for foliage plants.

Repotting and growing medium: repot in spring in ordinary compost.

Cultivation tip: if you want your plant to thrive from one year to the next, cut it hard back and repot it in early spring. Do not pinch out the tips of the shoots as they are naturally branching. In winter, keep your plant in a cool, bright spot at a temperature of 55° to 59° F (13° to 15° C).

Acalypha hispida ▶

▼ *Acalypha wilkesiana*

▼ *Acalypha hamiltonianum*

Achimenes

A. hybrids
Achimenes

Decorative interest

This perennial with a rhizomatous root structure and bushy habit produces mid green, dentate, downy, oval to lanceolate leaves, and open, trumpet-shaped flowers. This attractive plant, which is native to Mexico, was discovered by gardeners around the middle of the nineteenth century. At that time the plant in question was *Achimenes coccinea*, which was of little commercial value. The discovery of other new species led to the creation of numerous hybrids and the production of plants in a variety of colors. Achimenes flower in summer and the plants overwinter in the form of scaly rhizomes.

Associates well with… chlorophytums and, during the summer, combine with asparagus.

Ease of cultivation

Growing achimenes requires a certain amount of skill. Tropical in origin, they need a warm, humid environment during the summer but then require a period of winter rest during which the rhizomatous root system must be kept completely dry.

Propagation: each rhizome can produce up to six offsets. At the end of winter, when the plant is coming back into growth, remove these and plant each young rhizome up in a separate pot.

▼ *Achimenes* hybrids

TROUBLE SHOOTING

◆ Young shoots can be attacked by aphids. The leaves become sticky and deformed: treat your plant with a suitable insecticide.
◆ The leaves turn yellow and drop. A fine white webbing appears on their underside. Red spider mites thrive in warm, dry conditions. Increase the humidity around the plant by standing the pot on damp gravel (but avoid spraying water on the flowers). If necessary, treat your plant with an acaricide.

CARING FOR YOUR PLANT

Watering and humidity: water moderately in the early stages of growth, then more generously as the plant develops. Water less frequently after flowering has occurred and stop watering altogether when you notice the leaves are beginning to dry out. Maintain a high level of humidity during the flowering period.

Light: bright conditions during the growing period, but keep out of direct sunlight. Keep in semi-darkness during the rest period.

Feeding: feed every two weeks with food for flowering plants from bud formation to the end of flowering.

Repotting and growing medium: repot the rhizome at the end of winter in a light compost composed of peat and coarse sand; cover with about ¾ inch (1 to 2 cm) of compost and place the pot in a warm, light position. Gradually increase watering.

Cultivation tip: if you want your plant to flower again, place the rhizomes in dry peat and store in a cool place at a temperature of 53° to 58° F (12° to 14° C) during the winter and start them off again in February to March. When watering, use soft, tepid water. Never leave water standing in the saucer.

● **RELATED SPECIES AND VARIETIES**

A wide range of hybrids is available with a quite compact growth habit and colored blooms, such as "**Paul Arnold**" (dark purple-blue) and "**Little Beauty**" (dark pink). *Achimenes longiflora* "Ambroise Verschaffelt" produces white flowers with ornate purple-reddish veins and spots in the yellowish throat of the flower.

▼ Blue and red *Achimenes*

Acorus

A. gramineus **"Variegatus"**   Variegated Acorus

Decorative interest

The genus *Acorus* is a member of the arum family and includes two species of rhizomatous perennials that grow in damp soil or shallow water. Native to Asia, *Acorus gramineus* reaches a height of 8 to 16 inches (20 to 40 cm) and has fine, upright, strap-like leaves, similar to those of grasses. The variety "**Variegatus**" is prized for its pale green leaves with two pale cream striations. The green inflorescences are insignificant.

Ease of cultivation

The acorus is not a difficult plant. Originating in wetland areas, it requires a high level of humidity.

Propagation: divide the rhizomes in spring and replant them individually in a suitable growing medium immediately.

● **RELATED SPECIES AND VARIETIES**

Acorus gramineus "Ogon" has dark green foliage with paler green and creamy-yellow variegation.

TROUBLE SHOOTING

◆ The tips of the leaves become dry and yellow: increase the ambient humidity by standing the pot on a saucer filled with damp gravel and spray the foliage more often.

CARING FOR YOUR PLANT

Watering and humidity: the roots must never be allowed to dry out. Water generously and leave a little water standing in the saucer. Maintain a humid atmosphere around the pot.

Light: bright, filtered, or semi-shade conditions.

Feeding: in spring and summer, feed every two weeks with a weak dilution of plant food.

Repotting and growing medium: repot in spring, if the plant has outgrown the pot, using a peat-based compost.

Cultivation tip: the acorus is able to tolerate a wide range of temperatures, from around 40° to 68° F (5° to 20° C). Your plant will benefit from spending the summer outdoors.

▼ *Acorus gramineus* "Variegatus"

Acorus gramineus "Variegatus" ▼

Adenium

A. obesum   False baobab, desert rose, impala lily

Decorative interest

The false baobab is a succulent perennial that grows in the desert regions of Africa. The swollen base of the plant is bottle-shaped and can be partially underground. The bare branches carry oval, gray-green leaves at their tips. In summer, flat, bowl-shaped flowers appear, either singly or in clusters; they are red, pink, or white. When cultivated indoors, the false baobab rarely grows taller than 20 inches (50 cm).

Ease of cultivation

The false baobab does not pose any particular problems providing its cultivation requirements are met.
Propagation: grown from seed in spring at 68° to 72° F (20° to 22° C), or cuttings taken from non-flowering stems in summer, kept warm but not covered.

Worth remembering

The milky sap is toxic and can cause skin irritation.

Adenium obesum ▼

CARING FOR YOUR PLANT

Watering and humidity: water moderately once a week during the growing period. Reduce watering in the fall and keep the plant almost dry in winter.
Light: full sunlight.
Feeding: feed once a month in spring and summer with plant food for cactuses and succulents.
Repotting and growing medium: repot in spring every two years using compost for cactuses and succulents.
Cultivation tip: allow your plant a period of dry winter rest. Do not expose to temperatures below 55° to 59° F (13° to 15° C).

▼ *Adenium obesum*

TROUBLE SHOOTING

◆ Deformed, sticky leaves reveal the presence of aphids: treat with a suitable insecticide.

Adiantum

A. raddianum   Maidenhair fern
synonym: *Adiantum cuneatum*

Decorative interest

Maidenhair ferns differ from other ferns by their dark, filiform leaf stalks, which carry numerous leaflets, known as pinnules, which are often fan-shaped and have lightly scalloped edges. Native to Brazil, *Adiantum raddianum* is the most popular commercial species. The pale green fronds—upright when young— arch gracefully as they mature. They are composed of hundreds of small pinnules on blackish-purple stalks. This plant grows to 12 to 16 inches (30 to 40 cm) in height but is often broader in habit.

Associates well with... your maidenhair fern will combine well with other, full-leaved ferns such as *Asplenium nidus*.

Ease of cultivation

The maidenhair fern is quite a delicate plant and requires plenty of humidity; avoid drafts and keep out of full sunlight.

Propagation: rhizome division is an easier option than sowing spores. In March to April, remove the plant from its pot and divide the root ball into two or more pieces, depending on the size of the plant. Pot each section up individually in a mixture consisting of equal parts peat, leaf mold, good yard soil, and coarse sand.

Adiantum raddianum ▶

CARING FOR YOUR PLANT

Watering and humidity: water your plant daily in summer when the weather is hot, using soft water, but don't leave water standing in the saucer. Avoid letting the pot get too dry. Stand the pot on damp gravel to provide good ambient humidity.

Light: shade lightly with a blind or curtain. Do not expose to direct sunlight as this will burn the foliage.

Feeding: feed every three or four weeks in spring and summer with half strength food for foliage plants.

Repotting and growing medium: repot in spring, if the plant is too large for the pot, using a light, peaty compost.

Cultivation tip: during the summer months, spray daily. Be sure not to move your plant once it has become acclimatized to its position indoors.

● RELATED SPECIES AND VARIETIES

Adiantum capillus-veneris (Southern Maidenhair Fern, Venus Hair Fern) is a species that is hardy in the south and west of France. Elsewhere it is grown indoors. Its finely divided fronds are composed of fan-shaped pinnules. The glossy, black leaf stalk is often hairy at the base.

Adiantum raddianum "Fragrantissimum" has dense foliage and is strongly aromatic.

A. "Fritz-Luthii" forms large pale green fronds.

A. "Goldelse" is characterized by its golden-yellow pinnules.

A. tenerum can grow to over 3 feet (1 meter) in height. Its pale green, triangular fronds are heavily divided. Some varieties, such as "**Scutum Roseum**," have pinkish fronds when young.

TROUBLE SHOOTING

◆ All the leaves have dried out: immerse the whole plant in a bucket of slightly tepid water for a few hours. When you take it out, drain it and cut off all the fronds with a sharp pair of scissors. New green shoots should start to appear after a few days.

◆ The leaves shrivel and turn brown: the atmosphere is too dry. Stand the pot on a bed of gravel soaking in water and spray the foliage more frequently.

▲ *Adiantum tenerum* "Scutum Roseum"

◀ *Adiantum hispidulum*

Adiantum tenerum ▶

Aechmea

A. fasciata
synonym: *Billbergia rhodocyanea*

Decorative interest

The aechmea is part of the bromeliad family (like ananas, guzmania, and vriesea). This plant is characterized by the rosette formation of its usually tough leaves. Native to Brazil, *Aechmea fasciata* produces very open, gray-green rosettes of leaves edged with black spines. This creates a natural, central reservoir which, in the wild, collects rainwater. Once mature, that is to say, after three to four years, the plant produces a flower spike with pink bracts concealing small flowers that are blue at first, then turn red. The inflorescence remains decorative for several months.

Associates well with... other aechmeas. Group several species of aechmea together in a bowl without removing them from their individual pots. Fill the gaps with pine bark and moss.

Ease of cultivation

Aechmea fasciata is not a difficult plant to grow. Make sure that water is not left standing in the rosette in winter.

Propagation: remove the offsets that appear at the base of the plant when they are about a third or half as tall as the mother plant. Separate with a sharp knife as close to the base as possible and leave them to dry for one or two days before potting them up in a medium identical to that of the adult plant.

Worth remembering

Once they have produced their splendid inflorescence, aechmeas will not survive. You will have to wait for the young shoot that appears at the base of the plant to replace it and flower in its turn.

● RELATED SPECIES AND VARIETIES

There are other species of aechmea, though less common than *Aechmea fasciata*.

Aechmea chantinii (synonym: *Billbergia chantinii*) produces dark green leaves with silvery-white stripes and a long, orangey-red and yellow inflorescence.

Aechmea fulgens var. *discolor* produces an open rosette of broad leaves, olive green on top, and reddish-brown on the underside. The inflorescence has small, red and violet flowers that become completely red as they fade.

CARING FOR YOUR PLANT

Watering and humidity: water moderately once a week with soft water. Keep the rosette filled throughout the summer. Increase ambient humidity when the weather is hot.

Light: enjoys a bright spot but make sure it is sheltered from the heat of the midday sun.

Feeding: feed every two to three weeks in spring and summer with half strength food for flowering plants.

Repotting and growing medium: it is rarely necessary to repot aechmeas as the plant dies after flowering. Most aechmeas are happy in small pots. Pot up the young offsets that the mother plant puts out in spring in a lime-free mixture consisting of equal parts peat, well-rotted leaf mold, and ericaceous compost.

Cultivation tip: in the fall, reduce watering and stop filling the rosette. In winter, keep your aechmea reasonably warm at a temperature of 61° to 64° F (16° to 18° C).

◀ *Aechmea fasciata* ▶

TROUBLE SHOOTING

◆ The leaves turn brown, the base of the rosette shows signs of rotting: the plant has been over-watered. Cut off the affected leaves and reduce watering. Never leave water standing in the saucer.

Aeschynanthus

A. marmoratus   Aeschynanthus
synonym: *Aeschynanthus zebrinus*

Decorative interest
A native of Burma, Thailand, and Malaysia, aeschynanthus is a semi-creeper producing long, trailing stems with pale green, oval leaves, mottled with dark green on the upper side and reddish-purple on the underside. It produces greenish-yellow axillary flowers, flecked with dark brown. The flowers are short-lived but continue appearing for several weeks from summer to fall. Aeschynanthus are especially decorative when grown as hanging plants.

Ease of cultivation
This is quite a difficult plant to cultivate. Aeschynanthus need heat and humidity during the growing period but a short period of rest in winter at around 59° F (15° C) if they are to flower again.

Propagation: cuttings require heat and humidity. In spring take 4 inch (10 cm) terminal cuttings and plant them in a moist mixture of equal parts peat and sand. Grow under some cover at 70° to 73° F (21° to 23° C).

Worth remembering
Aeschynanthus do not like to be moved during the flowering period. Avoid buying a plant already heavily in bloom as the flowers are liable to drop prematurely.

● RELATED SPECIES AND VARIETIES
The different species of *Aeschynanthus* and their hybrid forms are cultivated for their trailing habit and flowers, which are usually in shades of scarlet to orange.

TROUBLE SHOOTING
◆ The young leaves are covered in aphids and become sticky: treat with a suitable insecticide.

CARING FOR YOUR PLANT
Watering and humidity: in summer, water your plant regularly to keep the compost permanently moist but don't allow it to get too wet. Reduce watering in winter, particularly during cool periods. Spray the leaves in hot weather.
Light: bright conditions. Place the plant near a window but keep out of direct sunlight.
Feeding: feed every two weeks in spring and summer with food for flowering plants.
Repotting and growing medium: repot every two or three years at the end of winter in a light, fibrous, peat-based compost.
Cultivation tip: keep your plant almost dry in winter and give it a period of rest in a cool place. Use tepid water for watering.

Aeschynanthus speciosus has opposed, dark green, fleshy, elliptical leaves. The tubular, bright orangey-red flowers with green calyxes appear in clusters of terminal inflorescences and are between 2 and 3 inches (5 and 7.5 cm) long.

A. pulcher has dark green, oval, slightly dentate leaves and scarlet flowers with greenish-yellow calyxes. *A. lobbianus* is similar but the calyx is the same color as the corolla.

Aeschynanthus "Rasta" ▼   *Aeschynanthus "Mona Lisa"* ▼

Aeschynanthus "Carina" ▼   Variegated *Aeschynanthus* ▼

◀ *Aeschynanthus lobbianus*

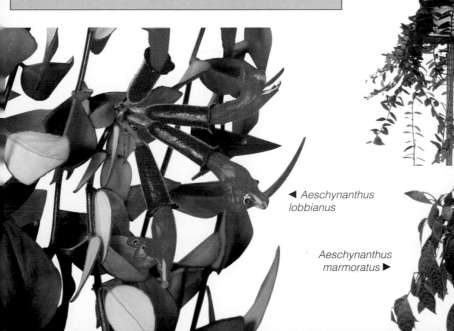
Aeschynanthus marmoratus ▶

Agave

A. americana   Agave

Decorative interest

Agaves produce succulent leaves in a rosette formation. The genus includes over 200 species, growing mainly in the desert regions of central America. *Agave americana* is a Mexican species that is very large when mature—between 9 and 13 feet (2 and 3 meters) across—and is widely naturalized on the Côte d'Azur. It is mainly young specimens that are used for indoor cultivation. The agave has bluish-green leaves and there are variegated varieties such as "**Mediopicta**," which has a broad central stripe, and "**Variegata**," whose leaves have creamy-yellow margins.

Ease of cultivation

Agaves do not present any particular difficulty, providing they are given maximum sunlight. Beware of overwatering.

Propagation: agaves can be increased by removing the offshoots when they are produced. They can also be grown from seed at 70° F (21° C) in a light growing medium.

● RELATED SPECIES AND VARIETIES

The smaller species are particularly suited to indoor cultivation. *Agave victoriae-reginae*, for example, forms a compact but quite open rosette of between 8 and 10 inches (20 and 25 cm) high. The leaves are dark green and triangular, with attractive white edges. They are not dentate but end in a very spiny tip.

A. parviflora is another small, decorative species with stiff, straight leaves edged with cottony filaments.

CARING FOR YOUR PLANT

Watering and humidity: water every week in summer and once a month in winter. Never pour water into the heart of the rosette. Agaves do not require a humid atmosphere.

Light: full sunlight.

Feeding: during the growing period, feed every three to four weeks with food for cactuses and succulents.

Repotting and growing medium: repot in spring every two or three years in ordinary compost with added coarse sand and a layer of gravel in the bottom of the pot to improve drainage.

Cultivation tip: agaves enjoy a period of winter rest in a cold or temperate greenhouse. If possible, move your agaves outdoors in full sunshine during the summer.

◄ *Agave americana* "Mediopicta"

Agave victoriae-reginae ▼

Agave potatorum ▼

Agave ferox ▼

Aglaonema

A. commutatum   Aglaonema

Decorative interest

Native to tropical Asia, aglaonemas have attractive variegated foliage. *Aglaonema commutatum* forms a clump of large, oblong, dark green leaves with silvery-gray or very pale green variegation, 12 to 16 inches (30 to 40 cm) tall. Mature plants sometimes flower, producing a rather dull inflorescence similar to that of arums.

Associates well with… other plants with decorative foliage such as philodendrons, crotons, and cordylines.

Ease of cultivation

Aglaonemas can be a little tricky to cultivate. They need good humidity and must be kept out of cold drafts. Use tepid water when watering.

Propagation: divide the clump in spring when repotting.

Worth remembering

The sap and berries of aglaonemas are toxic.

Aglaonema commutatum ▶

● RELATED SPECIES AND VARIETIES

Aglaonema commutatum "Silver Queen" has gray-green leaves with silvery-gray variegation. "Silver King" is a closely related cultivar with more marked variegation and a more upright habit.

Aglaonema crispum has thick, broader, gray-green leaves, with dark green margins. After a few years the plant forms a thick stem marked by foliar scarring.

Aglaonema "Pattaya Beauty" ▶

CARING FOR YOUR PLANT

Watering and humidity: water moderately in spring and summer, using tepid water. Water sparingly in winter and keep at a lower temperature: 59° to 61° F (15° to 16° C).

Light: enjoys filtered light; keep out of direct sunlight.

Feeding: from spring to the end of summer, feed every two weeks with food for foliage plants.

Repotting and growing medium: if necessary, repot in spring in ordinary compost enriched with a little fibrous peat.

Cultivation tip: avoid moving your plant. Remove dust from the leaves regularly by wiping with a damp sponge. Aglaonemas do not tolerate cigarette smoke.

Aglaonema "Silver Queen" ▼   *Aglaonema* "Compact Maria" ▼

TROUBLE SHOOTING

◆ Small brown lumps appear on the leaves, which become sticky: under their protective shells, scale bugs can be difficult to eradicate. Remove them using a Q-tip dipped in alcohol, or treat your plant with a systemic insecticide.

◆ The leaves become pale and covered in small, whitish dots: red spider mites thrive in hot, dry conditions. Increase the ambient humidity and spray the foliage more often. If necessary, treat the plant with an appropriate acaricide.

➤ *Ajania* see *Chrysanthemum*

Allamanda

A. *cathartica*   Allamanda

Decorative interest

This vigorous, soft-stemmed plant is native to central and South America. It produces dark green, glossy, oval leaves 3 to 5 inches (8 to 12 cm) long. From late spring to fall, open, funnel-shaped, yellow flowers appear; they are 2 to 4 inches (5 to 10 cm) in diameter. Allamandas can be trained over hoops but will later require a larger support.

Ease of cultivation

Allamandas need plenty of light and high ambient humidity. They must be cut back once a year to stop the stems becoming leggy and the long, soft branches need to be regularly trained on to supports.

Propagation: in spring take 3 to 4 inch (8 to 10 cm) terminal cuttings and insert them into cutting compost. Grow under cover at 70° to 72° F (21° to 22° C).

● **RELATED SPECIES AND VARIETIES**

Allamanda cathartica "Hendersonii" has bronze-tinted buds and yellow flowers with white markings in the base of the throat.

Allamanda cathartica "Silver Dwarf" ▼▶

TROUBLE SHOOTING

◆ The leaves become sticky and deformed: aphids mainly attack young shoots; treat with an appropriate insecticide..

CARING FOR YOUR PLANT

Watering and humidity: water moderately during the growing period; reduce watering in winter. Maintain a high level of humidity throughout the summer.

Light: bright conditions with three or four hours of sunlight daily, but keep out of the hot midday sun in summer.

Feeding: feed every ten or fifteen days in spring and fall, with food for flowering plants.

Repotting and growing medium: repot in spring every year or two using ordinary compost enriched with good yard soil.

Cultivation tip: at the end of winter, cut back stems, by half, that are too long. Allamandas are ideally suited to cultivation in a conservatory or heated greenhouse, being trained on a trellis fixed to the wall.

Alocasia

A. macrorrhiza   Taro, elephant ear

Decorative interest

Native to India, Sri Lanka, and Malaysia, the taro is an imposing, rhizomatous perennial that can grow to over 16 feet (5 meters) tall in its natural habitat. When pot-grown, this handsome, tropical plant rarely exceeds 6½ feet (2 meters) high and 3 feet (1 meter) wide—which is still quite impressive. A greenhouse or heated conservatory will provide it with the space it needs. Its huge, entire, oval leaves are mid-green with striking pale green veins.

CARING FOR YOUR PLANT

Watering and humidity: during the growing period, water regularly, keeping the compost moist at all times. Reduce watering in winter. Use soft water at room temperature. The plants require a high level of humidity. Maintain this by standing the pot on wet gravel. In hot weather, spray the foliage frequently.

Light: enjoys bright conditions but make sure you keep the plant out of direct sunlight.

Feeding: feed every two weeks in spring and summer, using a plant food rich in potassium to promote firm leaf growth.

Repotting and growing medium: repot every two or three years in early spring, using ordinary compost with added peat.

Cultivation tip: give your plant growing conditions that are as constant as possible, preferably in a greenhouse or heated conservatory. The rhizomes are susceptible to rotting if the temperature is too low (minimum of 61° F/16° C).

Flowering is typical of the arum family and consists of yellow-green spathes. These rarely occur in pot-grown plants. Taros are cultivated in the tropics of Asia for their rhizomes, which are edible once cooked.

Ease of cultivation

Taros can be quite tricky to cultivate as they require high humidity.

Propagation: divide the rhizome in spring: separate leaf-bearing sections and pot them up individually. Plants can also be grown from seed at 73° F (23 ° C).

Alocasia "Black Velvet" ▼

Alocasia macrorrhiza ▼

Alocasia sanderiana ▼

◀ *Alocasia cucullata*

TROUBLE SHOOTING

◆ Small, brown lumps appear on the leaves, which become sticky: these are scale bugs. Remove them with a Q-tip dipped in alcohol or treat the plant with a systemic insecticide.

● **RELATED SPECIES AND VARIETIES**

Alocasia sanderiana, a species native to Asia, is valued for its striking, dark green leaves with silvery-white veins. The large, arrow-shaped leaves with wavy edges are 12 to 16 inches (30 to 40 cm) long and emerge from the rhizome in a large clump. The plant grows to a height of 20 to 24 inches (50 to 60 cm), with a spread of 12 to 20 inches (30 to 50 cm). There are a number of hybrids, such as *A.* "**Black Velvet**," which has rounder, dark green leaves with silvery-white veins.

A. cuprea produces leaves that are coppery-purple on the surface with dark green veins, while the undersides are a violety-red.

Alocasia cuprea ▼

◀ *Alocasia lowi* "Ventii"

Alocasia "Calidora" ▼

Alocasia "Portodora" ▼

Alocasia "Polly" ▼

Aloe

A. arborescens   Aloe

Decorative interest

This aloe, native to South Africa, is sometimes known as the tree aloe or
candelabra aloe. It has tough leaves carried at the ends of branching, bare, woody
stems. The leaves, which are 4 to 6 inches (10 to 15 cm) long, are narrow, pale
green, and edged with white, spiny teeth. In spring, the plant produces
inflorescences of tubular flowers in shades of orangey-red or greenish-yellow.
In the wild, this species forms thick bushes that can reach as much as 13 feet
(4 meters) in height.

Ease of cultivation

Extremely drought resistant, this succulent is well suited to indoor cultivation in
a position with plenty of light.

Worth remembering

Aloes belong to the family Lilacaea, whereas agaves are members of the family
Agavaceae. The leafy rosette of agaves lies flat on the ground while that of aloes
often has a small aerial axis. Agave leaves are stiff, whereas aloe leaves are more
brittle and easily broken. And unlike agaves, aloes do not die after flowering.

● RELATED SPECIES AND VARIETIES

The variegated aloe, *Aloe variegata* (synonym: *A. punctata*) produces rosettes
of thick, dark green, triangular leaves with white markings. In spring, it can
produce a scape bearing spikes of orangey-pink flowers.

Aloe arborescens ▲

A. aristata forms a compact rosette of green leaves covered in small, white
lumps; *A. brevifolia* has pale green leaves edged with teeth, and pale pink
flowers. Both these species remain small.

A. mitriformis and *A. ferox* are large aloes with leaves reaching to over 3 feet
(1 meter) in length.

A. plicatilis produces long, bluish, strap-like leaves that are fleshy but not spiny,
arranged in the shape of a fan.

Aloe variegata ▲

▲ *Aloe* inflorescence

Aloe ferox ▼

Aloe plicatilis ▼

CARING FOR YOUR PLANT

Watering and humidity: water moderately in spring and summer.
In winter, keep the compost barely damp. Aloes are quite tolerant of
dry air.

Light: keep tough-leaved aloes in a sunny position. Aloes with tenderer
leaves prefer bright but filtered light.

Feeding: feed every two or three weeks in spring and summer with plant
food for cactuses and succulents.

Repotting and growing medium: repot in spring, if necessary, using
a light, free-draining compost suitable for succulents.

Cultivation tip: to encourage flowering, keep your plant in a cold
greenhouse during the winter (this aloe can even withstand light frost).
In summer, if you are able to do so, you may put your plant outdoors in
a position that allows full sunlight.

TROUBLE SHOOTING

◆ White, cottony clusters appear at the base of the leaves: mealy bugs
can be difficult to eradicate. If there are only a few, remove them with
a Q-tip dipped in alcohol. Otherwise, treat the plant with a systemic
insecticide.

Alpinia

A. zerumbet "Variegata"   Ornamental ginger

Decorative interest

This plant is the variegated form of *Alpinia zerumbet*, a rhizomatous perennial native to the open woodlands of tropical Asia. It produces a large clump of upright stems. The smooth, tough, lanceolate leaves are arranged in two rows. Pale green in the type species, they are shorter with attractive, yellow variegation in the "Variegata" form. The plant can grow 5 to 6½ feet (1.5 to 2 meters) tall. In summer, hanging clusters of yellow, purple-tinted flowers with ivory bracts appear.

Ease of cultivation

Alpinias are not easy to grow in pots as they have very vigorous roots. They also need a high level of ambient humidity.

Propagation: once the seeds are ripe, sow at 68° F (20° C), or increase by clump division in early spring.

● RELATED SPECIES AND VARIETIES

Alpinia calcarata produces yellow flowers with dark red veins in more or less upright clusters.

Alpinia purpurata, the red ginger, produces long bunches of small white flowers with bright red, evergreen bracts.

Alpinia vittata forms hanging clusters of small, pale green flowers with pink bracts, and has leaves with bright yellow variegation.

TROUBLE SHOOTING
◆ The leaves become pale and dry: red spider mites thrive in a warm, dry atmosphere. Increase the ambient humidity and spray the foliage more often. If necessary, treat with an acaricide.

CARING FOR YOUR PLANT

Watering and humidity: the plants require a high level of ambient humidity. Water twice a week during the growing period, allowing the surface of the compost to dry out between waterings. Water moderately in winter, when the temperature is cooler. Spray the foliage daily when conditions are dry.

Light: bright conditions, but keep out of direct sunlight.

Feeding: feed once a week in spring and summer with food for flowering plants.

Repotting and growing medium: repot each year in spring, using deep pots and potting compost enriched with good yard soil. For larger specimens grown in containers, a top dressing will suffice.

Cultivation tip: ornamental gingers are best grown direct in the soil in a greenhouse or heated conservatory. In winter, do not allow the temperature to drop below 15° C.

▼▲ *Alpinia zerumbet* 'Variegata'

 ➤➤ *Amaryllis* see *Hippeastrum*

Ampelopsis

A. brevipedunculata "Variegata"
synonym: *Ampelopsis brevipendunculata* "Elegans"

Variegated porcelain berry vine

Decorative interest

Ampelopsis is a deciduous climber that belongs to the same family as Parthenocissus. The species most commonly cultivated indoors is *Ampelopsis brevipedunculata* "Variegata." Less vigorous than the type species, and native to north-east Asia, this variety has dark green leaves divided into three or five lobes, tinged with pink and cream in the spring. The flowers are insignificant but produce violet-blue berries in the fall.

Ease of cultivation

This climber is easy to grow indoors if the temperature is not too warm. Provide it with support to help it climb.

Propagation: grow from seed in spring, after stratification in the cold, or take herbaceous cuttings in spring.

Worth remembering

When it starts to put out new growth, cut back the stems by a third to encourage new leaves to form.

CARING FOR YOUR PLANT

Watering and humidity: water abundantly during the summer months but reduce watering as fall begins. Water sparingly in winter, during the plant's period of rest. In summer, spray the foliage with water from time to time.

Light: enjoys bright conditions, but keep out of the hot midday sun in summer.

Feeding: feed every three or four weeks in spring and summer with food for foliage plants.

Repotting and growing medium: repot every two years in spring, in a mixture of ordinary compost and good yard soil. Use a deep pot.

Cultivation tip: the plant needs a period of winter rest in a cool place—a greenhouse or cool conservatory is ideal—make sure the temperature is not too warm. It will drop its leaves during this time.

TROUBLE SHOOTING

◆ Small, brown lumps appear on the stems and leaves, and they become sticky: scale bugs are more common in fall and winter. Remove them with a Q-tip dipped in alcohol or treat the plant with an appropriate systemic insecticide.

▼ *Ampelopsis brevipedunculata*

Ampelopsis brevipedunculata "Variegata" ▶

Ananas

A. comosus 'Variegatus'   Variegated pineapple
synonym: *Ananas sativus* "Variegatus"

Decorative interest
The variegated pineapple is an ornamental variety of the cultivated pineapple. It produces a dense rosette of long, tough leaves that are green with pale cream edges and very spiny. After a few years' cultivation, the plant may produce a short, sturdy flower stem bearing small flowers, which are surrounded by very colorful bracts. A small, pink fruit then appears, topped by a tuft of short leaves. When cultivated indoors, the fruit will not ripen.

Ease of cultivation
The variegated pineapple is easy to grow, providing it receives sufficient light and is correctly watered over the course of the year. It requires warmth in winter.
Propagation: remove the lateral offsets when they are about 6 inches (15 cm) high or cut the flower crown from the top of the fruit (leaving it to dry for one or two days), and plant it in a mixture of peat and sand, and grow under cover at 77° F (25° C).

Worth remembering
Too much humidity is more harmful than temporary dryness.

CARING FOR YOUR PLANT

Watering and humidity: water once a week during the growing period. Reduce watering significantly during the winter.
Light: give this plant as much sunlight as possible.
Feeding: feed every two or three weeks during the growing period with food for flowering plants.
Repotting and growing medium: repot in spring approximately every two years, using ordinary compost. Pineapples prefer small pots.
Cultivation tip: temperature is the key factor affecting growth. Below 68° F (20° C), growth slows down markedly.

TROUBLE SHOOTING

◆ White, cottony clusters appear at the base of the leaves: mealy bugs are particularly difficult to eradicate. If there are only a few, remove them with a Q-tip dipped in alcohol. Otherwise, treat the plant with a systemic insecticide.

● RELATED SPECIES AND VARIETIES
Ananas bracteatus "Striatus" (synonym: "Tricolor") has dark green leaves with yellow stripes.
Ananas nanus is like a miniature version of *Ananas comosus*. Its dark green leaves, edged with upright spines, reach a length of 4 inches (10 cm).

Ananas "Champaca" ▶

Ananas comosus "Variegatus" ▶

Ananas comosus ▼

Anigozanthos

Kangaroo paws

Decorative interest

This genus, native to Australia, includes a dozen species of evergreen perennials. The species most commonly cultivated indoors is *Anigozanthos flavidus* and its hybrids. The plant produces a clump of linear leaves, bright green in some varieties, bluish in others, and reaching almost 20 inches (50 cm) in height. In summer, curious, upright inflorescences appear; the tubular flowers come in a variable range of colors including yellow, green, and orange, and grow in clusters at the tips of long, stiff stems.

Ease of cultivation

As a houseplant, the anigozanthus is not long-lived. It is better suited to cultivation in a greenhouse or cold conservatory.

Propagation: not if you discard the plant after flowering. However, the clumps can be divided in spring.

TROUBLE SHOOTING

◆ Marks appear on the leaves: these plants are particularly susceptible to fungal diseases. Avoid water getting into the heart of the clump. If necessary, treat with a fungicide.

CARING FOR YOUR PLANT

Watering and humidity: water twice a week while in flower, then water less frequently. Keep your plant almost dry in winter.

Light: full sunlight.

Feeding: feed every two or three weeks in spring and summer with food for succulents.

Repotting and growing medium: repot in spring every year, if necessary. Use potting compost enriched with good yard soil and sand.

Cultivation tip: the plant is best treated as a greenhouse or conservatory plant. You can put your plant out in the yard or on a terrace during the summer.

Anigozanthos hybrid ▶

◀ *Anigozanthos*

Anthurium

A. andraeanum — Anthurium, flamingo flower

Decorative interest

This species, native to Colombia, has given rise to numerous hybrids. The inflorescences keep for a long time as cut flowers, and are highly prized by florists. Typical of the arum family, anthuriums have a slightly curved, yellow to ivory spadix and crinkled, pink, red, or white spathes, depending on the variety. The flower stems emerge from the center of the clump of dark green, heart-shaped leaves, which are carried on long stalks.

Anthurium andraeanum ▶

CARING FOR YOUR PLANT

Watering and humidity: from spring to fall, water sufficiently to keep the compost constantly moist, preferably using soft water. In winter, allow the compost to dry out slightly before watering. Provide a humid atmosphere for your plant by standing it on damp gravel. In warm, dry weather, spray the foliage (not the flowers) regularly with soft water.

Light: enjoys bright conditions, but keep out of direct sunlight.

Feeding: feed every two weeks in spring and summer with food for flowering plants.

Repotting and growing medium: initially repot each year, then every two years in spring, in a light mixture of compost and peat, with a good drainage layer in the bottom of the pot.

Cultivation tip: keep the atmosphere humid and the temperature as constant as possible. The temperature should not drop below 59° F (15° C) in winter.

Ease of cultivation

Anthuriums can be a little tricky to grow as they require good heat and humidity.
Propagation: in spring, divide the clump and plant each piece in a pot with a light mixture of compost and peat. Keep them warm (75° F/24° C) and under cover until they begin to put out growth.

Tip

Support the inflorescences with a light stake.

Anthurium andraeanum ▼

TROUBLE SHOOTING

◆ The leaves become sticky and deformed: aphids are attacking the shoots. Treat with an appropriate insecticide.
◆ Brown marks with yellow rings appear on the leaves: fungal septoriosis slows down the growth of the plant. This fungus thrives in warm, damp conditions. Remove the affected leaves if there are not too many. If the damage is more extensive, treat the plant with a fungicide.
◆ White, cottony clusters appear on the leaves: mealy bugs are difficult to eradicate. If there are only a few, remove them with a Q-tip dipped in alcohol. In cases of severe attack, treat the plant with a systemic insecticide.

Anthurium scherzerianum ▼

● RELATED SPECIES AND VARIETIES

Anthurium scherzerianum is the easiest anthurium to cultivate indoors. It produces dark green, lanceolate leaves that can grow to 8 to 12 inches (20 to 30 cm) in length. The inflorescence is composed of a yellow to reddish, sinuous spadix and a scarlet, oval spathe, sometimes with white markings.

Unlike other anthuriums, *A. crystallinum* is cultivated for its decorative foliage. The large, smooth, heart-shaped leaves, 12 to 20 inches (30 to 50 cm) long, are first tinged with violet, before becoming deep green as they mature. The veins on the upper surface are ivory, and pale pink on the underside. The green inflorescence is of limited interest. This plant can grow to about 24 inches (60 cm) in height and width.

There are other hybrids with very attractive, glossy, green leaves.

Anthurium ellipticum "Jungle Bush" ▼

Anthurium scherzerianum ▼   *Anthurium hookeri* ▼

Aphelandra

A. squarrosa　　　　　　　　Zebra plant

Aphelandra squarrosa ▲

Aphelandra aurantiaca ▲

Decorative interest

This surprising, bushy plant, native to the American tropics, is characterized by its large, dark green, glossy, elliptical leaves with white markings along the veins. The inflorescence consists of a bright yellow, terminal spike composed of bright yellow, overlapping bracts from which short-lived, pale yellow, tubular flowers emerge in spring. The plant grows to 12 to 24 inches (30 to 60 cm) in height. It is tricky to get it to flower a second time, but it is worth keeping for its attractive foliage.

TROUBLE SHOOTING

◆ The zebra plant is susceptible to attack from aphids and scale bugs: keep an eye on your plant. If necessary, treat immediately with an insecticide.

CARING FOR YOUR PLANT

Watering and humidity: water abundantly during the flowering period but do not allow the plant to stand in water. Reduce watering once flowering has finished. Maintain a high level of humidity by standing the pot on damp gravel. In warm weather, spray the foliage regularly but avoid wetting the flowers.
Light: enjoys bright conditions, but keep out of direct sunlight.
Feeding: feed every two weeks in spring and summer with food for flowering plants.
Repotting and growing medium: repot every year in early spring, in ordinary compost enriched with peat.
Cultivation tip: in winter, keep your plant in a cool, bright spot at 53° to 59° F (12° to 15° C). Protect it from cold drafts.

◀ *Aphelandra squarrosa*

Ease of cultivation

The zebra plant is a rather delicate species. It is often considered to be a seasonal plant.
Propagation: in spring, take 3 to 4 inch (8 to 10 cm) long cuttings from side shoots and insert them in a moist mixture of equal parts peat and sand. Grow under cover at between 70° and 75° F (21° and 24° C).

Worth remembering

If you keep your plant from one year to another, cut the stems quite short when repotting.

● RELATED SPECIES AND VARIETIES

Aphelandra squarrosa "Brockfeld" has dark green leaves and a compact habit.
Aphelandra squarrosa "Dania" has shorter leaves speckled with silver, and an orangey-yellow inflorescence.
Aphelandra squarrosa "Louisae" is the variety most commonly cultivated. It has long leaves with striking ivory-white veins.

Aphelandra squarrosa "Dania" ▶

Araucaria

A. heterophylla   Araucaria pine, Norfolk Island pine
synonym: *Araucaria excelsa*

Decorative interest

Araucaria are trees that grow to a height of about 165 feet (50 meters) in their native regions of Australia and Norfolk Island. When pot-grown, *Araucaria heterophylla* only reaches 3 to 6½ feet (1 to 2 meters). Its evergreen, needle-like leaves have a tough, darkish green, flattened limb. Its attractive, tiered silhouette makes it particularly decorative. To achieve this balanced shape, the plant must have sufficient space and receive uniform light. It is related to the monkey puzzle tree (*Araucaria araucana*), which is cultivated as a decorative outdoor species in temperate climates.

Ease of cultivation

This araucaria likes to spend the winter in a cool, bright, unheated room at a temperature of no more than 44° to 50° F (6° to 10° C). Even in summer it needs good ventilation and can happily be placed near an open window.
Propagation: this is best left to the experts, who grow the plant from seed or head cuttings.

CARING FOR YOUR PLANT

Watering and humidity: water quite generously during the growing season. Keep the root ball almost dry in winter.
Light: choose a spot with plenty of light, but keep out of the midday sun in summer.
Feeding: feed every two weeks in spring and summer with food for foliage plants.
Repotting and growing medium: repot every two years when the tree is still young. Once it has reached 3 feet (1 meter), a top dressing will suffice. Use a mixture of ordinary compost, peat, and sand.
Cultivation tip: keep araucarias away from radiators. As they mature, araucarias lose their leaves and become less attractive.

TROUBLE SHOOTING

◆ White, cottony clusters appear on the needles and stems: mealy bugs are difficult to eradicate. Remove them with a Q-tip dipped in alcohol, or treat the plant with a systemic insecticide.

Araucaria heterophylla ▶

Araucaria heterophylla ▼

Ardisia

A. crenata
synonym: *Ardisia crispa*

Ardisia

Decorative interest

This shrub, native to east Asia, can reach a height of 30 to 40 inches (0.8 to 1 meter) when grown indoors. It produces an upright trunk and tough, glossy, dark green, lanceolate leaves with scalloped edges. Clusters of starry, pinkish-white flowers appear at the leaf joints in early summer. They are followed by berries which are green at first and then turn bright red. Highly decorative, these last until the next flowering and even longer in good conditions.

Ease of cultivation

Ardisias do best in a cool room at 59° to 62° F (15° to 16° C); if the room is warmer, they require a lot of humidity.

Propagation: sow the seeds in early spring at 62° to 64° F (16° to 18° C). In early summer you can remove side shoots together with a small piece of bark, and root them under cover in a slightly damp mixture of equal parts peat and sand.

Worth remembering

As it matures, the plant becomes less vigorous. You can replace it by taking cuttings or improve it by cutting it back to 4 inches (10 cm) in February.

TROUBLE SHOOTING

◆ White, cottony clusters appear on the leaves: mealy bugs are difficult to eradicate. Remove them with a Q-tip dipped in alcohol, or treat the plant with a systemic insecticide.

CARING FOR YOUR PLANT

Watering and humidity: water your plant generously during the growing season, so that the compost remains moist but do not allow it to get too wet. In winter, water less often, according to the temperature. If temperatures are below 59° F (15° C), water very lightly and allow the compost to dry to a certain depth between waterings. Maintain a high level of humidity around the plant.

Light: enjoys bright conditions with some direct sunlight, except at the hottest time of day.

Feeding: feed every two weeks in spring and summer with food for flowering plants.

Repotting and growing medium: with young plants, repot every year in spring in a mixture of equal parts ordinary compost, peat, and sand.

Cultivation tip: during the winter, keep your ardisia in a bright, cool room at temperatures of 45° to 59° F (7° to 15° C)—in a conservatory, for example.

Ardisia crenata ▼

Variegated *Ardisia crenata* ▼

Aristolochia

A. littoralis
Aristolochia, Dutchman's pipe

synonym: *Aristolochia elegans*

Decorative interest

Aristolochias are climbers with twining stems and are found in the temperate and tropical regions of the world. Some species are completely hardy. *Aristolochia littoralis* is the species most commonly cultivated as a houseplant. It is an evergreen climber that produces pale green, heart-shaped leaves. In summer, large, unusual flowers appear. These have no petals but a tubular peduncle that broadens into a pipe shape and is brownish-purple with white veins.

Ease of cultivation

Aristolochias are demanding in terms of heat and humidity.

Propagation: in early spring, take 4 inch (10 cm) cuttings and insert them into a barely moist mixture of equal parts sand and peat. Keep under cover at 70° to 75° F (21° to 24° C). Using hormone rooting powder will encourage rooting. You can also grow from seed in spring at 72° F (22° C).

● RELATED SPECIES AND VARIETIES

Aristolochia gigantea has large, dark green, triangular leaves and very large flowers speckled with white or cream.

TROUBLE SHOOTING

◆ The leaves become pale and dry: red spider mites thrive in warm, dry conditions. Increase the ambient humidity and spray the foliage. If necessary, treat the plant with an acaricide.

◆ Small white bugs fly away when you touch the plant: whitefly are small, sap-sucking bugs that are difficult to eradicate. Treat the plant repeatedly with insecticide every eight to ten days.

CARING FOR YOUR PLANT

Watering and humidity: water generously during the growing period. Reduce watering in winter, according to the temperature. Maintain a high level of humidity.

Light: enjoys bright but filtered light conditions.

Feeding: feed every two weeks in spring and summer, using food for flowering plants.

Repotting and growing medium: repot in spring, if necessary, using a mixture of compost and good yard soil.

Cultivation tip: lightly cut back the stems in early spring. Maintain a minimum temperature of 50° F (10° C) in winter. This plant is particularly suited to cultivation in a warm or temperate greenhouse.

Aristolochia gigantea ▲   *Aristolochia littoralis* ▲

Aristolochia grandiflora ▲

Aristolochia littoralis ▶

➤ *Ascocenda* see *Vanda*

Asparagus

A. densiflorus "Sprengeri"

synonym: *Asparagus sprengeri*

Asparagus fern

Decorative interest

A native of South Africa, this species is not commonly cultivated as a houseplant. However, it has given rise to the well-known cultivar "Sprengeri," with its bushy, branching, trailing stems covered in small, needle-like, modified branches (known as cladodes) arranged in whorls of three. The stems are slightly spiny. The asparagus fern makes a very attractive hanging plant.

Associates well with... planted in a large bowl, this slender-leaved plant will work well with other species that enjoy slightly damp soil, such as variegated ivies and chlorophytums.

TROUBLE SHOOTING

◆ The leaves become pale and dry: red spider mites thrive in warm, dry conditions. Increase the ambient humidity and spray the foliage. If necessary, treat the plant with an acaricide.

◆ Small brown lumps appear on the leaves, which become sticky: scale bugs are difficult to eradicate. Remove them with a Q-tip dipped in alcohol, or treat the plant with a systemic insecticide.

◀ *Asparagus densiflorus* "Sprengeri"

Ease of cultivation

This is an easy plant for a beginner, providing hot, dry conditions are avoided.
Propagation: by clump division in March or April, when repotting. Can also be grown from seed in spring, at 61° F (16° C), but the young plantlets can be slow to develop.

Worth remembering

The asparagus fern will often bear fruit when grown indoors, producing small, poisonous, red berries.

CARING FOR YOUR PLANT

Watering and humidity: water abundantly during the growing period but do not leave water standing in the saucer. In winter, keep the compost almost dry. Spray the foliage in hot, dry weather.
Light: enjoys a light position, out of direct sunlight.
Feeding: feed every two weeks in spring and summer, using food for foliage plants.
Repotting and growing medium: repot in spring, in ordinary compost, if the plant becomes pot-bound.
Cultivation tip: the asparagus fern tolerates quite low temperatures in winter, down to 45° F (8° C), but it does not tolerate hot, dry conditions. In summer, keep the room ventilated if the temperature rises above 70° F (21° C), or move the plant out into the yard but keep out of direct sunlight.

● RELATED SPECIES AND VARIETIES

Asparagus densiflorus "Myrsii" (synonym: *A. meyeri*) has soft stems covered in fine, green "branches" that look like long bottle brushes.

A. falcatus is a climbing species, native to India and Sri Lanka. Its long shoots resemble fine asparagus tips and develop into slender, spiny stems covered in long, falciform leaves. As a pot plant, it can grow to 5 to 6½ feet (1.5 to 2 meters) in height.

A. setaceous (synonym: *A. plumosus*) produces upright, filiform stems covered not with leaves, but with small, light, modified branches (cladodes). This species is highly prized by florists, who often slip one or two stems into an arrangement.

Asparagus falcatus ▶

Asparagus setaceus "Pyramidalis" ▼

◀ *Asparagus densiflorus* "Myrsii"

Aspidistra

A. eliator
Aspidistra, mother-in-law's tongue

Decorative interest
This robust plant, with its handsome, glossy foliage, is a very attractive option for beginners. Its scaly rhizome produces long, shiny, dark green, lanceolate leaves that are 24 to 32 inches (60 to 80 cm) in length. It sometimes produces modest purple flowers that are followed by small red berries. The aspidistra is native to the forests of the Himalayas, China, and Japan.

Ease of cultivation
The aspidistra is an extremely robust plant that can withstand pollution, smoke, poor light, and changes of temperature. This makes an ideal houseplant.
Propagation: by clump division in spring.

Worth remembering
A slow-growing plant, on average the aspidistra produces only two to four leaves a year.

● RELATED SPECIES AND VARIETIES
Aspidistra eliator "Variegata" is a form with white-striped leaves which requires brighter light conditions and a compost low in nutrients.

▼▲ *Aspidistra elatior* 'Variegata'

CARING FOR YOUR PLANT

Watering and humidity: water moderately during the growing period and reduce watering in winter. Do not leave water standing in the saucer.
Light: can tolerate almost any light conditions except full sunlight. However, dark conditions will slow down growth.
Feeding: feed every two to three weeks in spring and summer with heavily diluted foliage plant food.
Repotting and growing medium: repot in spring if the plant has become pot-bound, using ordinary compost. Provide a good layer of drainage at the bottom of the pot.
Cultivation tip: avoid full sunlight and over-watering. Remove dust from the leaves regularly with a damp sponge.

TROUBLE SHOOTING

◆ The leaves become pale and dry: red spider mites thrive in warm, dry conditions. Increase the ambient humidity and spray the foliage. If necessary, treat the plant with an acaricide.
◆ Small brown lumps appear under the leaves which become sticky and yellow: scale bugs are difficult to eradicate. Remove them with a Q-tip dipped in alcohol, or treat the plant with a systemic insecticide.

Asplenium

A. nidus   Bird's nest fern

Decorative interest

A native of tropical south-east Asia, this fern produces long, bright green, glossy fronds with wavy edges and a central brown vein. The delicate young fronds develop from the fibrous center of the dark brown rosette. When mature, the undersides of the fronds have brown lines containing spores. When grown as a pot plant, the fronds do not generally grow longer than 20 inches (50 cm).

Associates well with… you can combine this fern with plants with divided leaves or a trailing habit such as cissus, pothos, and creeping fig (*Ficus pumila*).

Ease of cultivation

This fern is easy to grow providing it is kept out of cold drafts and is not moved too often.

Propagation: can be grown from spores, but this is a difficult technique to master.

● RELATED SPECIES AND VARIETIES

Asplenium bulbiferum is native to Australia; its finely divided fronds produce bulbils which give rise to numerous small plantlets.

Asplenium antiquum is similar in appearance but has slenderer fronds with wavy edges.

CARING FOR YOUR PLANT

Watering and humidity: water very regularly during the growing period so that the compost remains moist. In winter, reduce watering at cooler temperatures. Spray the foliage in hot weather.
Light: average light conditions.
Feeding: feed every three to four weeks in spring and summer with diluted half strength foliage plant food.
Repotting and growing medium: repot in spring every year or two according to the age of the plant, using a mixture of equal parts leaf mold, peat, and coarse sand.
Cultivation tip: do not move your plant, and keep it protected from drafts.

TROUBLE SHOOTING

◆ Small brown lumps appear on the fronds: scale bugs are commonly seen on this fern. Keep an eye out for them and remove them with your fingernail as soon as they appear. Bird's nest ferns respond badly to products such as insecticides.

Asplenium antiquum "Osaka" ▲

Asplenium nidus ▶

Bambusa

B. vulgaris   Indoor bamboo

Decorative interest

This bamboo, native to the tropics, is ideal for indoor cultivation. It forms a tuft of smooth, yellow canes with bright green, slender, oblong, pointed leaves. The variety "Vittata" (synonym: *"Striata"*) produces beautiful, golden-yellow canes with bright green striations. In its native habitat, this bamboo can grow to almost 100 feet (30 meters) tall. As a pot plant it rarely exceeds 6½ feet (2 meters).

Ease of cultivation

This bamboo requires very good light. Stand it in front of a large window or glass door, or in a temperate conservatory.

Propagation: in spring, divide the clump when it has become thick. Transplant the divisions immediately to prevent them drying out.

CARING FOR YOUR PLANT

Watering and humidity: water moderately throughout the year but be careful not to let the compost dry out, especially in summer. Water the foliage daily in hot weather.

Light: bright light conditions, but keep out of direct sunlight in summer.

Feeding: feed once a month during the growing period with foliage plant food.

Repotting and growing medium: repot in spring, in a mixture of equal parts ordinary compost, yard soil, and coarse sand.

Cultivation tip: move your bamboo outdoors during the summer; position the pot in partial shade in case of hot weather.

● **RELATED SPECIES AND VARIETIES**

Bambusa ventricosa is a species native to southern China. It produces thick canes with whorls of ten to twenty, dark green, linear leaves. The internodes are often strangely swollen, earning this bamboo the name "Buddha's Belly." When pot-grown it can reach a height of 6½ to 10 feet (2 to 3 meters). It is very tolerant of pruning and makes an ideal bonsai specimen.

TROUBLE SHOOTING

◆ Deformed, sticky leaves reveal the presence of aphids: treat the plant with a suitable insecticide.

◆ White, cottony clusters appear at the base of the leaves: these are mealy bugs. Remove them with a Q-tip dipped in alcohol, or treat the plant with a suitable insecticide.

◆ The leaves become pale and dry: red spider mites thrive in warm, dry conditions. Increase the ambient humidity and spray the foliage. If necessary, treat the plant with an acaricide.

Bambusa vulgaris ▶

Bambusa ventricosa ▼

Beaucarnea

B. recurvata
Elephant's foot

synonym: *Nolina recurvata*

Decorative interest

This unusual plant owes its name to the swollen, woody, fissured base of its upright trunk. Branching in its upper part, the trunk is topped by several tufts of very long and slender, dark green, strap-like leaves that arch and trail. Elephant's foot is slow to grow but can eventually reach a height of 6½ feet (2 meters) or more. The striking structural lines of elephant's foot make it suitable for growing on its own as a feature plant.

Ease of cultivation

Providing it is put in a room with plenty of light, elephant's foot is relatively easy to grow.

Propagation: difficult to propagate indoors. It is propagated either from seed or by removing the offsets which form (only rarely) at the base of the trunk.

Worth remembering

Elephant's foot is attractive to cats, who enjoy chewing the ends of the leaves and scratching their claws on its trunk!

Beaucarnea recurvata ▼

Beaucarnea recurvata ▼

CARING FOR YOUR PLANT

Watering and humidity: water moderately, allowing the surface of the compost to dry out between waterings. Water less frequently in winter, especially if the temperature is low.

Light: enjoys bright light conditions, but filter out the summer sun during the hottest part of the day.

Feeding: feed every three to four weeks in spring and summer with half strength foliage plant food.

Repotting and growing medium: repot in spring if the roots are pot-bound, using a free-draining mixture of the type used for cactuses and succulents.

Cultivation tip: give your plant plenty of light and don't overwater. In winter, move it to a cooler room at 59° to 64° F (15° to 18° C).

Begonia

B. x *hiemalis*

Flowering begonia

Decorative interest

These fibrous-rooted begonias, depending on their parentage, can be either short-day (winter flowering) or long-day (summer flowering) types. So it is possible to find begonias on sale all year long. They are very floriferous, producing single or double flowers 1½ to 2 inches (4 to 5 cm) in diameter in shades of red, pink, orange, and yellow. The short, fleshy, upright, or slightly trailing stems have heart-shaped, green, or bronze leaves.

Associates well with… begonias are often sold planted up in pots of several different-colored hybrids.

Ease of cultivation

It is easy to grow flowering begonias in a brightly-lit room at 64° to 68° F (18° to 20° C).

Propagation: growing from seed is difficult. It is best to buy young plants.

Begonia x *hiemalis* ▼   *Begonia* x *hiemalis* ▶

▼ *Begonia* x *hiemalis*

● **RELATED SPECIES AND VARIETIES**

Begonia "Lucernae" and *B.* "Comte de Miribel" are examples of "cane" begonias—so-called because they have upright stems which resemble bamboo canes. Their green, lanceolate leaves have silvery-white markings on the upper surface. From spring to fall they produce large clusters of bright pink flowers. The tamaya is a stem-grown, cane begonia presented in a square pot; at one time this type of begonia was very popular.

Worth remembering

The begonias used as flowering pot plants have complex origins. Cheimantha begonias (*Begonia* x *cheimantha*), *B.* "Gloire de Lorraine," for example, are the result of crossing *B. socotrana*—a bulbous begonia native to the island of Socotra—and *B. dregei*—a semi-tuberous species from southern Africa. The eliator begonias (*B.* x *eliator*) are produced by crossing *B. socotrana* and hybrids of tuberous species native to the Andes (*B.* x *tuberhybrida*). Cheimantha and eliator begonias are known collectively as hiemalis begonias (or *B.* x *hiemalis*).

Begonia x *hiemalis* ▼   ▼ *Begonia* x *hiemalis*

TROUBLE SHOOTING

◆ The leaves become covered in a light, white, powdery deposit: oidium thrives in a humid atmosphere or if there is a sudden drop in temperature. Treat with a suitable fungicide.
◆ The leaves shrivel up: the room is too warm. Find a cooler spot in which to position your plant.
◆ The leaves are mottled with black marks: water less frequently if the temperature is cooler.

CARING FOR YOUR PLANT

Watering and humidity: throughout the flowering period, make sure that the compost remains slightly moist but not wet. Don't spray the leaves.
Light: bright conditions, but keep out of direct sunlight.
Feeding: feed every two to three weeks during the flowering period with food for flowering plants.
Repotting and growing medium: these are seasonal plants; there is no point in repotting them.
Cultivation tip: make sure your plant has a cool, bright spot when in flower.

Begonia x *hiemalis* ▼

Begonia "Lucernae" ▼

Begonia (tamaya) ▲

Begonia (with decorative foliage)

B. x rex-cultorum

Begonia rex

Decorative interest

The type species *Begonia rex* is not cultivated but it has given rise to numerous hybrids with extremely decorative foliage, known collectively as rex-cultorum begonias. These have large, rounded, pointed leaves with concentric zones of color in shades of green, bronze, brown, white, and red. In summer, they sometimes produce pale pink flowers.

Ease of cultivation

These begonias are easy to grow but require a bright spot out of direct sunlight. They will be happy at normal room temperature.

Propagation: between May and June, cut off mature leaves together with a piece of stem. Place them on the surface of a seed tray filled with a moist mixture of equal parts sand and peat. Cover with transparent plastic film and keep at a temperature of between 64° and 70° F (18° and 21° C). The roots will form first and then plantlets will appear. Once the plantlets have produced two or three leaves, prick them out and pot them up individually.

▼ *Begonia* x *rex-cultorum*

▲ *Begonia* x *rex-cultorum*

● **RELATED SPECIES AND VARIETIES**

Begonia x *rex-cultorum* "Comtesse Louise Erdoedy" has interesting spiral leaves that resemble a snail's shell.

Begonia Iron Cross, *B. masoniana* is a rhizomatous species native to New Guinea. Its mid-green, crinkled leaves have dark brown central markings that bear a certain resemblance to a cross.

B. boweri "Tiger" produces bronze leaves with bright green markings, edged with fine hairs.

B. "Erythrophylla" is an easy to cultivate hybrid with large, fleshy, glossy leaves, dark green on top and dark red on the underside. It produces small clusters of pale pink flowers.

▼ *Begonia boweri* "Tiger"

CARING FOR YOUR PLANT

Watering and humidity: water moderately at all times, preferably with soft water.
Light: to obtain good color, keep your begonias close to a window, but out of direct sunlight.
Feeding: feed every two weeks in spring and summer with food for foliage plants.
Repotting and growing medium: repot every two years in March, in a wide, shallow pot in peat-based compost.
Cultivation tip: water your plant regularly but not excessively, and be sure to avoid cold drafts.

TROUBLE SHOOTING

◆ The leaves become covered in a light, white, powdery deposit: oidium thrives in a humid atmosphere or if there is a sudden drop in temperature. Treat with a suitable fungicide.

Begonia venosa ▼

▼ *Begonia venosa*

◀ *Begonia masoniana*

Billbergia

B. x windii   Billbergia

Decorative interest

This bromeliad is the result of crossing *Billbergia nutans* and *B. decora*. It forms rosettes of stiff, strap-like leaves, between 20 and 28 inches (50 and 70 cm) in length, covered in gray scales which give the plant a powdery appearance. In summer, it produces arching inflorescences composed of small, green flowers with purple-red edges and bright pink bracts.

Ease of cultivation

This is an easy plant to cultivate but needs a bright position if it is to flower.
Propagation: remove offsets when they are 4 to 6 inches (10 to 15 cm) tall. Allow them to dry for one or two days before planting them in a bromeliad compost. Support with a stake until rooting is complete.

▼ *Billbergia x windii*

CARING FOR YOUR PLANT

Watering and humidity: water generously in summer with soft water, but make sure that no water is left standing under the pot. Reduce watering in winter, particularly in unusually cool temperatures. A humid atmosphere is required throughout the year.
Light: position your plant at a sunny window, but filter out the hot, midday sun in summer.
Feeding: feed every two weeks in spring and summer with half strength food for foliage plants.
Repotting and growing medium: repot in spring in a free-draining, lime-free, bromeliad compost.
Cultivation tip: allow billbergias to form a clump; they will flower much better.

TROUBLE SHOOTING

◆ White, cottony clusters appear under the leaves: remove these mealy bugs with a Q-tip dipped in alcohol. If necessary, treat the plant with a systemic insecticide.

● RELATED SPECIES AND VARIETIES

Native to South America, *Billbergia nutans* is the species most commonly cultivated. It forms large, quite tight rosettes of long, dark green, strap-like, arching leaves with dentate edges. The trailing inflorescences are composed of pink or red bracts, from which green and violet flowers emerge.

B. pyramidalis has an open rosette surrounding a woolly flower stem.

▼ *Billbergia nutans*

Blechnum

B. gibbum　　　　　　　　Blechnum
synonym: *Lomaria gibba*

Decorative interest
This compact, bushy fern, native to New Caledonia, produces large, deeply divided fronds that can grow to over 3 feet (1 meter) long. They emerge from an upright rhizome which is covered in black scales.

Ease of cultivation
Slightly tricky to grow, blechnums like a high ambient humidity, particularly during the growing period.
Propagation: grown from spores by professionals.

Blechnum brasiliense "Fire Leaf" ▼

◄ *Blechnum gibbum*

CARING FOR YOUR PLANT

Watering and humidity: water abundantly in summer and more moderately in winter. Maintain good ambient humidity. A bathroom with plenty of natural light would be ideal for this plant. Stand the pot on a thick layer of gravel and keep this damp at all times.
Light: a brightly lit spot, but out of direct sunlight.
Feeding: feed every two weeks in spring and summer with half strength food for foliage plants.
Repotting and growing medium: repot in spring in a mixture of equal parts ericaceous compost and leaf mold.
Cultivation tip: place this fern in a humid position but make sure it is out of direct sunlight and that you protect it from sudden changes of temperature, and drafts.

TROUBLE SHOOTING

◆ Small brown lumps appear under the fronds which become sticky: scale bugs are particularly difficult to eradicate. Remove them with a Q-tip dipped in alcohol, or, if necessary, treat the plant with a systemic insecticide.

Bouvardia

Bouvardia

Decorative interest

With this genus, native to the tropical regions of the American continent, it is mainly the hybrid forms of the species *Bouvardia longiflora* (synonym: *B. humboldtii*) that are cultivated. Bouvardias are shrubs with a bushy habit and long, oval, evergreen leaves 1 to 2 inches (3 to 5 cm) long. When pot-grown the bouvardia rarely exceeds 28 inches (70 cm) in height. The flowers bloom in the fall; they are tubular, solitary or in clusters, white or pink, and scented.

Ease of cultivation

Bouvardias need a winter rest period if they are to flower again. They are best suited to greenhouse cultivation.

Propagation: take cuttings 3 to 4 inches (7 to 10 cm) long in spring and root them under cover with bottom heat. Getting cuttings to root can be difficult.

Tip

In spring, cut back flowering branches to half their length.

Bouvardia longiflora ▶

CARING FOR YOUR PLANT

Watering and humidity: water moderately during the growing period. Water very lightly in winter, particularly at unusually cool temperatures.
Light: bright conditions, but keep out of direct sunlight.
Feeding: feed every two weeks in spring and summer with heavily diluted plant food.
Repotting and growing medium: repot every year in spring, in potting compost with added peat.
Cultivation tip: avoid overwatering. During the winter months, keep your plant in a cool place (minimum temperature 41° F/5° C)—ideally in a greenhouse.

TROUBLE SHOOTING

◆ White, cottony clusters appear at the base of the leaves: mealy bugs can be difficult to eradicate. If there are only a few, remove them with a Q-tip dipped in alcohol. Otherwise, treat the plant with a suitable insecticide.
◆ Small white bugs fly away when you touch the plant: whitefly are small, sap-sucking bugs that are also particularly difficult to eradicate. Treat the plant repeatedly with an appropriate insecticide every eight to ten days.

◀ *Bouvardia longiflora*

Brachychiton

B. rupestris   Bottle tree

Decorative interest

The genus *Brachychiton* includes some thirty trees native to Australia and New Guinea. Many develop a swollen, bottle-shaped trunk. *Brachychiton rupestris* is the species most commonly cultivated as a houseplant. Its strangely shaped trunk, its long, tapering green leaves with their paler central vein, and its tolerance of heavy pruning make it an ideal choice for bonsai cultivation. When pot-grown, and with a light winter pruning, the bottle tree can reach a height of just over 3 feet (1 meter)—but it is a slow grower.

Ease of cultivation

This plant is relatively easy to grow indoors but will respond badly if left standing in a saucer of water.

Propagation: propagation from cuttings is difficult; take semi-woody cuttings at the end of summer, dip the ends in hormone rooting powder, and root them under cover, with bottom heat. It is also possible to grow bottle trees from fresh seed.

Brachychiton rupestris ▲

TROUBLE SHOOTING

◆ The leaves become pale and dry: red spider mites thrive in warm, dry conditions. Increase the ambient humidity and spray the foliage. If necessary, treat the plant with an acaricide.

◆ Small brown lumps appear on the stems, the leaves become sticky: these are scale bugs. Remove them with a Q-tip dipped in alcohol, or treat the plant with a systemic insecticide.

Brachychiton rupestris ▶

CARING FOR YOUR PLANT

Watering and humidity: water your plant abundantly during the growing period but allow the surface of the compost to dry out between waterings. Never leave water standing in the saucer. Water less frequently in winter.

Light: enjoys bright conditions, but keep out of direct sunlight.

Feeding: feed every two to three weeks in spring and summer with food for foliage plants.

Repotting and growing medium: repot every two or three years in spring, in a mixture of compost and good yard soil, with a little added sand to improve drainage.

Cultivation tip: do not overwater. Keep your plant in a heated room in winter (minimum temperature 50° to 54° F/10° to 12° C).

Brighamia

B. insignis   Hawaiian palm

Decorative interest

This genus of the campanula family includes two species native to Hawaii. *Brighamia insignis*, often sold commercially under the name "vulcan palm," is an endangered species in its natural habitat, the island of Kaua'i. A campaign to save it is under way with a view to reintroducing it into its original habitat. In fact it is not a palm at all and owes its common name to the way its soft, green, oval leaves are arranged in a clump at the top of a slender trunk. After a few years, the plant may produce some pale yellow, starry flowers in winter.

Ease of cultivation

Hawaiian palms must not be exposed to damp, waterlogged conditions.

Propagation: experts propagate this plant from seed.

Worth remembering

Young leaves form at the top of the plant. It is normal for the leaves at the base to turn yellow and eventually drop. If leaf fall seems excessive, the plant may be suffering from damp, or parasite attack.

● RELATED SPECIES AND VARIETIES

Brighamia rockii is the other species of this genus; it is only found on the Hawaiian island of Molokai.

CARING FOR YOUR PLANT

Watering and humidity: water regularly but not excessively during the growing period. This plant does not require a significant period of winter rest, but water less frequently in winter.

Light: enjoys bright conditions, but keep out of direct sunlight.

Feeding: feed every two weeks in spring and summer with food for foliage plants.

Repotting and growing medium: repot in spring, if necessary, in potting compost with added sand to improve drainage.

Cultivation tip: do not expose your plant to temperatures lower than 54° to 55° F (12° to 13° C) and never leave water standing in the saucer as the plant does not tolerate damp, waterlogged conditions, which will cause excessive leaf fall.

TROUBLE SHOOTING

◆ The leaves become pale and dry: red spider mites thrive in warm, dry conditions. Increase the ambient humidity and spray the foliage. If necessary, treat the plant with an acaricide.

➤➤ **Bromeliaceae** see *Aechmea, Ananas, Billbergia, Cryptanthus, Guzmania, Neoregelia, Nidularium, Tillandsia, Vriesea*

◀ *Brighamia insignis*

Browallia

Amethyst flower, bush violet

Decorative interest

This genus includes six annual species and subshrubs native to tropical America. *Browallia speciosa* is a woody perennial, often cultivated as an annual, which has given rise to varieties in different shades of blue, violet, and white. The browallia is a seasonal plant that is discarded after flowering. The spindly, oval leaves are bright green and pointed. The star-shaped flowers are 2 inches (5 cm) in diameter and have five large, uneven lobes. They are blue in the species. Flowering normally occurs in summer but it is possible to make the plant flower at other times of year depending on when the seed is sown.

Ease of cultivation

Browallias are easy to grow but their flowers will last longer at a cool temperature.

Propagation: grow from seed. To obtain pot plants that will flower in winter, sow seeds in August in trays of seed compost. Prick out the plantlets and pot them up individually.

Worth remembering

Browallias are poisonous if ingested.

Tip

Regularly pinch out the tips of the branches to get a more compact plant.

Browallia speciosa ▶

CARING FOR YOUR PLANT

Watering and humidity: water moderately, allowing the surface of the compost to dry out between waterings.
Light: enjoys bright conditions and direct sunlight in winter.
Feeding: feed every two weeks during the flowering period with food for flowering plants.
Repotting and growing medium: this is a seasonal plant; discard after flowering.
Cultivation tip: keep your plant in a cool, bright room at around 59° F (15° C); the flowers will last longer.

TROUBLE SHOOTING

◆ The leaves become sticky and deformed: aphids are attacking the shoots. Treat with a suitable insecticide.
◆ Small white bugs fly away when you touch the plant: whitefly are small, sap-sucking bugs that are difficult to eradicate. Treat the plant repeatedly with insecticide every eight to ten days.

Brunfelsia

B. pauciflora   Brunfelsia, Yesterday-today-and-tomorrow
synonym: *Brunfelsia calycina*

Decorative interest

This shrub, native to Brazil, reaches a height of about 24 inches (60 cm) when pot-grown. It has dark green, glossy, oval leaves. From spring to fall it produces a succession of scented flowers with flat corollas. Purple on opening, the petals become pale blue the next day, then white the day after, before eventually fading. If kept at a temperature of between 55° and 61° F (13° and 16° C), flowering will continue for much of the year.

Ease of cultivation

Brunfelsias like a cool, humid atmosphere, which is not always compatible with heated interiors.

Propagation: take 2½ inch (6 cm) cuttings in spring and root them under cover in a moist mixture of equal parts peat and sand, at 68° to 72° F (20 to 22° C). Rooting can take a long time and is erratic.

Tip

In spring, cut back the side stems by two-thirds to promote the formation of flower-bearing shoots. Regularly pinch out the tips of the shoots to maintain a compact appearance.

Brunfelsia pauciflora ▲

◀ *Brunfelsia pauciflora*

CARING FOR YOUR PLANT

Watering and humidity: water regularly during the growing period to keep the compost moist but not wet. After flowering, reduce watering, and water very little during the period of winter rest. In warm weather, increase the ambient humidity by standing the pot on a bed of damp gravel.

Light: enjoys bright conditions, but keep out of direct sunlight.

Feeding: feed every three to four weeks in spring and summer with food for flowering plants.

Repotting and growing medium: repot in early spring or after flowering in a mixture of equal parts ordinary compost and peat.

Cultivation tip: in winter, move your plant to a cool, bright place—a conservatory, for example—at 50° to 53° F (10° to 12° C).

TROUBLE SHOOTING

◆ The leaves become pale and dry: red spider mites thrive in warm, dry conditions. Increase the ambient humidity and spray the foliage more often. If necessary, treat the plant with an acaricide.

Caladium

C. bicolor   Caladium

synonym: *Caladium* x *hortulanum*

Decorative interest

Native to tropical America, these tuberous plants are prized for the beauty of their foliage. Their rounded tubers produce large, handsome, spearhead-shaped leaves, that are deeply divided at the base and 6 to 12 inches (15 to 30 cm) long on slender, 6-inch (15-cm) leaf stalks. They are brightly colored green and purple, often with cream and pink variegation. Their flowers are insignificant. In the fall, the leaves turn yellow, then gradually drop, and the plant enters a period of winter rest.

Ease of cultivation

Caladiums can be quite difficult to keep for more than one season. The overwintering period is critical.

Propagation: in March, when repotting, remove a piece of the tuber and plant it in moist peat at 70° F (21° C).

Worth remembering

Caladiums are sensitive to drafts. Contact with the sap can produce skin irritation. Ingestion of any part of the plant will cause mild stomach problems.

● RELATED SPECIES AND VARIETIES

Most of the hybrids of *Caladium bicolor* are known collectively under the name *Caladium* x *hortulanum*.

"**Pink Beauty**" has leaves that are pink in the center and green speckled with pink on the edges.

"**Lord Derby**" has leaves delicately tinged with pink.

"**Red Flare**" has bright pink to purple leaves with bright red veins.

"**Aaron**" is a spectacular hybrid that has leaves with milky-white centers and dark green edges.

TROUBLE SHOOTING

◆ The leaves become dry and shriveled: the air is too dry. Stand the plant on a saucer filled with damp gravel.
◆ The leaves become soft and collapse: the temperature is too cold.
◆ Deformed, sticky leaves reveal the presence of aphids: treat your plant with a suitable insecticide.

CARING FOR YOUR PLANT

Watering and humidity: keep the compost slightly damp throughout the growing period and maintain a good level of humidity—do not allow the soil to dry out. At the end of the summer, gradually reduce watering and stop altogether when the leaves have faded.

Light: enjoys good light, but keep out of direct sunlight. If the light is too strong it will harm the delicate colors of the foliage.

Feeding: feed every two to four weeks in spring and summer with half strength food for foliage plants.

Repotting and growing medium: in March, start the tubers off on the surface of a pot filled with slightly moist peat at a temperature of 70° F (21° C). Once the first shoots appear, plant up the tubers in a mixture of equal parts peat and compost at a depth of 1 inch (2 cm). Increase watering as the leaves develop.

Cultivation tip: in winter, store the tubers in dry peat at a temperature of between 55° and 61° F (13° and 16° C).

▼ *Caladium bicolor*

Caladium bicolor ▼

Caladium bicolor ▼

Calanthe

Calanthe

Decorative interest

Calanthes are essentially terrestrial orchids and are native to different temperate and tropical regions of Asia. The foliage can be evergreen or deciduous—temperature requirements will vary accordingly, so find out about this before making your purchase. The species and hybrids with deciduous foliage are more widely cultivated. *Calanthe vestita* is a beautiful species with ovoid, silver to pale green pseudo-bulbs. The large, deciduous leaves are narrow and lanceolate, and grow to a length of over 36 inches (1 meter). The flower spikes appear in the fall, usually just after the leaves have fallen. They bear clusters of white or pale pink flowers with purple-tinged pink labella in the center.

Ease of cultivation

Calanthes are robust orchids that are quite undemanding but do require a lot of space when in leaf.

Propagation: when repotting, separate the old pseudo-bulb if it is still firm, and repot it separately.

CARING FOR YOUR PLANT

Watering and humidity: water freely during the growing period. Reduce watering when the leaves turn yellow in the fall, then stop altogether in winter. Calanthes enjoy high levels of humidity, but spraying can mark the leaves.

Light: enjoys quite bright conditions, but keep the plant out of direct sunlight.

Feeding: feed every two weeks in spring and summer with special food for orchids.

Repotting and growing medium: every year when growth begins, repot in orchid compost.

Cultivation tip: calanthes with deciduous leaves should be kept at a temperature of 64° to 68° F (18° to 20° C) in summer; after flowering, move them to a cool room at 50° to 54° F (10° to 12° C). Species with evergreen leaves need a regular temperature of 59° to 72° F (15° to 22° C) throughout the year.

TROUBLE SHOOTING

◆ The leaves become pale and dry: red spider mites thrive in warm, dry conditions. Increase the ambient humidity. If necessary, treat the plant with an acaricide.

◀ *Calanthe veratrifolia*

Calanthe veratrifolia ▶

Calanthe harrisii ▼

Calathea

C. makoyana
Calathea, peacock plant
synonym: *Maranta makoyana*

Decorative interest
The peacock plant has exceptionally striking, handsome leaves. Measuring 6 to 8 inches (15 to 20 cm) in length, the fine, oval, upright leaves are carried on leaf stalks that rise directly from the root. On the upper side they are silvery-green edged with mid-green, and have large, irregular, dark green markings along the median vein. On the underside, the markings are red or purple. The plant grows to a height of 16 to 24 inches (40 to 60 cm) with a spread of 12 to 16 inches (30 to 40 cm). This splendid plant is native to Brazil.

Associates well with… combine your peacock plant with *Aglaonema commutatum* "Silver Queen," which has silvery foliage.

Calathea makoyana ▼

▼ *Calathea rufibarba*

Ease of cultivation

Calatheas require a certain amount of attention in terms of watering and maintaining a high level of humidity, but the results will more than compensate your efforts.

Propagation: the most common method used is clump division. This can only be done after a few years of cultivation, when the roots are sufficiently well developed. New plants can take a long time to become established and this method is not always successful.

Tip

Spray the leaves regularly in warm weather.

● RELATED SPECIES AND VARIETIES

Calathea lancifolia has upright, linear leaves with wavy edges and the limb can grow to 18 inches (45 cm) long. The green upper side of the leaf has dark green markings, while the underside is reddish-brown.

C. sanderiana (synonyms: *C. ornata* "Sanderiana," *C. majestica* "Sanderiana") has leaves 8 inches (20 cm) long which are bright green on the upper surface and pale purple-red on the underside. The young leaves have fine pink striations along the lateral veins, becoming ivory as the plant matures. It can reach a height and spread of between 16 and 32 inches (40 and 80 cm).

C. picturata "Argentea" has silvery-white, oval leaves edged with green on the upper surface and bright purple on the underside.

C. rufibarba has long, slender, lanceolate leaves with wavy edges that are dark olive-green on top and purple underneath.

Calathea "Medallion" ▶

Calathea picturata "Argentea" ▶

Calathea lancifolia ▶

Calathea orbifolia ▼

Calathea zebrina ▼

Calathea sanderiana ▼

Calathea albertii ▼

Calathea

C. crocata
Flowering calathea

Decorative interest

This species forms clumps of leaves, veined on their upper sides and pinkish-purple on the underside. It is decorative mainly for its flower spikes with their large, orange-yellow bracts. Calatheas usually bloom in late winter as flowering is brought on by shorter daylight hours. They grow to 6 to 12 inches (15 to 30 cm) tall and 8 to 16 inches (20 to 40 cm) wide. Calatheas are native to the tropical rainforests of America and many are cultivated for their attractive foliage.

Associates well with... grow this calathea at the base of *Aglaonema commutatum* "Silver Queen," whose heavily variegated foliage forms an attractive contrast.

Calathea crocata ▶

TROUBLE SHOOTING

◆ The leaves become pale and lots of whitish spots appear: red spider mites thrive in warm, dry conditions, so increase the ambient humidity to try and eliminate them. If necessary, treat the plant with an appropriate acaricide.

Ease of cultivation

This flowering calathea needs a high level of ambient humidity and will not tolerate too much brightness.

Propagation: this can be done by clump division at the end of spring.

CARING FOR YOUR PLANT

Watering and humidity: during the growing period, water your plant with soft water (rainwater if possible) at room temperature. Maintain a high level of ambient humidity.

Light: provide good light but filter it with a blind or curtain.

Feeding: feed approximately every two weeks in spring and summer with food for foliage plants.

Repotting and growing medium: repot in spring or early summer in a mixture of peat, ericaceous compost, and sand.

Cultivation tip: the ideal growing temperature for this plant is between 61° and 70° F (16° and 21° C). It is important to avoid exposing the plant to sudden changes of temperature and drafts, and to too much brightness.

▼ *Calathea warscewiczii*

Calceolaria

C. x herbeohybrida   Calceolaria

Decorative interest

This cheerfully colored, charming biennial produces upright, branching stems with soft, slightly hairy, petiolated, pale green leaves. Its abundant yellow, orange, and red flowers with purple spots appear from November to May. They are puffy, round, or ovoid. This group of hybrids includes numerous cultivars. The genus *Calceolaria* is native to South America.

Associates well with… try putting several different-colored plants together in the same bowl.

Ease of cultivation

Calceolarias are plants to buy for a single season and discard after flowering. A cool temperature will ensure abundant flowers.

Propagation: from seed in June to flower the following spring, with a winter temperature of 45° to 50° F (7° to 10° C).

Tip

At night in summer put your plant on a window ledge or balcony; the cool of the night will improve flowering.

● RELATED SPECIES AND VARIETIES

"Atlas" is a type 14 inches (35 cm) high, producing large flowers, but is not widely available as its inflorescences are easily damaged when transported. Nevertheless, it is recommended to plant lovers who can get hold of the seeds and successfully germinate them.

"Mona" is a type 10 inches (25 cm) high, which has flowers 2½ inches (6 cm) across in a wide range of colors, often with markings.

"Cosette" is a dwarf plant 6 to 10 inches (15 to 25 cm) tall, which produces a profusion of flowers just over 1 inch (3 cm) in diameter, in shades of red and yellow with purple markings.

Calceolaria x *herbeohybrida* ▼

Calceolaria x *herbeohybrida* ▼

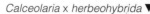

CARING FOR YOUR PLANT

Watering and humidity: water generously while in flower, but never leave water standing in the saucer. Try not to wet the leaves as they are liable to rot.

Light: bright conditions, but keep out of direct sunlight.

Feeding: feed every two weeks while in flower, with food for flowering plants.

Repotting and growing medium: there is no point in repotting calceolarias as they are seasonal plants.

Cultivation tip: this is an accommodating plant but it cannot tolerate dry heat—the flower buds will drop. Stand the pot on a saucer filled with damp gravel and try to maintain a temperature of around 59° to 64° F (15° to 18° C).

Callisia

C. warszewicziana   Callisia

Decorative interest

Callisia are related to spiderworts (*Tradescantia*). Most are cultivated for their creeping habit and their foliage, which is often variegated, but this plant—only recently available commercially—is prized essentially for its flowers. It produces a compact clump of lanceolate leaves that are green, tinged with purple. From the center of these, flower stems emerge carrying tight clusters of small, rounded, purple-blue flowers. Callisias produce numerous side shoots.

Ease of cultivation

Callisias are not difficult to grow but they do require a bright position; they benefit from spending the summer outdoors.

Propagation: separate off the side shoots and root them in a moist mixture of peat and sand.

Tip

Don't keep these plants in transit areas as callisias break easily.

● RELATED SPECIES AND VARIETIES

Callisias with decorative foliage are dealt with under spiderworts (see *Tradescantia*).

TROUBLE SHOOTING

◆ Fine webs develop between the leaves: red spider mites thrive in warm, dry conditions. Increase the ambient humidity. In cases of heavy infestation, treat the plant with an acaricide.

CARING FOR YOUR PLANT

Watering and humidity: water moderately during the growing period and never leave water standing in the saucer. Water less frequently in winter.

Light: full sunlight or filtered bright conditions. In the sun the plant will develop a more compact shape and the leaves will take on a beautiful purple tint.

Feeding: feed every two to three weeks in spring and summer with food for flowering plants.

Repotting and growing medium: repot in spring, in ordinary compost for foliage plants.

Cultivation tip: in summer, move your plant out into the yard or on to a terrace in a sunny position. In winter, bring it back in and keep it in a conservatory or temperate greenhouse.

▼ *Callisia warszewicziana* "Safira"

Callisia warszewiciana "Safira" ▼

Callistemon

C. citrinus   Bottle brush plant

Decorative interest

Calllistemon are evergreen trees and shrubs native to Australia. Remarkable for its striking flowers, the species *C. citrinus* is hardy in sheltered situations in the south of France. This small shrub can reach a height of over 6 feet (2 meters) when grown in a container. Its gray-green, straight, lanceolate leaves give off a citron fragrance when rubbed. The flower spikes, with flowers reduced to tufts of long stamens, form brilliant red bottle brushes in summer. There are other species and varieties, mostly with red flowers, though some are yellow.

▼ *Callistemon citrinus*

CARING FOR YOUR PLANT

Watering and humidity: water generously during the growing period, with soft water if possible, but never leave water standing in the saucer. Reduce watering in winter according to the temperature.

Light: several hours of direct sunlight daily.

Feeding: feed every two weeks in spring and summer with food for flowering plants.

Repotting and growing medium: repot young plants at the end of winter in a lime-free, ericaceous compost.

Cultivation tip: in order to flower, the bottle brush plant needs to spend the winter months in a cool, bright place at temperatures of 41° to 53° F (5° to 12° C)—a cold conservatory or greenhouse are ideal locations.

Ease of cultivation

Bottle brush plants are easy to grow in a cold greenhouse. If you have a yard or terrace, move your plant outdoors in summer.

Propagation: take semi-woody cuttings at the end of summer and root them in a mixture of peat and sand.

● RELATED GENUS

Metrosideros is a closely related genus with around thirty species and is native to New Zealand and Polynesia. *Metrosideros excelsa* (sometimes known as *M. tomentosa*) is a small, slow-growing shrub. Its leaves are dark green and downy-white on the underside, and it has abundant crimson flowers.

Metrosideros excelsa ▼

Campanula

C. isophylla

Campanula, Mary's star

Decorative interest

Mary's star (also known as star of Bethlehem) produces creeping stems with heart-shaped leaves on leaf stalks 1½ to 2 inches (4 to 6 cm) long. In summer, it produces numerous violet-blue flowers on flat-topped inflorescences that almost conceal the foliage. The plant grows to 4 to 6 inches (10 to 15 cm) high and about 10 inches (25 cm) across. It is a species native to northern Italy and can be grown in a pot on a windowsill or in a hanging basket.

Associates well with... campanulas combine well with various species of ivies and begonias.

Ease of cultivation

Campanulas need to be cool during the summer and have a period of winter rest in a cool place.

Propagation: the easiest method of propagation is to take cuttings during the summer. Take 1 to 2 inch (2 to 5 cm) cuttings from non-flowering shoots and insert them in a light, free-draining mixture of three parts coarse sand to one part peat, and root them in a cold frame.

Tip

Deadhead regularly to prolong flowering.

TROUBLE SHOOTING

◆ The leaves become pale and dry: red spider mites thrive in warm, dry conditions. Maintain a high level of humidity and spray the foliage regularly.

CARING FOR YOUR PLANT

Watering and humidity: water every day in summer, twice a week when the temperature drops to 59° to 64° F (15° to 18° C), and only once a week when it drops below 59° F (15° C). On very hot days, give the foliage a good spray.

Light: this campanula requires very good light, but no direct sunlight in summer.

Feeding: feed every two weeks in spring and summer with food for flowering plants.

Repotting and growing medium: repot at the end of winter if the plant is pot-bound, using houseplant potting compost.

Cultivation tip: at the end of fall, reduce watering; cut long stems back to the roots and move the plant to a cool spot (45° to 50° F (7° to 10° C) is sufficient).

● **RELATED SPECIES AND VARIETIES**

Campanula isophylla "Alba" is a superb variety with white flowers.
Campanula isophylla "Mayi" has light blue flowers with white centers.

Campanula isophylla "Napoli" ▼

Campanula medium ▶

Campanula carpatica ▶

Capsicum

C. annuum   Ornamental pepper

Decorative interest

The ornamental pepper is a short-lived plant cultivated for its decorative fruit. It has a bushy habit and produces slender stems and dark green, pointed, lanceolate leaves. Small, white, insignificant flowers give rise in the fall to colorful fruit, the shape and color of which varies according to the variety: they can be cylindrical, pointed, square, green, yellow, orange, red, or violet. The fruits can last for two or three months on the plant before dropping. As the plant is an annual it is then discarded.

Ease of cultivation

The ornamental pepper is usually treated as a decorative, seasonal plant.
Propagation: can be grown from seed, but this is not easy to achieve in indoor conditions.

CARING FOR YOUR PLANT

Watering and humidity: water moderately, keeping the compost slightly moist but never leave water standing in the saucer.
Light: a bright, sunny position.
Feeding: there is no point in feeding plants bought in the fall.
Repotting and growing medium: repotting is not necessary as the plant is discarded at the end of the season.
Cultivation tip: give your ornamental pepper as much sunlight as possible when the fruit are developing. Fruit will last longer at a cool temperature of approximately 59° F (15° C), although the plant will tolerate up to 68° F (20° C).

Worth remembering

If you don't have a greenhouse, capsicums can be difficult to cultivate. It is better to buy a plant from July onwards, when it will already have fruit.

▼ *Capsicum annuum*

Capsicum annuum ▶

▼ *Capsicum annuum*

Carex

C. brunnea "Variegata"
Sedge

Decorative interest

This extensive genus includes numerous perennial, rhizomatous species, both evergreen and deciduous, that grow in the wetlands in a range of varying climates. *Carex brunnea* "Variegata," native to Asia, is the species most commonly cultivated as a houseplant. It produces a clump of green, grass-like leaves with white stripes, from 12 to 16 inches (30 to 40 cm) in length. The flowers are of little interest.

Ease of cultivation

This sedge is easy to grow in a cool room.

Propagation: by clump division in spring, when the plant has become pot-bound.

CARING FOR YOUR PLANT

Watering and humidity: water abundantly during the growing period and more moderately in winter. You can leave a little water in the saucer in very hot weather.

Light: bright light, but filtered during the hottest part of the day.

Feeding: feed every two weeks in spring and summer with food for foliage plants.

Repotting and growing medium: repot in spring, if necessary, in a mixture of compost and good yard soil.

Cultivation tip: in winter, keep your plant at between 50° and 59° F (10° and 15° C) in a spot with plenty of natural light.

TROUBLE SHOOTING

◆ The leaves become sticky and deformed: aphids are attacking the shoots. Treat with a suitable insecticide.

Carex brunnea "Variegata" ▼

Caryota

C. mitis

Caryota

Decorative interest

This palm is characterized by large, bipennate leaves. The angular form of the leaflets has earned it the name "fishtail palm." It forms several trunks (stipes) and grows to a height of 16 to 23 feet (5 to 7 meters) in the tropics. As a pot plant it rarely exceeds 6½ feet (2 meters). It grows slowly and does not produce flowers when cultivated indoors.

Ease of cultivation

The fishtail palm requires a constant temperature and a high level of ambient humidity.

Propagation: growing from seed is best left to the professionals. You can try propagating the plant from offsets: remove offsets with a few roots and place them in pots filled with moist compost. Keep warm but out of direct sunlight until growth begins.

Caryota mitis ▶

TROUBLE SHOOTING

◆ The leaves become pale and dry: red spider mites thrive in warm, dry conditions. Increase the ambient humidity and spray the foliage. If necessary, treat the plant with an acaricide.

▲ *Caryota mitis* inflorescence

CARING FOR YOUR PLANT

Watering and humidity: water abundantly during the active growing period but never leave water standing in the saucer. In fall and winter, growth slows down: water a little less frequently. Spray the foliage regularly in hot weather.

Light: bright but filtered light.

Feeding: feed every two to three weeks in spring and summer with food for foliage plants.

Repotting and growing medium: repot every two or three years in early spring, in a mixture of yard soil and potting compost, with a good layer of drainage material at the bottom of the pot. For large specimens, a top dressing will suffice.

Cultivation tip: avoid dry atmospheres and keep your palm warm, maintaining a minimum temperature of 55° to 59° F (13° to 15° C).

Castanospermum

C. australe
Moreton Bay chestnut, blackbean

Decorative interest
This genus of the family leguminacaea has only one tree species—*Castanospermum australe*—which is native to the tropical rainforests of Australia. It is planted along the edges of roads and is a much-valued source of timber. It grows slowly but can reach a height of 66 feet (20 meters) in its natural habitat. Young specimens are grown as houseplants for the decorative quality of their leaves. The large, dark green, glossy, pennate leaves have lanceolate leaflets. Mature trees produce butterfly-shaped, yellow and red flowers, followed by large pods containing three to five seeds, similar to chestnuts.

Ease of cultivation
Castanospermums need to be watered very regularly, but never leave water standing in the saucer.
Propagation: grow from fresh seed at 64° to 77° F (18° to 25° C).

Worth remembering
The seeds, which look like chestnuts, are poisonous.

CARING FOR YOUR PLANT

Watering and humidity: water regularly and allow the surface of the compost to dry out between waterings. In dry weather, spray the foliage regularly.
Light: bright conditions, but keep out of the hot midday sun in summer.
Feeding: feed every two to three weeks in spring and summer with food for foliage plants.
Repotting and growing medium: repot in spring, if necessary, in ordinary potting compost.
Cultivation tip: the Moreton Bay chestnut can tolerate temperatures close to 32° F (0° C), in which case the foliage is semi-deciduous, and can be planted outdoors in a mild climate.

Castanospermum australe ▶

TROUBLE SHOOTING

◆ Small brown lumps appear on the stems and the leaves become sticky: these are scale bugs. Remove them with a Q-tip dipped in alcohol, or treat the plant with a systemic insecticide.

Cattleya

Cattleya

Decorative interest

These orchids are epiphytes, which means that in their natural habitat (the American tropics), they grow on the trunks of trees. They produce very colorful flowers at various times of year, depending on the species. Certain botanical species of *Cattleya* and numerous hybrids are suitable for indoor cultivation, preferably in a warm greenhouse or at a large window. Cattleyas produce pseudo-bulbs with one or two thick, fleshy, bright green leaves. The flower-scapes appear from the tips of the pseudo-bulbs and bear one or more flowers, which are characterized by a broad, tongue-shaped labellum. Their colors are very varied.

Cattleya aurantiaca: bears small flowers in summer. They are 1 to 2 inches (3 to 5 cm) in diameter and bright orange or pale yellow with dark red spots or stripes.

Cattleya bowringiana: flowers in the fall. The blooms are 4 inches (10 cm) in diameter and pale purple-red with a white-yellow base and the labellum edged in dark purple.

Cattleya forbesii: blooms in summer. The fragrant flowers are 2 to 2¾ inches (5 to 7 cm) in diameter, pink to pale green, and the labellum has yellow stripes.

Cattleya guttata: blooms in winter. The flowers are 2¾ inches (7 cm) in diameter and yellow to lime green, with purple-red markings or purple stripes.

Cattleya labiata: flowers in the fall and winter. The flowers are pale pink with a yellow-throated, crimson labellum.

▲ Cattleya

Cattleya mossiae: flowers in early summer. The scented blooms are 6 inches (15 cm) in diameter and pink to magenta, with a yellow-throated, white or lilac labellum.

Cattleya skinneri: blooms from winter to spring. The flowers are 2½ to 4 inches (6 to 10 cm) in diameter and purple-pink to bright purple, with a white or cream labellum.

There are countless other hybrids produced by crossing cattleyas with other close genera such as *Laelia*, *Sophronitis*, and *Brassavola*.

Ease of cultivation

Cattleyas are difficult plants to cultivate. A night temperature of about 7° to 9° F (4° to 5° C) below the daytime temperature is essential for flower formation.

Propagation: divide the clump, but only if you can obtain pieces with at least three pseudo-bulbs.

Worth remembering

If kept at a constant temperature, your cattleya will not flower.

Cattleya leopoldii ▼

CARING FOR YOUR PLANT

Watering and humidity: water abundantly with soft water in summer but allow the fibrous growing medium to dry out almost completely between waterings. Reduce watering after flowering and in winter. Spray the foliage daily with soft water when the weather is hot.

Light: enjoys bright conditions, but keep out of direct sunlight during the summer.

Feeding: feed at every third or fourth watering with plant food for orchids.

Repotting and growing medium: repot after the rest period, when the new shoots have reached the rim of the pot, using a special orchid compost.

Cultivation tip: plant your cattleyas in wooden baskets or in open-sided pots to ensure the roots are well ventilated. Give your plant its rest period: two months, during which watering is almost completely suspended.

TROUBLE SHOOTING

◆ The leaves turn black: this is due to overwatering or a lack of ventilation, causing the plant to rot.

◆ Small brown lumps appear on the leaves and pseudo-bulbs: these are scale bugs. Remove them with a Q-tip dipped in alcohol, or treat the plant with a suitable insecticide.

◆ The young shoots become deformed and sticky: aphids develop in colonies. Treat your plant with an insecticide.

Ceropegia

C. linearis ssp. woodii
String of hearts

Decorative interest

This small, tuberous succulent native to South Africa is quite unusual. It produces long, thin, trailing stems that can grow to 6 or 7 feet (2 meters) in length. These carry strings of small, opposed, heart-shaped leaves that are dark gray-green with silver variegation on the upper sides and purple-pink on the undersides. In summer, the plant sometimes produces small, modest, pink tubular flowers, swollen at the base and between ½ and 1 inch (1 to 2 cm) long.

Ease of cultivation

Ceropegia is easy to grow as a hanging plant.

Propagation: remove the bulbils that develop along the stems and plant them on the surface of some sandy compost.

Worth remembering

The stems of the string of hearts are extremely brittle and break easily.

CARING FOR YOUR PLANT

Watering and humidity: water during the growing period, but moderately. Allow the compost to dry out to a certain depth between waterings. In winter, reduce watering even further.

Light: requires at least three to four hours of sunshine daily or the foliage will lose its color.

Feeding: feed once a month in spring and summer with a weak dilution of plant food.

Repotting and growing medium: repot every three to four years in ordinary compost enriched with coarse sand, or in compost for cactuses and succulents.

Cultivation tip: plenty of sun and very little water are the golden rules for this plant. It can be kept in the cool in winter at 50° to 53° F (10° to 12° C).

Ceropegia sandersonii ▼   ▼ Ceropegia barkleyi

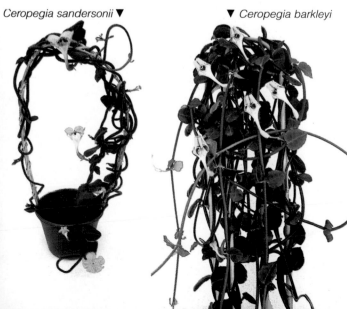

▲ Ceropegia linearis ssp. woodii

TROUBLE SHOOTING

◆ Small brown, sticky lumps appear on the stems and leaves: these are scale bugs. Remove them with a Q-tip dipped in alcohol, or treat the plant with a systemic insecticide.

Chamaedorea

C. elegans — Dwarf palm

Decorative interest

Native to Mexico and Guatemala, this small palm, which rarely grows above 3 feet (1 meter), is prized for its elegant appearance. It produces arching, pennate palms composed of mid-green, lanceolate leaflets. As it matures, the lower palms drop, revealing a thin, upright stipe. Mature plants produce spikes of small, yellow, insignificant flowers.

Associates well with... for a fuller effect, group several specimens together in the same pot.

Ease of cultivation

This is an accommodating plant but it will be at its best if you can provide good humidity.

Propagation: from seed, but the process is a slow one and best left to the professionals.

Chamaedorea elegans ▼

CARING FOR YOUR PLANT

Watering and humidity: keep the growing medium moist at all times, but not wet, during the growing season. In winter, water less frequently, depending on the temperature. In warm weather, spray the foliage frequently.

Light: bright conditions, but keep out of direct sunlight. The dwarf palm tolerates shade but its growth will be noticeably slower in poor light.

Feeding: feed every two to three weeks in spring and summer with half strength food for foliage plants.

Repotting and growing medium: repot in early spring if the plant has become pot-bound, using ordinary compost with a little added sand.

Cultivation tip: although the dwarf palm tolerates temperatures as low as 55° F (13° C), it is happier at temperatures of between 64° and 72° F (18° and 22° C).

TROUBLE SHOOTING

◆ The leaves become pale and are covered in small, whitish spots: red spider mites thrive in warm, dry conditions. Increase the ambient humidity and spray the foliage frequently. If necessary, treat the plant with an appropriate acaricide.

● **RELATED SPECIES AND VARIETIES**

Chamaedorea metallica has simple (undivided) palms, deeply indented at the top; it is bluish-green with a metallic sheen.

◀ *Chamaedorea metallica*

▼ *Chamaedorea tepejilote* (fruits)

Chlorophytum

C. comosum "Vittatum"

Chlorophytum, spider plant

Decorative interest

This vigorous plant, also known as the spider plant, is a favorite among novice plant lovers. It forms a large clump of linear, arching leaves 10 to 12 inches (25 to 30 cm) long and pale green with a central, white or cream, sometimes broad stripe. In spring and especially in summer, flower stems appear, carrying small, white flowers at their tips and then plantlets; the weight of these causes the stems to arch downwards toward the soil where the plantlets quickly form roots.

Associates well with... this accommodating plant combines well with many other species. Chlorophytums are ideal as underplanting for species that tend to lose their lower leaves, such as *Dracaena marginata*.

Ease of cultivation

Extremely easy to cultivate. There are few other species as willing to grow as the spider plant.

Propagation: remove well-developed plantlets and root them in water or in a small pot.

Worth remembering

Spider plants can tolerate short periods at 45° F (7° C) in a dry growing medium.

● RELATED SPECIES AND VARIETIES

Chlorophytum comosum "Variegatum" has green leaves edged with white. *C. orchidastrum* "Green Orange" is a recent variety. It produces green, lanceolate leaves carried on orange-colored, sheathed stalks. The veins are also orange-tinged. The small, white flowers grow in clusters in dense, cylindrical panicles at the base of the foliage.

◀ *Chlorophytum comosum* "Vittatum"

TROUBLE SHOOTING

◆ The leaves become sticky and deformed: aphids are attacking the shoots. Treat with a suitable insecticide.

◆ The tips of the leaves turn brown: the air is too dry. Cut off the brown tips, leaving a little dead tissue behind. Spray the leaves more often.

Chlorophytum orchidastrum "Green Orange" ▼

Chlorophytum comosum "Vittatum" ▼

CARING FOR YOUR PLANT

Watering and humidity: water regularly during the growing period to keep the compost moist. Reduce watering in winter, particularly when the temperature is unusually low.

Light: enjoys bright conditions, with a little sun in winter. Will tolerate semi-shade but the variegation will be less striking.

Feeding: feed every ten to fifteen days in spring and summer with food for foliage plants.

Repotting and growing medium: repot in spring when the plant has become pot-bound, using ordinary compost.

Cultivation tip: spider plants are tolerant of dry indoor conditions but enjoy regular spraying in summer. Once the plant becomes less attractive, do not hesitate to replace it through propagation.

Chrysalidocarpus

C. lutescens
synonym: *Areca lutescens*

Areca palm

Decorative interest

The areca palm forms a clump of bright green palms, 3 to 10 feet (1 to 3 meters) in length; carried on a yellowish petiole, these are pennate and arching. A native of Madagascar, the areca palm can reach a height of between 5 and 13 feet (1.5 and 4 meters) when grown in a pot.

Associates well with... it is difficult to combine a palm with other plants. However, a number of young areca palms grouped together in the same pot can be very attractive.

Ease of cultivation

The areca palm is easy to cultivate but will appreciate some ambient humidity.

Propagation: it is possible to grow this plant from seed but it can be quite complicated. It is easier to divide the lateral offsets that develop at the base of the plant.

Chrysalidocarpus lutescens ▼

CARING FOR YOUR PLANT

Watering and humidity: water abundantly during the growing period to keep the compost very moist, but do not leave water standing in the saucer. Reduce watering in winter. Spray the foliage every day.

Light: enjoys conditions that are as bright as possible, but keep out of direct sunlight.

Feeding: feed every two weeks in spring and summer with food for foliage plants.

Repotting and growing medium: repot every two years in spring, with a mixture of compost, peat, and sand, and put a good layer of drainage in the bottom of the pot.

Cultivation tip: the winter temperature should not be allowed to drop below 55° F (13° C).

◄ *Chrysalidocarpus lutescens*

Chrysanthemum

C. hortorum

Florists' chrysanthemum, fall chrysanthemum

Decorative interest

Although fall is the main season for pot chrysanthemums, "forced" plants are available all year round (this is achieved by artificially altering the number of daylight hours to which the plants are exposed). Hybrids come in a wide range of forms and different colors. Small single and double daisy-like blooms are often preferred to larger flowers.

Chrysanthemum hortorum ▶

CARING FOR YOUR PLANT

Watering and humidity: water regularly, keeping the compost slightly moist at all times.

Light: bright conditions with some sunlight, but not at the hottest part of the day.

Feeding: feed every ten to fifteen days during the flowering season with food for flowering plants.

Repotting and growing medium: this plant is generally discarded after flowering, so does not need repotting.

Cultivation tip: in order to prolong flowering, stand the pot on wet gravel in a warm room. This will also increase the ambient humidity.

Ease of cultivation

This seasonal plant will flower longer if you give it a cool, light, and airy position at around 54° to 61° F (12° to 16° C).

Propagation: best left to the experts.

Worth remembering

When buying a chrysanthemum, choose one in which the flower buds are already showing some color. Small buds that are still green do not always open.

TROUBLE SHOOTING

◆ The leaves become sticky and deformed: aphids are attacking the plant. Treat it with a suitable insecticide.

◆ The leaves become pale and dry: red spider mites thrive in warm, dry conditions. Increase the ambient humidity. If necessary, treat the plant with an acaricide.

Daisy-type flowers ▲

Spider chrysanthemum with tube-like petals ▲

Small semi-double blooms ▲

Small double blooms ▲

● RELATED GENUS

Ajanias, which are similar to chrysanthemums, are cultivated mainly for their decorative foliage: green, lobed leaves delicately edged with silvery-gray. *Ajania pacifica* (synonyms: *Chrysanthemum pacificum*, *Dendranthema pacificum*) produces large, glossy, yellow flower buds in the fall which last for several weeks before opening.

The variety "**Pink Ice**" has clusters of pink blooms with yellow centers. This is a short-day plant so flowering naturally occurs in the fall, although horticulturalists manage to make them flower at different times of year by controlling the plants' exposure to daylight. These plants are native to central and eastern Asia and are hardy so they can also be planted outside in flower borders.

Ajania pacifica "Pink Ice" ▼

Cissus

C. rhombifolia
synonym: *Cissus rhomboidea*

Cissus, grape ivy

Decorative interest
Native to the American tropics, this cissus has long, slender, trailing, or climbing stems bearing dark green, rhomboidal leaves with toothed edges in groups of three. Trained on a support, it forms a dense, green column. Young plants are ideal for growing in hanging containers.

Ease of cultivation
This vine is happy almost anywhere.
Propagation: from terminal cuttings taken in spring or early summer.

● RELATED SPECIES AND VARIETIES
Cissus rhombifolia "Ellen Danica" has heavily divided leaflets.
C. antarctica is a very vigorous, twining, Australian species. Its bright green, oval leaves are strongly dentate. It can easily grow to 6½ to 10 feet (2 to 3 meters). Young plants can be cultivated in hanging containers.
C. discolor has large, dark green, pointed leaves with attractive silvery-white and purple variegation.
C. striata produces slender stems bearing leaves composed of three to five bright green, tough, obovate leaflets.

▼ *Cissus rhombifolia*

◀ *Cissus rhombifolia* "Ellen Danica"

● **RELATED GENUS**

Tetrastigma voinierianum is a vigorous, twining vine from the tropical forests of Laos. The brown, velvety stems bear leaves divided into three or five leaflets; these are glossy and dark green on the upper side and reddish-brown and downy on the underside. The plant is a quick grower, rapidly gaining in size and needing a very sturdy support. It requires warmth (55° to 59° F/13° to 15° C) and plenty of humidity.

Cissus striata
(trained as climber) ▶

Cissus antarctica ▶

Cissus rotundifolia ▼

Cissus striata (as hanging plant) ▼

Tetrastigma voinierianum ▼

Citrus

C. limon — Lemon tree

Decorative interest

The cultivated lemon tree is spiny and very branching and can grow to a height of 10 to 20 feet (3 to 6 meters). For pot cultivation more compact species are preferred, such as *Citrus limon* "**Meyer**," which only grows to 4 feet (1.2 meters). This shrub has dark green, oval leaves carried on spiny stems. The fragrant white blossom is followed by yellowish, thin-skinned, rounded fruit. This type of lemon tree is grown essentially for its decorative qualities.

Ease of cultivation

Lemon trees are best grown in a cool conservatory as they need a period of cool winter rest.

Propagation: between April and June, take stem cuttings 4 to 6 inches (10 to 15 cm) long, dip them in hormone rooting powder, and insert them in cutting compost at 70° F (21° C).

◄ x *citrofortunella microcarpa*

▼ *Citrus limon*

Citrus limon blossom ▲

● RELATED SPECIES AND VARIETIES

The citron tree, ***Citrus medica***, produces very large, oblong, lemon-yellow fruits with a coarse skin. *C. medica* var. *sarcodactylis* (synonym: *C. medica* "Sarcodactylis") produces unusual, strongly flavored fruit with curious, finger-like appendages that have earned it the name Buddha's hand.

TROUBLE SHOOTING

◆ Small brown lumps appear on the stems and leaves, which become sticky: lemon trees are very susceptible to attack from scale bugs. Remove these bugs with a Q-tip dipped in alcohol, or treat the plant with a systemic insecticide.

◆ The leaves become covered in a black, sooty deposit: fumagin is a fungus that develops on the sticky honeydew secreted by sap-sucking parasites such as scale bugs and aphids. Identify the cause and treat the problem accordingly.

CARING FOR YOUR PLANT

Watering and humidity: water once a week during the growing period, taking care not to leave water standing in the saucer. In winter, when it is cooler, only water sufficiently to prevent the compost drying out altogether. Spray the leaves occasionally in summer.

Light: at least four hours of sunlight per day. In summer, move your plant outdoors into full sunlight.

Feeding: feed every two weeks in spring and summer with citrus plant food.

Repotting and growing medium: repot your plant every two to three years in spring, in ordinary compost to which a little peat or sand has been added.

Cultivation tip: give your lemon tree plenty of sunlight and a definite period of cool winter rest in a cool conservatory at temperatures of 41° to 50° F (5° to 10° C).

Citrus medica var. *sarcodactylis* ▼

◄ *Citrus paradisi*

● **RELATED GENERA**

The genus ***Fortunella*** (kumquat) includes four or five species of shrubs that grow in the rainforests of Asia. The branches, which are often spiny, bear small, oval, evergreen leaves and small, white flowers followed by small, thick-skinned, rounded fruit which are eaten candied, in syrup or as jelly, mainly in China and Japan.

Fortunella japonica (sometimes sold under the name *Citrus japonica*) has spiny branches with elliptical leaves and produces round, orangey-yellow fruit just over an inch (3 to 4 cm) in diameter. It is also known by the name marumi. There is also a variety with speckled-white leaves.

F. margarita "Nagami" has spine-free branches, lanceolate leaves, and dark orange, oval fruit 1½ inches (4 cm) long and ¾ inch (2 cm) wide.

F. "Fukushu" produces small, bright orange fruit that are completely edible. This small, symmetrical tree has attractive, bright green leaves.

▲ *Fortunella japonica*

◄ *Fortunella* "Fukushu"

The calamondin, x *Citronella microcarpa* (synonym: x *Citrofortunella mitis*, *Citrus mitis*) is a hybrid created by crossing the two genera, *Citrus* and *Fortunella*. This large shrub, or small, bushy tree, produces bright green, oval leaves and axillary white flowers followed by rounded fruit that are yellow and then turn orange and that are ¾ to 1½ inches (2 to 4 cm) in diameter.

▼ x *Citrofortunella microcarpa*

◄ x *Citrofortunella microcarpa*

Clerodendrum

C. thomsoniae   Clerodendron

Decorative interest

This twining plant has simple, deep green leaves, either entire or dentate, with long stalks. The pleasantly scented flowers appear between June and September in terminal clusters. They have a swollen, white calyx enclosing a very bright scarlet corolla. The clerodendron is usually sold as a short-stemmed plant and requires regular cutting back to maintain its compact appearance.

Ease of cultivation

This can be a rather difficult plant to grow as very high humidity is essential during the growing period and it also requires a period of cool winter rest.
Propagation: in May or June take 4 to 6 inch (10 to 15 cm) cuttings and insert them in a moist mixture of equal parts sand and peat. Grow under cover at 70° to 73° F (21° to 23° C).

Worth remembering

You can plant this clerodendron directly into open soil in a greenhouse or conservatory: the stems can grow to 6½ to 10 feet (2 to 3 meters) in length.

Clerodendrum thomsoniae ▲

Clerodendrum thomsoniae ▼

CARING FOR YOUR PLANT

Watering and humidity: water generously during the growing period with soft water, but do not overwater. In winter, only water sufficiently to stop the growing medium drying out completely. In summer, regularly spray the leaves.

Light: bright conditions, but keep out of direct sunlight in summer.

Feeding: feed every ten to fifteen days in spring and summer with food for flowering plants.

Repotting and growing medium: repot in April in ordinary compost with added peat.

Cultivation tip: requires a period of winter rest in a cool spot at 55° to 59° F (13° to 15° C) to flower again the following year.

● RELATED SPECIES AND VARIETIES

Clerodendron thomsoniae "Delectum" is characterized by its pink to magenta flowers.

C. speciosissimum is an upright, woody-stemmed shrub with rounded, slightly lobed leaves and terminal clusters of scarlet flowers.

C. ugandense is a climber that produces terminal clusters of small blue and violet flowers.

C. wallichii has narrow, dark green, lanceolate leaves with wavy edges and trailing clusters of white flowers.

Clerodendrum paniculatum ▶

TROUBLE SHOOTING

◆ The leaves become pale and dry: red spider mites thrive in warm, dry conditions. Increase the ambient humidity and spray the foliage more often. If necessary, treat the plant with an acaricide.

◆ Small white bugs fly away when you touch the plant: whitefly are small, sap-sucking bugs that are difficult to eradicate. Treat the plant repeatedly with insecticide every eight to ten days.

▼ *Clerodendrum thomsoniae*

Clerodendrum wallichii ▼

Clerodendrum ugandense ▼

Clerodendrum speciosissimum ▼

Clivia

C. miniata   Clivia

Decorative interest
This handsome, fleshy-rooted plant produces long, dark green, glossy, strap-like leaves. They grow in the same direction, the bases stacked one above the other. Toward the end of winter, clivias produce a flower-scape topped by one or more inflorescences of orangey, trumpet-shaped flowers. There are also hybrids with yellow or red flowers.

Ease of cultivation
Clivias can be a little tricky to grow as they need a period of fall rest in order for flower buds to form.
Propagation: remove the offsets that appear at the base of the plant when they have at least three leaves 8 to 10 inches (20 to 25 cm) long.

Worth remembering
The fleshy roots of clivias are brittle and break easily.

● RELATED SPECIES AND VARIETIES
Clivia nobilis has drooping orangey-red flowers with green tips.
C. miniata var. *citrina* is a natural variety with yellow flowers.

CARING FOR YOUR PLANT

Watering and humidity: water moderately from the end of winter to summer; reduce watering in fall and early winter.
Light: enjoys bright conditions, but keep out of direct sunlight in summer.
Feeding: feed every two weeks in spring and summer with food for flowering plants.
Repotting and growing medium: repot every three to four years in ordinary compost when the roots have filled the pot. Terracotta pots are best as they are more stable, but choose pots that are not too big, as clivias flower better when relatively confined.
Cultivation tip: be careful with temperature control: cool conditions (50° to 54° F/10° to 12° C) are essential in early fall for the flower-scapes to form.

TROUBLE SHOOTING

◆ White, cottony clusters appear at the base of the leaves: mealy bugs can be difficult to eradicate. If there are only a few, remove them with a Q-tip dipped in alcohol. In cases of severe attack, treat the plant with a systemic insecticide.
◆ The plant fails to flower a second time: it has spent the fall in a room that was too warm or watering began too early in winter.

Clivia citrina hybrid ▼

Clivia nobilis ▼

◀ *Clivia miniata*

Clusia

C. rosea
Clusia

synonym: *Clusia major*

Decorative interest

The clusia is a shrub or small tree native to tropical America and is cultivated for its handsome, decorative foliage which resembles that of the rubber plant (*Ficus elastica*). The large, oval, opposed leaves, which are 8 to 12 inches (20 to 30 cm) long, are a bright, dark green, tapering near the base. The leaf stalk is striped and very short. When grown in a pot clusias can grow up to 6½ feet (2 meters) in height but do not usually flower. There are also varieties with variegated leaves.

Ease of cultivation

This tropical plant requires high levels of humidity.

Propagation: you can sow seeds in spring at 68° to 72° F (20° to 22° C), or take semi-woody cuttings in summer, growing them under cover with bottom heat.

Clusia rosea ▶

CARING FOR YOUR PLANT

Watering and humidity: water your plant abundantly during the growing period but never leave water standing in the saucer. Reduce watering during the winter months. Make sure you keep the humidity high by spraying the foliage twice a day.

Light: filtered.

Feeding: feed every two to three weeks in spring and summer with food for foliage plants.

Repotting and growing medium: repot every three or four years in spring in a mixture of compost and good yard soil, with added sand to improve drainage.

Cultivation tip: in winter, make sure the temperature does not drop below 61° F (16° C) and protect from sudden changes in temperature as these can cause leaf drop.

Cocos

C. nucifera   Coconut palm

Decorative interest

The coconut palms sold commercially are very young specimens. This palm can in fact grow as tall as 65 feet (20 meters) in its natural habitat in the tropics. From the half-buried nut there emerge elegant leaves in a beautiful, glossy green which are different from the pennate leaves that form later (though rarely when grown as a houseplant).

Ease of cultivation

It can be difficult to grow coconut palms indoors because they need a great deal of light, warmth, and humidity.

Propagation: grow from seed at 77° to 82° F (25° to 28° C), though this can be difficult for non-professionals.

CARING FOR YOUR PLANT

Watering and humidity: water moderately throughout the year so that the compost remains moist but not waterlogged. Stand the pot on a bed of wet gravel and spray the leaves daily.
Light: needs bright conditions, with as much sun as possible.
Feeding: feed every two weeks in spring and summer with half strength food for foliage plants.
Repotting and growing medium: there is often no point in repotting coconut palms as they are short-lived as houseplants. However, if appropriate, repot in spring every two to three years in fibrous compost, with added sand and ericaceous compost.
Cultivation tip: due to their need for light, warmth, and humidity, it is difficult to cultivate this sculptural plant for any length of time except in a tropical greenhouse.

TROUBLE SHOOTING

◆ The leaves turn pale and lots of small, whitish spots appear: red spider mites thrive in warm, dry conditions. Increase the ambient humidity and spray the foliage more often. If necessary, treat the plant with an appropriate acaricide.
◆ Small brown lumps appear on the leaves, which become sticky: these are scale bugs. Remove them with a Q-tip dipped in alcohol, or treat the plant with a systemic insecticide.

Cocos nucifera ▼

◀ *Cocos nucifera*

Codiaeum

C. variegatum   Croton

Decorative interest

Native to Malaysia, crotons are vigorous shrubs with entire or lobed leaves. They are very polymorphous, passing through various shades of red, orange, bronze, green, and pink, and are sometimes speckled or have white or yellow markings. Their flowers are insignificant. There are two natural varieties, one of which—*C. variegatum* var. *pictum*—is the source of most forms grown commercially. There are many commercial forms and they usually have broad, oval leaves, though the leaves can also be long and narrow or have wavy edges.

CARING FOR YOUR PLANT

Watering and humidity: water generously but not excessively during the growing period with soft, tepid water. Reduce watering in winter. In warm weather, spray the foliage frequently with soft water. Stand the pot on a bed of damp gravel and keep this moist.

Light: requires a very light position, but keep out of direct sunlight. Crotons need a lot of natural light to maintain good leaf coloring.

Feeding: feed every ten to fifteen days in spring and summer with food for foliage plants.

Repotting and growing medium: repot in early spring, if necessary, in ordinary compost with a little added sand.

Cultivation tip: do not expose your plant to temperatures below 64° F (18° C) and protect it from cold drafts and sudden changes of temperature.

◄ *Codiaeum variegatum* "Aucubaefolia"

◄ *Codiaeum variegatum* "Excellent"

◄ *Codiaeum variegatum* "Petra"

Associates well with… crotons combine well with green foliage plants, such as the bird's nest fern or a small philodendron.

Ease of cultivation

The main reasons why crotons tend to be short-lived when grown as houseplants are sudden changes in temperature or a definite lack of humidity. They can be difficult to grow successfully except in a warm greenhouse or a very humid conservatory.

Propagation: take 3 to 4 inch (8 to 12 cm) terminal cuttings from the lateral stems. Sprinkle the exposed area with a little wood charcoal to stop the latex seeping out. Insert the cuttings in a moist mixture of equal parts sand and peat and grow them under cover at 72° F (22° C).

Worth remembering

The sap produced by crotons is an irritant.

● RELATED SPECIES AND VARIETIES

Codiaeum variegatum var. *pictum* has given rise to numerous hybrids with a wide range of leaf forms and variegation.

Codiaeum variegatum "Mammi" ▼

Codiaeum variegatum var. *pictum* ▼

Codiaeum variegatum "Goldmoon" ▼

Breynia disticha ▼

Breynia disticha "Nana" ▼

● RELATED GENUS

Like crotons, the genus **Breynia** is a member of the Euphorbia family. Breynias are evergreen shrubs that grow in the tropical forests of Asia, Australia, and some Pacific islands. *Breynia disticha* (synonyms: *B. nivosa, Phyllanthus nivosus*) grows to a height of 3 to 6½ feet(1 to 2 meters) and produces dark red, zigzag leaves. The oval leaves, arranged one above the other, are dark green with white variegation, and are white and red when young.

Codonanthe

Codonanthe

Decorative interest

Codonanthes are perennial shrubs or plants with evergreen foliage and are native to central and South America. The most commonly cultivated species is *Codonanthe crassifolia*, a small, epiphytic plant, prized for its decorative trailing habit and abundant flowers, which are sometimes followed by colored fruits. The dark green, oval, pointed leaves are thick and waxy. The plant bears plentiful small, white, tubular flowers with purple-pink centers almost all year long. Orange berries may appear if the flowers have been pollinated. Codonanthes are excellent grown as hanging plants. *C. gracilis* is a related species producing trailing stems covered in lanceolate leaves. Its flowers are white with yellow centers.

Ease of cultivation

Codonanthes need regular watering and a constant temperature in order to grow well.

Propagation: take 4 to 6 inch (10 to 15 cm) terminal stem cuttings; remove the lower leaves and root them under cover in a moist mixture of peat and sand.

Codonanthe crassifolia ▼

Coffea

C. *arabica* "Nana"   Dwarf coffee

Decorative interest

Dwarf coffee plants grow no more than 3 feet (1 meter) tall. They are valued for their decorative, dark green foliage. Their opposed, glossy leaves are elliptical, with wavy edges, and are pointed at the tips. After a few years of cultivation they may produce small, white, starry flowers with a fragrance similar to orange blossom; these are followed by green berries which turn red and eventually brown as they ripen. However, plants grown indoors rarely produce flowers and fruit.

Ease of cultivation

Dwarf coffee plants are not difficult to grow, but they must be protected from cold and drafts.

Propagation: grow from seed in spring, using fresh seed; germinate under cover at 75° F (24° C).

CARING FOR YOUR PLANT

Watering and humidity: keep the compost moist during the growing period, but avoid overwatering. Reduce watering in fall and winter. Coffee plants enjoy high levels of humidity: stand the pot on damp gravel and spray the leaves regularly.

Light: medium light conditions, but keep out of direct sunlight.

Feeding: feed every two weeks in spring and summer with food for foliage plants.

Repotting and growing medium: repot in spring, if necessary, using ordinary compost.

Cultivation tip: the ideal temperature for these plants is between 64° and 70° F (18° and 21° C). Avoid drafts as these can cause sudden changes in temperature.

TROUBLE SHOOTING

◆ The ends of the leaves become dry: the air in the room is too dry. Spray the foliage more often.

◆ Small brown lumps appear on the stems and the underside of the leaves, which become sticky: these are scale bugs. Remove them with a Q-tip dipped in alcohol, or, if you are unsuccessful, treat the plant with a systemic insecticide.

▼ *Coffea arabica*

Coffea arabica ▶

Coffea arabica ▼

Coffea arabica ▼

Columnea

Columnea

Decorative interest

Several species and hybrids of columnea are cultivated as houseplants. They are long-stemmed, trailing plants (or climbing, if trained), covered in small, usually dark, opposed leaves. They light up when they come into bloom, producing tubular flowers in yellow or orange to scarlet, depending on the variety. Some can flower several times during the course of the year, others only in fall and winter. Flowering lasts for a number of weeks with flowers often opening along the entire length of the stem.

Columnea gloriosa produces long, trailing stems with simple, dark green, oval leaves and scarlet flowers with a small, yellow mark at the bottom of the throat. *C. microphylla* has very small leaves, less than ½ inch (1 cm) long, covered in reddish-brown hairs and orange-red flowers with yellow throats. *C.* x *banksii* has dark green, oval, smooth, glossy leaves, ¾ to 1½ inches (2 to 4 cm) long and slightly downy on the underside; it produces scarlet flowers.

Columnea ▼

CARING FOR YOUR PLANT

Watering and humidity: water your plant moderately but regularly during the summer months, with soft, tepid water. Reduce watering in winter. In warm weather, spray the foliage of smooth-leaved species frequently; in the case of plants with hairy leaves, stand the pot on wet gravel to increase humidity.

Light: bright conditions, but keep out of direct sunlight.

Feeding: feed every two weeks in spring and summer with half strength food for flowering plants.

Repotting and growing medium: repot every two years after flowering, in compost enriched with fibrous peat.

Cultivation tip: remove any weak branches and maintain good ambient humidity. Columneas grow well in hanging baskets, but keep them away from drafts.

Columnea ▼

TROUBLE SHOOTING

◆ Your plant no longer flowers: to encourage flowering, certain species, such as *Columnea microphylla*, need a period of rest in a cool spot—at temperatures of 55° to 61° F (13° to 16° C)—for at least a month. During this period, reduce watering and keep the compost almost dry. Once flower buds appear, gradually increase watering and move the plant into a warmer room.

Ease of cultivation

Columneas are sensitive to dry air. They also need protection from cold drafts. Avoid watering with cold water.

Propagation: take cuttings from non-flowering stems between March and May. Place them in a propagator or cover them with transparent plastic film. Grow them at a temperature of 68° to 72° F (20° to 22° C).

Worth remembering

Smooth-leaved species of columnea are easier to cultivate successfully than those with hairy leaves, which are more susceptible to rotting.

Columnea "Heckla" ▲

Columnea "Hostag" ▲

Columnea "Sanne" ▲

Columnea "Sanne" ▼

▼ *Columnea arguta*

▼ *Columnea hirta*

Cordyline

C. terminalis
Cordyline

synonym: *Cordyline fruticosa*

Decorative interest

Cordylines, which are similar to dracaenas, have leaves arranged in clumps. As they mature they eventually form a short trunk. The lanceolate leaves, which are 12 to 20 inches (30 to 50 cm) long, range from mid- to dark green and sometimes have cream, red, or purple variegation. As a houseplant, this cordyline, which is native to south-east Asia, will not grow more than 3 to 5 feet (1 to 1.5 meters) tall.

Associates well with... you can combine several species of cordylines and dracaenas. When the cordylines begin to lose their lower leaves, you can plant other trailing plants, such as ivy or cissus, around the base.

Ease of cultivation

This cordyline can be a little tricky to cultivate as it requires a high level of ambient humidity. *Cordyline australis*, with its narrower, tougher leaves, is more tolerant of dry air conditions.

Propagation: take terminal cuttings or stem sections and insert them in a light mixture of sand and peat. Keep under cover at approximately 68° F (20° C).

Cordyline terminalis ▼

◀ *Cordyline terminalis* "Atoom"

● RELATED SPECIES AND VARIETIES

Cordyline terminalis "Red Edge" has red and green striped leaves.
C. terminalis "Prince Albert" has handsome bright red and dark green leaves.
C. terminalis "Tricolor" has pale green leaves with red, pink, and cream variegation.
Cordyline australis has long, tough, narrow, pointed leaves which are pale green in the species but often variegated in cultivated varieties. This cordyline is more tolerant of cooler temperatures.
C. stricta has an elegant form, with long, deep green, linear leaves.

Cordyline terminalis "Red Edge" ▲

TROUBLE SHOOTING

◆ The edges of the leaves turn brown and curl up: the air is too dry. Spray the leaves daily.
◆ Deformed, sticky leaves reveal the presence of aphids: treat with a suitable insecticide.

Cordyline australis ▶

Cordyline australis "Red Star" ▶

Cordyline stricta ▶

Cordyline terminalis "Tango" ▼

Cordyline terminalis "Glauca" ▼

Cordyline terminalis "Kiwi" ▼

Corynocarpus

C. laevigatus
Corynocarpus, New Zealand laurel
synonym: *Corynocarpus laevigata*

Decorative interest
This evergreen tree, native to New Zealand, is grown for its decorative foliage. Its large, tough, oval leaves are dark green and glossy. In its natural habitat the corynocarpus can grow to a height of over 32 feet(10 meters), but when grown as a pot plant it takes on a bushy habit and grows to 6½ to 10 feet (2 to 3 meters). It produces small, greenish flowers but rarely when cultivated as a houseplant.

Ease of cultivation
The corynocarpus is easy to grow but it must spend the winter in the cool, in a greenhouse or temperate conservatory.
Propagation: take semi-woody cuttings at the end of summer and root them under cover in a moist mixture of peat and sand. Hormone rooting powder will encourage rooting.

Corynocarpus laevigatus "Variegatus" ▼

CARING FOR YOUR PLANT

Watering and humidity: water your plant moderately during the growing season. Reduce watering in winter, according to the ambient temperature.
Light: full sunlight.
Feeding: feed every three to four weeks in spring and summer with food for foliage plants.
Repotting and growing medium: repot in spring, if necessary, in a mixture of compost and good yard soil. Put a good layer of drainage material in the bottom of the pot.
Cultivation tip: you can move your plant outdoors in summer. In winter, give it a very light position at temperatures of 50° to 55° F (10° to 13° C).

TROUBLE SHOOTING

◆ Small brown lumps appear on the stems and the leaves become sticky: these are scale bugs. Remove them with a Q-tip dipped in alcohol, or treat the plant with a systemic insecticide.

● RELATED SPECIES AND VARIETIES
Corynocarpus laevigatus "Variegatus" produces green leaves with yellow variegation.

Corynocarpus laevigatus ▼

Crassula

Crassula

Decorative interest

This genus includes numerous succulents which are very different from one another in form, size, and cultivation requirements. They grow mainly in the arid and semi-arid areas of southern Africa.

Crassula arborescens is a strongly branching succulent that can grow to over 3 feet (1 meter) in height. Its fleshy, rounded leaves are 1¼ to 2½ inches (3 to 7 cm) long and silvery-green, often edged with red. Mature specimens can produce a few whitish-pink flowers in spring.

C. ovata also produces branching stems, with elliptical leaves ¾ to 1½ inches (2 to 4 cm) long; they are mid-green and glossy, sometimes edged with red. This crassula is sometimes sold under the name *C. arborescens*, which can lead to confusion.

C. perfoliata var. *minor* (synonym: *C. falcata*) has a thick, fleshy stem which bears numerous flat, fleshy, falcate, dull blue-green leaves, 2½ to 4 inches (6 to 10 cm) long. It produces small, red flowers in summer.

C. rosularis (synonym: *C. orbicularis*) produces rosettes of flattened leaves from which green flower stems tinged with red emerge, bearing light clusters of small flowers.

C. rupestris var. *marnieriana* (synonym: *C. marnieriana*) produces branching stems with fleshy, angular leaves, tightly stacked, each pair at a 90° angle from the previous one.

Ease of cultivation

Crassulas are undemanding plants but do require good light.

Propagation: take 2 to 3 inch (5 to 8 cm) terminal cuttings with at least two pairs of leaves and insert them in a compost for cactuses and succulents.

CARING FOR YOUR PLANT

Watering and humidity: water once a week during the growing period, but only every two weeks in fall and winter.

Light: enjoys bright conditions, with as much sun as possible, throughout the year.

Feeding: feed every three to four weeks in spring and summer with food for succulents.

Repotting and growing medium: repot every two years, in spring, in compost for cactuses and succulents, with a good layer of drainage material at the bottom of the pot.

Cultivation tip: plenty of light but moderate watering. Crassulas can spend the summer outdoors in a bright, sheltered position. The minimum winter temperature they will tolerate is 41° to 45° F (5° to 7° C).

Crassula ovata "Tricolor" ▼

Crassula "Isabelle" ▼

◀ *Crassula arborescens*

Crassula "Schmidtii" ▼

Crassula rosularis ▼

Crassula rupestris subsp.
marnieriana "Hottentot" ▼

TROUBLE SHOOTING

◆ White, cottony clusters appear at the base of the leaves: mealy bugs can be difficult to eradicate. If there are only a few, remove them with a Q-tip dipped in alcohol. In cases of severe attack, treat the plant with a suitable insecticide.

▲ *Crassula ovata*

Crassula ovata
"Horn tree" ▶

Crassula ovata
"Horn tree" ▶

Crocus

Crocus

Decorative interest

These small, bulbous plants, commonly seen in yards, can also be grown in pots and used for indoor decoration. Crocus "bulbs" are in fact corms, and from them emerge a number of open, cup-shaped flowers in a bright and varied range of colors, including some with stripes. The linear leaves develop at the same time as the flowers or shortly afterwards. There are numerous hybrids.

Plant the corms in September in ordinary compost with added coarse sand and place the pots in a dark, cool spot, such as a basement, at 41° to 50° F (5° to 10° C). When the flower buds begin to open, move the pots to a warm, bright room. You can also buy pre-planted pots, which are available in stores from November.

Crocus vernus "Joan of Arc" ▲

Ease of cultivation

Once they have flowered, crocuses need to return to a cool environment. The flowering period can be very short in a heated room.

Propagation: crocuses are propagated by separating off the new baby corms.

CARING FOR YOUR PLANT

Watering and humidity: water moderately, just enough to keep the growing medium slightly moist.

Light: bright conditions, but don't let your crocuses become overheated at a window if the room temperature is warm.

Feeding: not required.

Repotting and growing medium: after flowering, plant your crocuses in open ground if you have a yard.

Cultivation tip: keep your plants in a cool place, at temperatures of between 46° and 53° F (8° and 12° C) if possible, and not more than 61° F (16° C). If they are overwatered, the corms will rot.

● RELATED GENUS

Muscaris (*Muscari*) can be cultivated in the same way. These small plants produce tight clusters of tubular flowers on a bare stem, mainly in shades of blue. Grow them in tight groups for the best effect.

▼ *Crocus vernus* "Remembrance"

◄ *Crocus chrysanthus*

Crossandra

C. infundibuliformis   Crossandra

Decorative interest

This sub-shrub, native to tropical Asia, has glossy, mid-green, lanceolate leaves with wavy edges. It flowers in spring and summer, producing axillary spikes 2½ to 4 inches (5 to 10 cm) long, in colors ranging from orange-red to salmon-pink. They open from the base of the spike. As a houseplant, crossandras rarely grow taller than 12 to 16 inches (30 to 40 cm).

Ease of cultivation

Crossandras need warmth and humidity.
Propagation: in spring, take 2½ to 3 inch (5 to 8 cm) cuttings and plant them in a moist mixture of equal parts peat and sand. Grow under cover at 70° F (21° C).

Tip

Pinch out the tips of young shoots to promote branching.

● RELATED SPECIES AND VARIETIES

Crossandra infundibuliformis "Mona Whaled," has salmon-pink flowers and is the most common variety.

CARING FOR YOUR PLANT

Watering and humidity: during the growing period, water your plant once or twice a week with soft, slightly tepid water. Water less during the winter months. Stand the pot on damp gravel to increase the ambient humidity.
Light: strong light, but keep out of direct sunlight.
Feeding: feed every two weeks in spring and summer with food for flowerings plants.
Repotting and growing medium: repot young plants in early spring, every two years, in a mixture of ordinary and ericaceous compost.
Cultivation tip: the temperature should not be allowed to drop below 61° to 64° F (16° to 18° C). If your plant becomes less attractive, replace it by taking cuttings.

Crossandra infundibuliformis ▼

TROUBLE SHOOTING

◆ The leaves become pale and lots of whitish spots appear on the underside: red spider mites thrive in warm, dry conditions. Increase the ambient humidity. If necessary, treat the plant with an acaricide.

Crossandra infundibuliformis ▼

Cryptanthus

C. zonatus   Cryptanth

Decorative interest

Cryptanths are bromeliads valued for their decorative rosettes of tough leaves. *Cryptanthus zonatus* produces brownish-green, wavy leaves with silvery-gray horizontal bands, covered in white scales on the underside. The rosette can grow to 16 inches (40 cm) in diameter. *C. zonatus* "Zebrinus" is a variety with more strikingly contrasting foliage—chocolate-brown leaves with silvery-white bands. **Associates well with…** try mixing different species of cryptanthus together in a wide, shallow bowl.

Ease of cultivation

Cryptanths appreciate some ambient humidity and are easier to grow in a terrarium or bottle garden.

Propagation: separate and plant up lateral offsets in April.

Worth remembering

Cryptanths die after flowering; offsets will take four or five years of cultivation before flowering.

● RELATED SPECIES AND VARIETIES

Cryptanthus bivittatus has green, wavy leaves with toothed edges and creamy-white, longitudinal stripes becoming pink under a bright light. The small flowers are insignificant. This plant grows no larger than 6 to 8 inches (15 to 20 cm) in diameter. *C. acaulis* has slightly wavy, mid-green leaves, covered in pale gray scales.

C. bromelioides has green leaves with longitudinal white variegation.

C. fosterianus has red-brown leaves with very wavy edges and gray stripes.

CARING FOR YOUR PLANT

Watering and humidity: water your plant moderately throughout the year, making sure you keep the compost just slightly moist. Maintain a good level of ambient humidity by spraying the rosettes frequently with soft, tepid water.

Light: enjoys bright but filtered conditions. Choose a west-facing window for preference.

Feeding: feed every two weeks in spring and summer with a weak dilution of food for foliage plants (or orchid fertilizer).

Repotting and growing medium: repot in early spring, if necessary, in a very fibrous compost mixture or special compost for terrestrial bromeliads.

Cultivation tip: give your plant growing conditions that are as constant as possible.

TROUBLE SHOOTING

◆ The leaves become crisp and dry: the air is too dry. Spray the foliage more often, especially in winter when you have the heating on.

Cryptanthus zonatus "Zebrinus" ▶

Cryptanthus bromelioides ▼

Cryptanthus fosterianus ▶

Cryptanthus bivittatus "Tricolor" ▼

Ctenanthe

Ctenanthe

Decorative interest

Native to Brazil and Costa Rica, ctenanthes are related to calatheas and marantas. Their narrower leaves are carried on slender leaf stalks. The leaves of *Ctenanthe lubbersiana* are lanceolate and bright green, with yellow markings on the upper sides and pale green on the undersides. They can grow to 12 inches (30 cm) long. The flowers are insignificant.

C. burle-marxii has shorter, pale green, oval leaves with dark green, chevron stripes on the upper side and purple on the underside.

C. oppenheimiana produces 16 inch (40 cm) long, dark green, lanceolate leaves with silvery variegation on the upper side and purple on the underside. The variety "**Tricolor**" has foliage with irregular, pale green, dark green, and cream variegation.

C. setosa has narrow, lanceolate leaves on slender, hairy leaf stalks; the green limb has broad, silvery, lateral bands.

C. pilosa "**Golden Mosaic**" is a variety with dark green, light green, and cream variegation.

Ease of cultivation

Ctenanthes are tricky plants to grow as they need warmth and a high level of ambient humidity. They will not tolerate having cold roots.

Propagation: divide the clump in spring when repotting.

CARING FOR YOUR PLANT

Watering and humidity: during the growing period, water moderately to keep the compost slightly moist; regularly spray the foliage. Reduce watering in winter if the temperature drops.

Light: bright conditions, but out of direct sunlight.

Feeding: feed every two weeks in spring and summer with food for foliage plants.

Repotting and growing medium: repot in spring, if necessary, in ordinary compost enriched with peat.

Cultivation tip: protect the plant from drafts and keep the temperature as constant as possible—a minimum temperature of 59° F (15° C) is sufficient.

Ctenanthe burle-marxii ▶

Ctenanthe setosa ▼

◀ *Ctenanthe pilosa* "Golden Mosaic"

TROUBLE SHOOTING

◆ The leaves turn dry and curl up: the air is too dry. Spray the leaves more frequently and stand the pot on damp gravel to increase the ambient humidity.

◆ The leaves become pale and dry: red spider mites thrive in warm, dry conditions. Increase the ambient humidity and spray the foliage more often. If necessary, treat the plant with an acaricide.

Curcuma

C. alismatifolia   Curcuma

Decorative interest
Native to the tropical regions of Asia and Australia, curcumas are perennials with fleshy roots and make very decorative houseplants. The bluish, oval to oblong leaves arise in a clump from the base of the plant. In late spring, thick flower-scapes appear with an inflorescence of small, insignificant flowers at their tip and large, bright pink bracts. There are also hybrids with inflorescences in various colors.

Ease of cultivation
The curcuma grows in a tropical climate with a marked dry season and therefore needs a period of winter rest.
Propagation: you can divide the rhizomes of large clumps in spring, when repotting.

Worth remembering
The rhizome of certain species of this genus is used as a spice.

CARING FOR YOUR PLANT

Watering and humidity: water generously while your plant is in flower, then reduce the amount of watering until you notice the leaves are beginning to fade. Begin watering again when the first stem appears. Spray the leaves in hot weather.
Light: enjoys bright conditions, but keep out of direct sunlight.
Feeding: feed every two weeks in spring and summer with food for flowering plants.
Repotting and growing medium: repot the rhizomes every year in spring, in a mixture of compost and good yard soil.
Cultivation tip: in winter, move your plant to a cool room at 59° F (15° C).

● **RELATED SPECIES AND VARIETIES**
Curcuma roscoeana produces long, mid-green, oval leaves with dark green veins. In summer, beautiful scarlet flowers appear.

Curcuma alismatifolia ▶

▼ *Curcuma* "Chocolate"

Curcuma "Siam Summer" ▼

Curcuma roscoeana ▼

Cycas

C. revoluta
Cycad

Decorative interest

Cycads, which look like palms, have a sort of trunk topped by a crown of pennate, green, arching leaves, which appear delicate but are in fact tough. They are slow growing and often produce only a single leaf per year. When grown as houseplants, they do not flower.

Ease of cultivation

Growing cycads is not difficult providing you can give them sufficient light.
Propagation: experts propagate cycads from seed but this is difficult for non-professionals.

TROUBLE SHOOTING

◆ Small brown lumps appear along the spines: these are scale bugs. Remove them with a soapy solution (cycads respond badly to the use of insecticides).

CARING FOR YOUR PLANT

Watering and humidity: water your plant moderately throughout the year. Reduce watering during the winter months when the temperature drops.
Light: enjoys bright conditions, with or without direct sunlight.
Feeding: feed once a month in spring and summer with food for foliage plants.
Repotting and growing medium: repot in spring every two to three years, in ordinary compost with added coarse sand to improve drainage.
Cultivation tip: cycads are very sensitive to overwatering; too much water will make their leaves turn yellow.

Worth remembering

Don't confuse *Zamias* with *Zamioculcas*: the latter belong to the family Araceae and are native to tropical Africa.

● RELATED SPECIES AND VARIETIES

Cycas rumphii is a slow growing plant. It produces handsome, slender, bright green leaves, 3 to 6½ feet (1 to 2 meters) long. It has a less open shape than *C. revoluta*, and looks more like a palm tree.

◀ *Cycas revoluta*

● RELATED GENUS

Like cycads, **Zamia** belong to the order Cycadales, a group of plants midway between ferns and palms. The genus comprises around thirty species growing in tropical and subtropical regions of America. *Zamia furfuracea* produces a short, cylindrical, partially buried trunk, crowned with long, pale green to olive, pennate leaves covered in reddish-brown hairs. The trunk of *Z. loddigesii* is almost entirely below ground and has bright green, pennate leaves.

◀ *Cycas rumphii*

Cyclamen

C. persicum hybrids

Florists' cyclamen, Persian cyclamen

Decorative interest

This very common plant is particularly valued for its colorful flowers. It grows from a tuber and has rounded, dark green, heart-shaped leaves, often with silvery-gray markings. The long-stemmed flowers have reflexed petals in tones of red, pink, white, and mauve, often with a darker throat. The flowering period is from fall to early spring, depending on when they are planted. There are also dwarf varieties.

Associates well with... this short-lived plant is often sold in pots containing three differently colored varieties.

Ease of cultivation

Cyclamens need cool temperatures. They are generally discarded after flowering.
Propagation: professionals grow cyclamens from seed.

Worth remembering

When purchasing a cyclamen, choose a plant with plenty of flower buds of which only a few are already open. Push back the leaves to check that the tuber is healthy and that the plant has new flowers forming.

TROUBLE SHOOTING

◆ The leaves turn yellow and droop: the plant is in a position that is too warm and dark. Move it to a brighter, cooler, and better ventilated spot.
◆ The leaves become sticky and deformed: aphids are attacking the plant. Treat it with a suitable insecticide.

CARING FOR YOUR PLANT

Watering and humidity: when the growing medium begins to feel dry, water it but don't wet the heart of the plant. It is better to water it from below (and empty the saucer after a quarter of an hour).
Light: bright conditions, but out of direct sunlight.
Feeding: feed it every two weeks while in flower with food for flowering plants.
Repotting and growing medium: discard after flowering.
Cultivation tip: keep your cyclamen in a cool room: the ideal temperature is between 53° and 64° F (12° and 18° C). The cooler the temperature, the longer the flowering period.

Cyclamen persicum ▼

Cyclamen persicum ▼

Cyclamen persicum ▼

Cymbidium

Cymbidium

Decorative interest

These orchids grow from oval pseudo-bulbs. They produce fleshy roots and long, strap-like, mid- to dark green leaves. One or more flower spikes emerge from the clump and carry a number of flowers, 1½ to 3 inches (3 to 7 cm) in diameter, in a variety of shades, depending on the hybrid: creamy-white to green, brown to red, yellow and pink, all usually with speckled throats. Cymbidiums normally flower in winter or spring, depending on the hybrid, and can continue in flower for several weeks.

Ease of cultivation

Cymbidiums already in flower are easy to keep as houseplants but require special treatment if they are to flower again.

Propagation: by division after flowering.

CARING FOR YOUR PLANT

Watering and humidity: water moderately but regularly from spring to the end of summer. When new pseudo-bulbs have formed, water less frequently. If kept indoors, spray the leaves once a day.

Light: cymbidiums require very bright conditions, but keep them out of direct sunlight during the hottest part of the day.

Feeding: feed every two to three weeks in spring and summer with special plant food for orchids.

Repotting and growing medium: repot every two years, immediately after flowering, in special orchid compost. After repotting, wait two or three weeks before watering (but spray the leaves daily).

Cultivation tip: to get your cymbidium to flower again, move it outside in the summer and put it in a sheltered spot in semi-shade. Bring it back indoors in October, before the frosts begin, and keep it in a cool, bright room. For flowers to form, it is essential that cymbidiums have a much lower temperature at night than during the day—a gap of approximately 18° F (10° C).

Cymbidium "Majolica Enzan" ▼

TROUBLE SHOOTING

◆ The leaves are attacked by aphids and become sticky: treat the plant with a suitable insecticide, but make sure you avoid spraying the flowers. If the flower spikes are affected, try to remove the aphids by running water over the flowers.

◆ The leaves become pale and lots of small, whitish spots appear on them: red spider mites thrive in warm, dry conditions. Increase the ambient humidity and spray the foliage more often. If necessary, treat the plant with an acaricide.

Cymbidium ▼

Cyperus

C. involucratus

Papyrus, umbrella plant

Decorative interest

Papyrus grows naturally in damp places and is valued for the structural beauty of its elegant, umbrella-like foliage. It produces long, slender, upright stems which can grow to over 3 feet (1 meter), crowned with tufts of radiating "leaves." These are in fact bracts, surrounding small, beige to brown, insignificant flowers. The true leaves are very modest and grow at the base of the stem.

▼ *Cyperus involucratus*

TROUBLE SHOOTING

◆ The leaves turn yellow and droop: the plant is in a position that is too warm and dark. Move it to a brighter, cooler and better ventilated spot.
◆ The leaves become sticky and deformed: aphids are attacking the plant. Treat it with a suitable insecticide.

Ease of cultivation

Papyrus is an easy plant to grow, providing both the roots and foliage are kept constantly humid.

Propagation: divide the clump in spring or take cuttings from the umbels of bracts: cut a tuft with 2 to 4 inches (5 to 10 cm) of stem, cut the bracts back by half, and place them upside down in a glass filled with water. Change the water once a week. After a few weeks, plantlets will appear at the axils of the bracts.

Worth remembering

Cats have a tendency to chew papyrus leaves.

Cyperus involucratus ▲

▼ *Cyperus kyllinga* "Alba"

CARING FOR YOUR PLANT

Watering and humidity: water abundantly to make sure that the growing medium remains constantly moist. You can leave the planter partly filled with water. Spray the foliage frequently.

Light: enjoys bright, sunny conditions, but keep out of the direct midday sun.

Feeding: feed every two weeks in spring and summer with food for foliage plants.

Repotting and growing medium: repot in early spring if the stems are filling the pot. Use ordinary compost enriched with good yard soil.

Cultivation tip: let your papyrus spend the summer out in the yard, in a semi-shaded spot. It can overwinter in a cool conservatory with a minimum temperature of 50° F (10° C).

● **RELATED SPECIES AND VARIETIES**

Cyperus involucratus "Gracilis" is a smaller variety with stiff, dark green bracts.

Cyperus papyrus, native to Egypt, grows much taller—6½ to 10 feet (2 to 3 meters). Its smooth stems are crowned by a few bracts and a radiating tuft of 100 to 200 thread-like stems, each bearing a small flower at its tip. This plant requires more warmth.

Cyperus papyrus "Green Gold" ▶

Cyperus diffusus ▼

Cyperus involucratus ▶

Dalechampia

Dalechampia

Decorative interest

Dalechampias belong to the same family as euphorbias. The genus includes around a hundred species of low-growing shrubs and twining creepers, native to different tropical areas of the world. The alternating leaves can be entire, lobed, or composite. The small, petal-less flowers, which grow in clusters at the leaf axils, have two colored bracts, often in shades of pink. Although the flowers are short-lived, the bracts last for several weeks.

Native to Mexico, *Dalechampia spathulata* is a low shrub, growing no more than 3 feet (1 meter) high, with lanceolate to spatulate, pointed leaves that are 6 to 8 inches (15 to 20 cm) long, and reddish-pink bracts.

D. dioscoreifolia is a climbing species of moderate growth which is native to Costa Rica; it has oval, pointed, velvety leaves, which are heart-shaped at the base, and pink, more rounded bracts. Give your plant a support on which the twining stems can be trained.

Ease of cultivation

Dalechampias are quite easy to grow in a conservatory or temperate greenhouse.

Propagation: professionals grow dalechampias from seed. It is also possible to take cuttings.

Worth remembering

There is a certain amount of confusion surrounding the names given to the plants sold commercially—though they are still not commonly available—and some climbing dalechampias are known as *D. spathulata*.

Dalechampia spathulata ▼

Dalechampia dioscoreifolia ▼

Davallia

D. mariesii
Rabbit's foot fern

Decorative interest
Native to Asia, this fern develops rhizomes covered in a reddish-brown down, which creep along the surface of the growing medium and resemble rabbit's feet. It produces finely divided, dark green fronds, 6 to 10 inches (15 to 25 cm) long, with dentate pinnules.

Ease of cultivation
This fern is easy to grow indoors; some species prefer a warm, humid environment.

Propagation: divide the rhizomes in spring, when repotting, making sure that each piece has at least two or three fronds. Pin these down on the surface of the growing medium and keep them warm and moist.

CARING FOR YOUR PLANT

Watering and humidity: water your plant moderately, enough to keep the root ball slightly moist, but no more. Use soft water at room temperature. Stand the pot on damp gravel and spray the foliage daily during periods of hot weather.

Light: medium to bright conditions, but keep out of direct sunlight.

Feeding: feed every three weeks in spring and summer with half strength food for foliage plants.

Repotting and growing medium: repot in spring every two years, using a light, fibrous compost suitable for epiphytes. Choose a large pot to give the rhizomes room to develop.

Cultivation tip: in winter, you can keep this semi-hardy species in a conservatory or a cold but frost-free greenhouse.

● RELATED SPECIES AND VARIETIES

Davallia fejeensis develops thick, brown, downy rhizomes with broad, pale green fronds, 12 to 20 inches (30 to 50 cm) in length, which are finely divided and serrated. With its light, trailing foliage, this fern is particularly suited to growing in a hanging container. Native to the Fiji Isles, it is more susceptible to cold than *D. mariesii* and enjoys a constant temperature of between 64° and 68° F (18° and 20° C) all year long, and a minimum temperature of 50° F (10° C).

D. canariensis has hairy, pale brown rhizomes and broad, mid-green fronds, 8 to 16 inches (20 to 50 cm) long, composed of triangular leaflets.

Davallia mariesii ▼

Dendrobium

Dendrobium

Decorative interest

The genus *Dendrobium* is very varied and includes over 1,000 species of orchid, mainly epiphytes, with deciduous or evergreen leaves, that are widely distributed in different regions of Asia and Oceania. A large number of species and hybrids are cultivated, each with its own characteristic dendrobium flower, with a lip formed by the fusion of two lateral sepals. It is easier to get to know this group of plants if you remember that there are two major groups of hybrids, identifiable, among other things, by their way of flowering: they are the hybrids of **Dendrobium nobile** and of *D. phalaenopsis*. If you are interested in keeping species, find out about their native habitat so that you know their cultivation requirements.

Dendrobium nobile is a species native to the Himalayas which has produced numerous hybrids valued for their diversity of color. These orchids have slender pseudo-bulbs that resemble bamboo stems. They have small, narrow, soft, alternating leaves along their entire length. The flowers appear in spring in groups of three or four along the whole length of the pseudo-bulb in shades of white, yellow, pink, and mauve. These hybrids grow rapidly during the summer but need a period of winter rest.

Dendrobium stratiotes ▲

Dendrobium phalaenopsis ▼

Dendrobium nobile ▼

Native to Australia, **Dendrobium phalaenopsis** (synonym: *Dendrobium bigibbum* var. *phalaenopsis*) has also produced numerous hybrids, some of which are cultivated for their cut flowers. Stiff, dark green leaves are borne along the whole length of their slender pseudo-bulbs. The flowers, often rounded in form, appear in spring in terminal clusters at the top of the pseudo-bulbs. Colors vary from white to yellow and also include purples and mauves.

Ease of cultivation

These orchids are not easy to cultivate. For *D. nobile* hybrids, a period of winter rest is essential. Hybrids of *D. phalaenopsis* need heat, humidity, and light; they are best grown in a conservatory or heated greenhouse.

Propagation: in spring, remove leafless pseudo-bulbs. Cut them into sections between the nodes or keep just the upper part. Plant each piece up to the level of the node in orchid compost. The new shoots that sometimes form at the top of old pseudo-bulbs can also be used for propagation.

Worth remembering

Some hybrids from deciduous species have a tendency to lose their leaves during the winter rest period.

▲ *Dendrobium lobbianum*

◄ *Dendrobium Thongchai*

CARING FOR YOUR PLANT

Watering and humidity: when growth begins at the end of winter, water *D. nobile* hybrids sparingly until the buds are well developed, then water moderately but regularly with soft water. At the end of summer, begin to reduce watering. In winter, only water enough to prevent the pseudo-bulbs from withering. With *D. phalaenopsis* hybrids, water abundantly in spring and summer while the pseudo-bulbs are flowering and growing, using soft water. When the pseudo-bulbs are well developed, gradually reduce watering. In winter, water moderately but make sure that the pseudo-bulbs do not shrink. Provide a high level of humidity throughout the year.

Light: bright conditions, but protect your plant from direct sunlight in spring and summer.

Feeding: feed every two weeks from spring to the end of summer with orchid food.

Repotting and growing medium: repot every two years in orchid compost, just after flowering for *D. nobile* hybrids, and when growth begins for *D. phalaenopsis*. Use small pots and leave the neck of the plant just showing on the surface.

Cultivation tip: during the period of winter rest, keep *D. nobile* hybrids at temperatures between 61° and 64° F (16° and 18° C) during the day and at 50° to 55° F (10° to 13° C) at night. For *D. phalaenopsis* hybrids, maintain a warm temperature throughout the year and a very high level of humidity: these orchids can cope with temperatures of up to 86° F (30° C); in winter, the temperature should not be allowed to drop below 59° F (15° C). All hybrids are best kept in a conservatory or heated greenhouse.

Dichorisandra

D. thyrsiflora   Blue ginger

Decorative interest

Blue ginger is not a member of the ginger family (Zingiber)—a spice plant that it resembles to some extent—but of the tradescantia family. This perennial from Brazil with short, rhizomatous roots, produces dark green, glossy lanceolate leaves, arranged in spirals. In late summer or early fall, a flower-scape emerges bearing a dense cluster of dark violet-blue flowers at its tip. Blue ginger can grow to 6½ feet (2 meters) in height.

Ease of cultivation

As it grows naturally in tropical forests, the blue ginger requires a high level of humidity.

Propagation: divide large clumps when repotting or take stem cuttings.

CARING FOR YOUR PLANT

Watering and humidity: water moderately but regularly during the growing period. Water less frequently in winter. Spray the leaves in hot weather.

Light: semi-shade.

Feeding: feed every two weeks in spring and summer with food for flowering plants.

Repotting and growing medium: repot in spring, if necessary, in a mixture of potting compost and good yard soil.

Cultivation tip: blue ginger can cope with indoor temperatures in winter but in this case will not enjoy a real period of winter rest. A room temperature of 59° F (15° C) is also suitable.

TROUBLE SHOOTING

◆ The leaves become pale and dry: red spider mites thrive in warm, dry conditions. Increase the ambient humidity and spray the foliage more often. If necessary, treat the plant with an acaricide.

Dichorisandra thyrsiflora ▼

Dichorisandra thyrsiflora ▼

Dicksonia

Tree fern

Decorative interest

Native to the mountain forests of various temperate and tropical regions, *Dicksonia* produce upright rhizomes resembling trunks, from the top of which emerge tough fronds, rolled up into crosiers when they first appear. Some of these ferns—such as *Dicksonia antarctica*, which can tolerate temperatures as low as 14° F (–10° C)—are sufficiently hardy to be grown outdoors in a mild climate. *Dicksonias* have fibrous roots along the length of the rhizome; the best way of watering is to trickle water slowly from the top of the "trunk."

The most commonly cultivated species is *D. antarctica*; *D. fibrosa* is closely related and sometimes confused with the former. In both these species, the stalks of the fronds are covered in stiff, russet hairs. *D. squarrosa* has very hairy, reddish-brown stalks.

Ease of cultivation

Dicksonia are intolerant of dry, overheated air. They are perfect for cultivating in an unheated greenhouse or conservatory.

Propagation: can be grown from spores, but this is a matter for experts.

Dicksonia squarrosa ▶

◀ *Dicksonia squarrosa*

CARING FOR YOUR PLANT

Watering and humidity: water your plant abundantly by pouring water down the "trunk," particularly in warm weather. Water less frequently in winter when the weather is cooler. Spray the fronds and the rhizome on a regular basis.

Light: quite bright light, but always filtered.

Feeding: feed every two to three weeks in spring and summer with food for foliage plants.

Repotting and growing medium: repot in spring every two or three years, in a mixture of equal parts good yard soil, compost, sand, and ericaceous compost.

Cultivation tip: install a drip watering system that delivers water to the top of the rhizome.

Didymochlaena

D. truncatula   Didymochlaena, mahogany fern
synonym: *Didymochlaena lunulata*

Decorative interest
This tropical fern produces upright rhizomes from which emerge large, double pennate, mid-green, glossy, triangular fronds, 3 to 5 feet (1 to 1.5 meters) in length. They are tinged with red when young. The spine is covered in brownish-red scales.

Ease of cultivation
Didymochlaenas benefit from regular watering in summer.
Propagation: large clumps can be divided in spring.

Didymochlaena truncatula ▲▼

CARING FOR YOUR PLANT

Watering and humidity: water regularly during the growing period, but only a little at a time. The compost should never be allowed to dry out. Maintain a good level of humidity by spraying the foliage frequently, especially in winter if your plant is in a heated room.
Light: medium light conditions, but keep out of direct sunlight.
Feeding: feed every two weeks in spring and summer with food for foliage plants.
Repotting and growing medium: repot in spring, if necessary, in ordinary compost with added peat and sand.
Cultivation tip: sudden changes of temperature will cause the pinnules to drop. The minimum winter temperature for this plant is 50° F (10° C).

TROUBLE SHOOTING

◆ Small brown lumps appear on the spine and the underside of the pinnules: these are scale bugs. Rub them off gently with a brush dipped in alcohol but be careful; the fronds are fragile. Do not use an aerosol insecticide.

Dieffenbachia

Dieffenbachia

Decorative interest

Dieffenbachias are traditional houseplants, valued for their handsome, variegated foliage. There are many varieties, some of which can grow to 6½ feet (2 meters) tall when grown indoors.

Most are varieties of *Dieffenbachia seguine*, a vigorous perennial producing dark green, glossy, oblong leaves, 12 to 16 inches (30 to 40 cm) long, with white markings.

"Tropic Snow" is a very popular variety, which has leaves with cream variegation, mainly in the center. "Amonea" (synonym: *D. amonea* hort.) is a very vigorous plant that has dark green leaves with creamy-white stripes between the lateral veins. "Camilla" is a variety with smaller leaves, just 8 inches (20 cm) long, with a lot of creamy-white variegation in the center.

Ease of cultivation

Although common, dieffenbachias are quite delicate plants: they require a good balance of warmth, watering, and humidity in order to thrive.

TROUBLE SHOOTING

◆ White, cottony clusters appear at the base of the leaves: mealy bugs can be difficult to eradicate. If there are only a few, remove them with a Q-tip dipped in alcohol. If you are unsuccessful, treat the plant with a systemic insecticide.

◆ The leaves become pale and dry: red spider mites thrive in warm, dry conditions. Increase the ambient humidity and spray the foliage more often. If necessary, treat the plant with an acaricide.

▲ *Dieffenbachia* "Tropic Snow"

▼ *Dieffenbachia* "Excellent"

◄ *Dieffenbachia* "Tropic Snow"

Propagation: take head cuttings in spring and root them under cover in water or in a mixture of peat and sand at 72° F (22° C). Stem sections with at least one eye can also be used as cuttings: place them flat and cover lightly in the same type of compost.

Warning, danger

The sap of dieffenbachias is highly toxic, as are all parts of the plant. Always wear gloves when handling them and keep them out of the reach of children and pets.

CARING FOR YOUR PLANT

Watering and humidity: water quite generously to keep the compost moist during the growing period. Reduce watering in winter, particularly in a heated room. Maintain a high level of humidity by spraying the foliage frequently.

Light: enjoys a light position but out of direct sunlight. If the room is too dark, the leaves will lose their variegation.

Feeding: feed every two weeks in spring and summer with liquid plant food for foliage plants.

Repotting and growing medium: repot young plants every year in spring, in ordinary compost with a little added peat.

Cultivation tip: maintain a good balance of warmth, watering, and humidity for your plant. Keep the temperature as constant as possible, allow a high level of humidity, and give your plant plenty of light. After a few years, when the plant becomes leggy, replace it by taking head cuttings.

Dieffenbachia "Vesuvius" ▼

◄ *Dieffenbachia* "Camilla"

◄ *Dieffenbachia* "Mars"

◄ *Dieffenbachia* "Hilo"

Dieffenbachia "Paco" ▶

Dieffenbachia "Sublime" ▶

Dionaea

D. muscipula
Dionea, Venus fly trap

Decorative interest
The dionea is a fascinating, carnivorous plant with leaf lobes that trap bugs inside by closing on them. Native to wetland areas of the United States (such as Carolina), it forms a rosette no more than 4 inches (10 cm) tall. The leaves consist of a long, flattened leaf stalk and a limb divided into two rounded lobes edged with long, stiff teeth. The inside of the leaves is covered in digestive glands and sensitive hairs. Once a bug has been caught, the glands secrete digestive juices that destroy their prey. After ten to thirty days of "digestion," the leaf opens again. Flower stems 4 to 12 inches (10 to 30 cm) long bear umbels of small, white flowers at the end of spring.

Ease of cultivation
Dioneas are best grown in a cold greenhouse. They need a high level of humidity during the growing period. In winter, they are best kept at a temperature of 41° to 50° F (5° to 10° C).
Propagation: by seed or division, but these are complicated techniques for non-professionals.

Tip
Use a glass cloche to maintain a humid atmosphere. Remove it from time to time to allow the plant to catch bugs.

Dionaea muscipula ▼

The dionea on the right has caught a spider. ▼

This dionea has caught a fly. ▼

Dischidia

D. pectenoides   Dischidia

Decorative interest

This rather uncommon climber, native to south-east Asia, is an epiphyte. It produces unusual fruit shaped like small balloons. In the wild, these swollen fruits provide shelter for ants. The small, red flowers that bloom in spring contribute to the decorative effect of the plant, which is best trained over a metal hoop.

Ease of cultivation

Dischidias require a high level of ambient humidity.
Propagation: grown from seed, but best left to the experts.

CARING FOR YOUR PLANT

Watering and humidity: water your plant moderately, but allow the growing medium to dry out between waterings. Spray the foliage on a regular basis.
Light: enjoys bright conditions, but make sure you keep out of direct sunlight.
Feeding: feed once a month in spring and summer with half strength food for foliage plants.
Repotting and growing medium: repot in spring, if necessary, in compost for epiphytic orchids. Use a small container.
Cultivation tip: average room temperature, with a minimum of 59° F (15° C) suits dischidias, which are cultivated in much the same way as orchids.

Dischidia pectenoides ▼▶

➤➤ *Doritaenopsis* see *Phalaenopsis*

Dracaena

synonym: *Pleomele*   Dracaena, dragon tree

Decorative interest

Dracaenas are popular foliage plants, valued particularly for their variegated foliage. Most are woody shrubs with upright, slightly branching stems and broad or narrow leaves, usually grouped in clusters at the top of the stems. Their flowers are without interest.

Dracaena fragrans can reach almost 5 feet (1.5 meters) when grown in a pot. It has green, strap-like, drooping leaves. It is the variegated varieties, such as "**Lindenii**" and "**Massangeana**," that are most commonly cultivated.

D. deremensis is a species with narrower leaves; the variety "**Warneckii**" has quite broad, lanceolate leaves, with attractive white, longitudinal stripes; "**Yellow Stripe**" has green leaves with creamy-yellow stripes.

D. marginata is prized for its slender silhouette and can reach over 3 feet (1 meter) in height. It is crowned with a tuft of very narrow, dark green leaves, 12 to 20 inches (30 to 50 cm) long and ¼ to ¾ inch (1 to 2 cm) wide, with dark red edges. "**Tricolor**" is a variety with pink and cream striped foliage.

D. reflexa produces an upright stem with compact tufts of strap-like leaves, dark green in the species and green with cream variegation in the variety "**Song of India**."

D. surculosa (synonym: *D. godseffiana*) has a more branching habit and elliptical, pointed leaves with quite rounded bases that are green with silvery-gray markings; in the variety "**Florida**," the limb is almost entirely covered in broad, creamy-white markings.

Sanders dracaena, *Dracaena sanderiana*, is a shrub with a slender, elegant habit. Its stems resemble bamboo canes. Its green, strap-like leaves are glossy and slightly wavy, with white edges. As a pot plant, Sanders dracaena rarely grows to over 3 feet (1 meter) tall. Its current popularity is due to its use in hydroculture. Sections of stem grown in water are grouped together decoratively, in upright, inclined, or spiral arrangements of different heights from 4 inches to 3 feet (10 cm to 1 meter). It is sold under the name of Chinese water bamboo or "Lucky Bamboo," and is said to bring happiness and harmony to your home.

Ease of cultivation

On the whole, dragon trees are easy to cultivate as they tolerate dry atmospheres and irregular watering.

Propagation: by cuttings at the end of spring or in summer. Take head cuttings (reducing the leaves by half) or stem sections and grow under cover in a moist mixture of peat and sand at 72° to 75° F (22° to 24° C).

Dracaena reflexa "Song of India" ▶

Worth remembering

If your dragon tree becomes too big, cut the stem back to the required height. After a while, some new shoots will appear.

Dracaena fragrans "Compacta" ▼

Dracaena fragrans "Massangeana" ▶

Dracaena fragrans "Janet Craig" ▼   *Dracaena fragrans* "Golden Coast" ▼

TROUBLE SHOOTING

◆ The leaves become pale and dry: red spider mites thrive in warm, dry conditions. Increase the ambient humidity and spray the foliage more often. If necessary, treat the plant with an acaricide.

Dracaena surculosa ▼

▲ *Dracaena sanderiana* "Lucky Bamboo"

▲ *Dracaena sanderiana* "Lucky Bamboo"

Dracaena marginata "Magenta" ▶

Dracaena reflexa "Song of India" ▶

Dracaena deremensis "White Jewel" ▼

Drosera

Drosera, sundew plant

Decorative interest

This genus includes around a hundred species of insectivorous perennials native to a variety of regions, but principally the wet peatlands of Australia and New Zealand. Three species, including ***Drosera rotundifolia***—the most common— grow in the peatlands of Europe. These plants catch and digest their prey by means of the glandulous hairs covering their leaves.

The cape sundew, ***D. capensis***, produces a leaf tuft 4 to 6 inches (10 to 15 cm) high. The narrow, elongated leaves are covered with striking, green and red, glandulous hairs. Flower-scapes 8 to 12 inches (20 to 30 cm) tall emerge from the center of the leaf rosettes with a single-sided spike of purple-pink flowers.

The Alice sundew, ***D. aliciae***, forms a rosette 1½ to 2½ inches (4 to 6 cm) across. The 16-inch (40-cm) tall flower-scapes bear small, dark pink flowers. ***D. binata*** produces forked leaves that can grow as long as 10 inches (25 cm), and white flowers.

◀ *Drosera capensis*

Ease of cultivation

Droseras are not easy plants to grow, as they have specific cultivation requirements.

Propagation: grow from fresh seed in spring at a temperature of 50° to 55° F (10° to 13° C), or by rhizome division.

Drosera capensis ▼

CARING FOR YOUR PLANT

Watering and humidity: water abundantly during the growing period so that the growing medium remains constantly damp. You can even stand the pot in a little water. Always use rainwater. Reduce watering in winter. Maintain a high level of humidity around the plant.

Light: the plant enjoys bright conditions, but make sure you keep it out of direct sunlight.

Feeding: does not require feeding.

Repotting and growing medium: repot at the end of winter, if necessary, in plain peat or a mixture of equal parts peat, sphagnum moss, and river sand.

Cultivation tip: a period of cool winter rest at temperatures between 41° and 59° F (5° and 15° C) is recommended, but you can normally grow cold-sensitive species at normal room temperature. At low temperatures the foliage will disappear completely but the plant will put on new growth in spring.

TROUBLE SHOOTING

◆ A gray mold appears on the leaves: *Botrytis* thrives in a confined, damp atmosphere, especially at cool temperatures. Ensure the plant is well ventilated and don't spray the leaves.

Duchesnea

D. indica

Mock strawberry, Indian strawberry

synonym: *Fragaria indica*

Decorative interest

A native of south and east Asia, the mock strawberry is a small, stoloniferous hardy perennial quite commonly seen in our yards. With its dentate, trifoliate leaves, and the red fruits which follow its yellow flowers—but are virtually tasteless—it resembles the strawberry plant. As a decorative houseplant, it is generally trained upwards on supports but can also be grown in a hanging container.

Ease of cultivation

The mock strawberry enjoys a light, cool position.

Propagation: divide large clumps when repotting; remove and plant up the plantlets that have formed on the runners. You can also sow seed in fall or early spring, in a cold frame.

CARING FOR YOUR PLANT

Watering and humidity: water generously during the summer. Water less frequently in winter, depending on the temperature.

Light: bright conditions, but keep out of direct sunlight in summer.

Feeding: feed every two weeks in spring and summer with food for flowering plants.

Repotting and growing medium: repot in spring, if necessary, in a mixture of good yard soil and compost.

Cultivation tip: in winter, keep your plant in a cool, bright place, such as a cold greenhouse or conservatory.

Duchesnea indica ▼

TROUBLE SHOOTING

◆ Your plant's leaves become sticky and deformed: aphids are attacking the shoots. Treat the plant with a suitable insecticide.

Echeveria

Echeveria

Decorative interest

This genus comprises around 150 species of succulents native to the semi-arid regions of America. The fleshy leaves are arranged in rosettes and the upright inflorescences have small, bell-shaped flowers in yellow, red, orange, or white. Many species and varieties are cultivated. Some are used in bedding arrangements.

Echeveria derenbergii, or **painted lady**, is a commonly cultivated species producing a tight rosette of fleshy, overlapping, gray-green leaves. New rosettes are constantly forming at the leaf axils. At the end of winter, flower-scapes about 3 inches (7 to 8 cm) long appear, bearing small, reddish-yellow flowers.

E. agavoides is distinguished by its fleshy, glabrous, triangular, pale green leaves. The 8- to 20-inch (20- to 50-cm) flower-scapes bear red flowers with yellow edges.

E. elegans forms a small rosette of pale bluish-yellow leaves covered in a white bloom. The 12-inch (30-cm) scapes carry pink flowers.

E. setosa produces a compact, regular rosette of small, thick, oval leaves covered in fine white hairs. Its red and yellow flowers bloom in summer.

E. leucotricha is a shrubby species with thick, pale green, lanceolate leaves covered in fine, white hair.

E. imbricata (synonyms: *E. imbricata*, *E. pumila* var. *glauca*, *E. glauca*, *E. secunda*) produces bluish-green, largely spatulate leaves and pinkish-red, elongated flowers with yellowish-orange tips.

E. rundelli produces small rosettes of flattened leaves in shades of red with quite long, scattered hairs toward the tip.

E. "Topsy-turvy" is a hybrid of *E. runyonii* with very curved, bluish-gray leaves and flowers with yellow centers and orangey-red petal tips.

E. gibbiflora is a tough plant with spatulate leaves 6 to 10 inches (15 to 25 cm) long, with wavy edges. They are gray-green with pink highlights and arranged in a rosette at the top of the stalk. In fall, this plant produces pale red flowers on leafy scapes.

Echeveria "Topsy-turvy" ▲

Echeveria "Imbricata" ▶

TROUBLE SHOOTING

◆ White, cottony clusters appear at the base of the leaves: mealy bugs can be difficult to eradicate. If there are only a few, remove them with a Q-tip dipped in alcohol. In cases of severe attack, treat the plant with a suitable insecticide.

CARING FOR YOUR PLANT

Watering and humidity: water sparingly in the growing period. Keep your plant almost dry in winter, particularly at low temperatures.

Light: as sunny a position as possible.

Feeding: feed every two weeks during the spring and summer months with cactus food.

Repotting and growing medium: repot young plants every year in spring, in special compost for cactuses and succulents, with a good layer of drainage material in the bottom of the pot.

Cultivation tip: avoid overwatering your plant. A period of cool winter rest at temperatures of 50° to 54° F (10° to 12° C) will encourage flower formation.

Echeveria rundellii ▼

Ease of cultivation

Echeverias are easy to grow indoors in a room with plenty of light.
Propagation: propagate from offsets or leaf cuttings.

● RELATED GENERA

Aeoniums Aeoniums are succulents similar to houseleeks (*Sempervivums*). Their leaves are arranged in attractive rosettes at the ends of bushy stems. Plants that reach maturity flower and then die. *A. arboreum* "Atropurpureum" produces a woody, branching stem no more than 3 feet (1 meter) high. The tough, spatulate leaves are an attractive shade of purple. *A. arboreum* "Schwarzkopf" has almost black foliage. *A. haworthii* is a branching species with terminal rosettes of fleshy, bluish-green leaves, edged with purple. *A. tabuliforme* has a very short stem. The rosettes are in the form of flat plates stacked tightly together.

A. undulatum produces a thick stem 24 to 36 inches (60 to 90 cm) tall, crowned by a large rosette of long, wavy, dark green leaves.

Graptopetalum bellum (synonym: *Tacitus bellum*) produces a flattened rosette of fleshy, reddish-brown leaves ½ to 1¼ inches (1 to 3 cm) long, arranged in a spiral on a very short stem, and branching inflorescences of carmine red flowers. This species was discovered in Mexico about thirty years ago.

Aeonium arboreum "Atropurpureum" ▼

Assorted *Echeveria* ▼

Echeveria leucotricha ▼

Echinocactus

E. grusonii Mother-in-law's cushion, golden barrel cactus

Decorative interest

This Mexican cactus, which is rounded and then elongated, produces a bright green stem with between twenty and forty very prominent ribs. The yellow areoles have golden-yellow spikes. Outdoors, if the plant reaches maturity, it produces bright yellow flowers 1½ to 2¼ inches (4 to 6 cm) long in summer. It grows slowly: as a houseplant it will grow to 6 inches (15 cm) in diameter over the course of ten years.

Associates well with... spherical cactuses form a good combination when planted with candle cactuses.

Ease of cultivation

Easy to grow in a bright position.

Propagation: in spring, sow seeds in seed trays over heat. Prick out the seedlings two months after sowing.

● RELATED SPECIES AND VARIETIES

Echinocactus horizonthalonius produces a flat, grayish-green stem with seven or eight ribs, often arranged spirally. The woolly areoles have strong, brownish spikes. Tubular pink flowers 2 inches (5 cm) long appear even on young plants.

E. platyacanthus is a variable species with very prominent ribs and gray areoles with grayish-brown spikes. The flowers are golden-yellow.

CARING FOR YOUR PLANT

Watering and humidity: water sufficiently to moisten the growing medium in spring and summer but allow it to dry out almost completely before watering again. In winter, only water your plant sufficiently to stop it drying out completely.

Light: this plant requires as much sunlight as possible in summer and in winter.

Feeding: feed every two to three weeks in spring and summer with cactus food.

Repotting and growing medium: repot in spring, if necessary, in compost for cactuses and succulents.

Cultivation tip: give your plant plenty of light but water sparingly. In winter, the echinocactus will tolerate temperatures as low as 41° F (5° C), but keep it dry until it begins to put on growth again.

◄ *Echinocactus grusonii* ▼▲

TROUBLE SHOOTING

◆ White, cottony clusters appear on the stem: mealy bugs can be difficult to eradicate. If there are only a few, remove them with a Q-tip dipped in alcohol. If you are unsuccessful, treat the plant with a systemic insecticide.

Epidendrum

Epidendron

Decorative interest

The *Epidendrum* genus is found widely throughout the tropical regions of America and comprises several hundred species of extremely varied orchids, the majority being epiphytes. Many botanical species are cultivated and there are also a number of interesting hybrids. Most produce upright stems similar to reeds, or short, thick stems. Others have pseudo-bulbs. The leaves are also very varied. The flowers, which are fragrant, appear in clusters at the tip of the stem, or from the base.

Ease of cultivation

Like orchids, epidendrons have special cultivation requirements where temperature and humidity are concerned.

Propagation: divide large clumps when repotting.

▲▼ *Epidendrum*

CARING FOR YOUR PLANT

Watering and humidity: water abundantly with soft water when the pseudo-bulbs are developing, then water less frequently. Stemmed epidendrons require more regular watering. Provide a high level of humidity all year round by standing the plant on a saucer of wet gravel; spray the foliage daily but avoid wetting the young shoots as they are susceptible to rotting.

Light: the plant enjoys bright conditions, but make sure you keep it out of direct sunlight.

Feeding: feed your plant every two weeks when the pseudo-bulbs are forming, with an orchid food rich in nitrogen; then use a special food for flowering orchids. Stop feeding it during the rest period.

Repotting and growing medium: repot every two years in spring, in compost for epiphytic orchids. Wait ten to fifteen days before starting to water again.

Cultivation tip: due to their special cultivation requirements, when buying an orchid, find out about its geographical origin: this will determine the temperature it requires. Generally speaking, orchids need a temperature difference of 9° to 14° F (5° to 8° C) between day and night.

TROUBLE SHOOTING

◆ The leaves become sticky and deformed: aphids are attacking the shoots. Treat your plant with a suitable insecticide.
◆ The leaves become pale and dry: red spider mites thrive in warm, dry conditions. Increase the ambient humidity and spray the foliage more often. If necessary, treat the plant with an acaricide.

Epipremnum

E. aureum
Pothos, ivy arum
synonyms: *Scindapsus aureus, Raphidophora aurea*

Decorative interest
This climber produces long, angular stems with oval leaves 4 to
6 inches (10 to 15 cm) long, which are pointed at the tip and
heart-shaped at the base. They are glossy and bright green
with yellow markings. Pothos are cultivated as hanging
plants or trained on a moss-covered pole. Mature
specimens develop fleshy, aerial roots. The variety
"Marble Queen" has white leaves with green
markings; it is more difficult to grow.

Ease of cultivation
When cultivated in a bright, humid
room, pothos will grow vigorously.
Propagation: take 4 inch (10 cm)
terminal cuttings; these will root
easily in water or in a mixture of
peat and sand.

Worth remembering
When cultivated in a greenhouse,
mature pothos will eventually develop
divided leaves that can grow as long as
24 to 32 inches (60 to 80 cm).

TROUBLE SHOOTING

◆ Brown marks appear on the leaves: your plant is probably suffering from
overwatering. Stop watering and allow the compost to dry out before
gradually beginning to water it again.

CARING FOR YOUR PLANT

Watering and humidity: water your plant moderately throughout
the year, but water less frequently in winter if the plant is situated in a
cool spot. Stand the pot on wet gravel. Frequently spray the moss-covered
pole with water.
Light: bright conditions and sun in winter. In a dark position the foliage
will lose its attractive variegation.
Feeding: feed every two weeks in spring and summer with food for
foliage plants.
Repotting and growing medium: repot young plants in spring
every year in ordinary compost with added sand or perlite in order to
improve drainage.
Cultivation tip: cut back the stems in spring to stop the plant becoming
too large. In winter, you can put your pothos in a cool room at 61° F
(16° C) to give it a period of rest.

Epipremnum aureum
"Marble Queen" ▶

● RELATED SPECIES AND VARIETIES

Epipremnum aureum "Marble Queen" has white leaves with green markings. It is more difficult to cultivate than other varieties.
E. pictus "Argyraeus" has smaller, matt green leaves with gray-green variegation.

Epipremnum aureum
"Marble Queen" ▶

◀ Epipremnum pinnatum

Scindapsus pictus
"Argyraeus" ▶

● RELATED GENUS

After various changes in plant classification, many species once classified as belonging to the genus **Scindapsus** have been moved to other genera. However, a climbing species (*Scindapsus pictus*), native to tropical Asia, remains in this genus. It is cultivated for its ornamental variety "**Argyraeus**" (synonym: *Pothos argyraeus*) which has dark green, very heart-shaped leaves, both rounded and pointed, with attractive silvery-gray markings.

Episcia

E. cupreata   Episcia

Decorative interest

Native to tropical America, this small plant forms rosettes of leaves 4 to 6 inches (10 to 15 cm) high and wide. The rosettes produce creeping or trailing stems (stolons) which themselves bear leaves. The leaves are oval to elliptical with dentate edges and are coppery on the upper surface. In spring, the plant produces scarlet flowers, either singly or in clusters of three or four. There are many hybrids with different-colored leaves and flowers.

Ease of cultivation

Episcias require warmth and a high level of humidity. Ideally they should be cultivated in a warm greenhouse or terrarium.

Propagation: cut a stolon next to a small rosette of leaves and transplant this plantlet into a pot.

TROUBLE SHOOTING

◆ The leaves become sticky and deformed: aphids are attacking the shoots. To treat your plant, use insecticide sticks that are pushed down into the compost. Avoid insecticide sprays, as episcias respond badly to them.

● **RELATED SPECIES AND VARIETIES**

Episcia cupreata "Acajou" has silvery-green leaves edged with dark tobacco-brown, and orangey-red flowers.

E. cupreata "Metallica" has coppery leaves with a central silvery band and pink margins.

E. cupreata "Tropical Topaz" has pale green leaves and yellow flowers.

E. dianthiflora has mid-green, velvety leaves with scalloped edges and solitary white flowers with fringed edges.

E. reptans has crinkly, brown-green, or bronze-green leaves with silver markings along the veins. The flowers are pinkish-red.

Episcia cupreata "Tropical Topaz" ▼

CARING FOR YOUR PLANT

Watering and humidity: water moderately yet regularly throughout the year, but slightly less in winter when the temperature is cooler. Maintain a good level of humidity by standing the pot on a bed of damp gravel.

Light: medium to bright conditions, but keep it out of direct sunlight.

Feeding: feed every two weeks in spring and summer with heavily diluted plant food.

Repotting and growing medium: repot in spring, if necessary, in a free-draining, peat-based compost.

Cultivation tip: give your plant warmth and good humidity in a place sheltered from cold drafts. In winter, the temperature should not be allowed to drop below 6° F (16° C).

Episcia dianthiflora ▼   *Episcia dianthiflora* ▼

Episcia cupreata "Neptune"▼

Erica

E. x *hiemalis*   Heather

synonyms: *E. hyemalis*, *E. hiemalis*

Decorative interest

This heather is valued for its late flowering habit. It has a shrubby form, with woody stems and can grow to 24 inches (60 cm) high and wide. The pale green, hairy, filiform leaves grow in dense tufts on upright branches. In fall and winter they bloom with compact clusters of pretty, tubular flowers, ¹⁄₂ to ³⁄₄ inch (1 to 2 cm) long, which are white, tinged with bright pink.

Ease of cultivation

It is not easy to keep heather for any length of time indoors as it needs a cool temperature. For this reason it is usually discarded after flowering.
Propagation: propagating heather is best left to specialists.

● RELATED SPECIES AND VARIETIES

Erica gracilis has a more compact habit, hairless leaves, and small, rounded flowers that are pale pink to crimson.
E. canaliculata produces small, pale pink to white, dish-shaped flowers with dark brown anthers.

CARING FOR YOUR PLANT

Watering and humidity: water regularly to keep the compost moist, using soft water. Spray the leaves daily with soft water if the atmosphere is warm and dry.
Light: enjoys bright conditions, but make sure you keep it out of very bright sunlight.
Feeding: not required.
Repotting and growing medium: not required as heathers are usually discarded after flowering.
Cultivation tip: keep your heather plant in a cool, well-lit room—a cool conservatory, for example.

Erica x *hiemalis* ▼

Erica persoluta ▼

Erica canaliculata ▼

TROUBLE SHOOTING

◆ The leaves are dropping: the air is too dry. Spray your heather every day with rainwater.

➤ *Euanthe* see *Vanda*

Eucharis

Amazon lily

Decorative interest

Amazon lilies are bulbous plants native to the woodlands of central and South America. The fragrant, white flowers, which resemble narcissi, are carried on a scape that can be as tall as 32 inches (50 cm). The dark green, elliptical, basal leaves have long stalks. These plants are sold commercially under two names, *Eucharis amazonica* and *E.* x *grandiflora*; considered to be identical by experts until quite recently, they are now treated as different species.

Ease of cultivation

Looking after this plant in flower is simple, but in order to get the plant to flower again, it needs exposure to cool temperatures with reduced watering for at least a month. If treated correctly it may reward you by flowering two or three times a year.
Propagation: when repotting, remove the bulbils that have formed on the main bulb and pot them up individually.

CARING FOR YOUR PLANT

Watering and humidity: during the growing period, water moderately when the surface of the compost is dry. Reduce watering in winter in accordance with the temperature.
Light: bright conditions, but keep it out of direct sunlight.
Feeding: feed every two weeks in spring and summer with food for foliage plants.
Repotting and growing medium: repot every two to three years in spring, in a mixture of good yard soil, compost, and coarse sand.
Cultivation tip: during the winter months, keep your plant in a cool, light room at temperatures of between 55° and 59° F (13° and 15° C).

● RELATED SPECIES AND VARIETIES

Ismene, or the **spider lily** (*Hymenocallis*), is cultivated in the same way. This genus is native to the continent of America and includes around forty bulbous species. In early summer, the plants produce fragrant umbels of scented flowers with long extensions to the petals. The basal leaves are strap-like in form.

Eucharis amazonica ▼

◄ *Eucharis amazonica*

Hymenocallis x *festalis* ▼

Euphorbia

E. milii
synonym: *Euphorbia splendens*

Crown of thorns, Christ thorn

Decorative interest
Like the poinsettia, the crown of thorns is a euphorbia. It is a small, branching, shrubby plant that often remains compact when grown indoors. The succulent stems have long spines and small, dark green, elliptical leaves. The flowers themselves are tiny and insignificant, but are surrounded by two red bracts. There are also forms with yellow flowers. Flowering can occur at any time of year but is most likely to be in winter.

Ease of cultivation
This euphorbia is definitely one of the easiest to grow indoors.
Propagation: in spring or early summer, take 2½ to 4 inch (7 to 10 cm) terminal cuttings. Rinse the cut ends in water to stop sap flowing. Leave the cuttings to dry for one or two days, then plant them up in a pot filled with a slightly moist mixture of peat and sand.

Worth remembering
The crown of thorns is poisonous. Its milky sap is a skin irritant.

Euphorbia milii ▶

Euphorbia milii ▼

Euphorbia milii ▶

CARING FOR YOUR PLANT

Watering and humidity: water moderately, allowing the compost to dry to a depth of about 1 inch (2 to 3 cm) between waterings. After flowering, water less frequently for a few weeks to give the plant a period of rest.

Light: a bright, sunny position.

Feeding: feed every two weeks between June and September with plant food for cactuses and succulents.

Repotting and growing medium: repot in spring, if necessary, in compost for cactuses and succulents. Use thick gloves when handling this plant.

Cultivation tip: make sure you avoid any excess humidity and give the plant plenty of light. The temperature should not be allowed to drop below 55° F (13° C).

Euphorbia caput-medusae ▲

● RELATED SPECIES AND VARIETIES

Of the thousands of species that belong to the genus *Euphorbia*, over half are succulents. Many are cultivated for their unusual shape. *Euphorbia caput-medusae* is a heavily branching plant with radiating, gray-green stems that can grow to a length of 28 inches (70 cm) and are crowned by small, mid-green, fleshy, linear leaves. *E. trigona* has an upright, branching habit, similar to a cactus; the leaves develop at the top of angular stems. *E. lactea* is the species that produces plants with flattened, wavy stems in a wide range of colors; these are grafted on to the stem of another euphorbia. These unusual plants are sometimes found under the name *Euphorbia lactea cristata*.

Euphorbia trigona ▲

Euphorbia cristata ▲

Euphorbia fiherenensis ▼

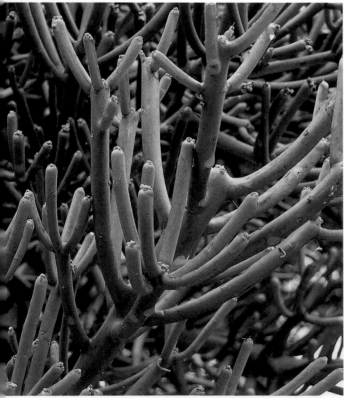

Euphorbia lactea (grafted plants) ▲

Euphorbia pulcherrima   Poinsettia, Christmas star

Decorative interest
This bushy plant, native to Mexico, is very popular at Christmas and New Year. Its large, oval, lanceolate leaves are mid- to dark green and sometimes lobed. In winter, tiny, insignificant, greenish-yellow flowers appear, surrounded by large, colorful bracts. These are usually bright red but can be creamy-white, creamy-yellow, or pale to salmon-pink, depending on the variety.

Ease of cultivation
The poinsettia is a "short day" plant and not difficult to cultivate, but it can be tricky to get it to flower again; it is usually treated as a seasonal plant and discarded after flowering.
Propagation: not of interest to non-professionals.

Worth remembering
The milky sap of this euphorbia can irritate the skin and mucous membranes.

CARING FOR YOUR PLANT

Watering and humidity: water generously while flowering, keeping the compost very moist.
Light: enjoys bright conditions; the poinsettia will tolerate winter sunshine.
Feeding: feed every two weeks with food for flowering plants.
Repotting and growing medium: repot in spring if you are keeping the plant, using ordinary compost with added sand.
Cultivation tip: cut the stems back hard after flowering; move the plant to a cool, light room and reduce watering. Repot in spring and start watering and feeding again. Pinch out the tips of the shoots. From mid-September onwards, give your poinsettia the "short day" treatment (i.e. more than twelve hours of complete darkness) for a period of six to eight weeks.

TROUBLE SHOOTING

◆ Deformed, sticky leaves reveal the presence of aphids: treat with a suitable insecticide.
◆ Small white bugs fly away when you touch the plant: whitefly are small, sap-sucking bugs that are difficult to eradicate. Treat the plant repeatedly with insecticide every eight to ten days.
◆ The leaves turn yellow and drop: the atmosphere is too warm and dry, or too dark.

▼*Euphorbia pulcherrima*

Euphorbia pulcherrima ▶

Euphorbia pulcherrima ▼

Eustoma

synonym: *Lisianthius*   Eustoma, lisianthus

Decorative interest

Eustomas are prized for their generous summer blooms. They are small biennials, usually grown as annuals and kept for only one season. Eustomas produce stems bearing opposed, oval, gray-green leaves and in summer are covered in attractive, deeply cupped flowers in a range of colors. The cultivated species, *Eustoma grandiflorum* (synonyms: *E. russellianum*, *Lisianthus russellianus*), has given rise to a whole range of varieties with constant new additions. There are also dwarf forms with a compact growth habit.

Ease of cultivation

Looking after a pot plant already in flower poses no problem, but growing the plant from seed is more difficult.
Propagation: growing from seed is quite tricky; sow in winter at 59° F (15° C).

TROUBLE SHOOTING
◆ The leaves wilt: the plant is reacting to a lack of water. Immerse the pot in water until the compost is completely soaked through.   ◆ The leaves become sticky and deformed: aphids are attacking the young shoots. Treat with a suitable insecticide.

CARING FOR YOUR PLANT
Watering and humidity: water regularly while in flower to keep the growing medium moist, but don't leave it standing in water.   **Light:** enjoys bright conditions, but keep the plant out of the midday summer sun.   **Feeding:** to maintain flowering, feed every two to three weeks with food for flowering plants.   **Repotting and growing medium:** not required—eustomas are discarded at the end of the season.   **Cultivation tip:** put your plant in a well ventilated room with plenty of light.

▲ *Eustoma grandiflorum*

Eustoma grandiflorum ▶

Euterpe

E. edulis
Euterpe

Decorative interest

This palm, which is native to tropical America, is a valuable houseplant as it has good shade tolerance. Its slender "trunk" (stipe) bears graceful, dark green, pennate leaves with long, pointed, pendant leaflets. In its natural habitat it can grow to 65 feet (20 meters) but when grown in a pot rarely exceeds 6½ feet (2 meters).

▼ *Euterpe edulis*

CARING FOR YOUR PLANT

Watering and humidity: water your plant freely during the growing season. Reduce watering a little in winter, even if the plant is not really resting. Water more sparingly if your plant is overwintering in a cool conservatory.

Light: enjoys bright conditions, but make sure you keep it out of strong, summer sunlight—shade lightly with a blind or curtain. This palm can cope with quite poor light levels.

Feeding: feed every two weeks in spring and summer with food for foliage plants.

Repotting and growing medium: repot young plants every year in spring, in a mixture of good yard soil and compost. A top dressing will suffice for larger plants grown in tubs.

Cultivation tip: keep a warm, constant temperature of over 59° F (15° C) throughout the year. Try not to move your plant. Remember not to cut back your palm or it will die.

Ease of cultivation

This palm is easy to grow but benefits from warmth and humidity.
Propagation: growing from seed is a matter for the professionals.

Worth remembering

Euterpes have an edible terminal bud (palm cabbage) and some species have been extensively cultivated for this. As these palms have only one terminal bud, the removal or destruction of it causes the plant to die. You can remove yellow leaves, but don't cut back your palm.

TROUBLE SHOOTING

◆ Small brown lumps appear on the stems and the leaves become sticky: these are scale bugs. Remove them with a Q-tip dipped in alcohol or treat the plant with a systemic insecticide.

◆ The leaves become pale and are covered in small, whitish spots: red spider mites thrive in warm, dry conditions. Increase the ambient humidity and spray the foliage. If necessary, treat the plant with an appropriate acaricide.

Exacum

E. affine   Exacum

Decorative interest

As a houseplant, this small perennial is cultivated as an annual, which is to say that it is discarded after flowering. Exacums are compact in habit, growing no taller than 8 inches (20 cm) high. They produce many small, bright green, fleshy, oval leaves. The violet-blue flowers with yellow stamens bloom in summer and fall, and stand out prettily against the foliage. There are also varieties with darker flowers and some with white flowers.

Associates well with... for an attractive color effect, combine several different-colored specimens in the same container.

Ease of cultivation

This is an easy plant to look after while in flower, but it is difficult to make it flower again.

Propagation: grown from seed but best left to the professionals.

TROUBLE SHOOTING
◆ The leaves become sticky and are invaded by aphids: treat the plant with a suitable insecticide.

CARING FOR YOUR PLANT
Watering and humidity: water regularly so that the compost remains slightly moist at all times, but avoid overwatering. **Light:** bright conditions, but keep it out of direct sunlight. **Feeding:** feed every two weeks while in flower with food for flowering plants. **Repotting and growing medium:** exacums are treated as annuals; there is no point in repotting them. **Cultivation tip:** deadhead regularly to encourage the formation of new flower buds.

▲ Variegated *Exacum affine*

Exacum affine ▶

Fatsia

F. japonica   Japanese aralia
synonym: *Aralia japonica*

Decorative interest

Native to Japan and Taiwan, this shrub can live outdoors in a mild climate. Its solid branches bear long-stemmed leaves, and the limb, which is divided into seven to nine very deep lobes, can grow to 6 to 16 inches (15 to 40 cm) in length. The leaves are pale green (though darker in plants grown outdoors) and glossy. In fall, mature specimens produce small, creamy-white flowers on branching umbels. Grown indoors, fatsias will reach a height of 5 feet (1.5 meters) in three years.

Ease of cultivation

The Japanese aralia is not difficult to grow, but benefits from cool temperatures, particularly in winter.

Propagation: in spring, take 2 to 3 inch (5 to 8 cm) long cuttings from the offsets around the root. Plant them in moist mixture of equal parts sand and peat. Grow under cover at 61° F (16° C).

Worth remembering

As the plant matures, the lower leaves drop and the stem becomes bare.

● RELATED SPECIES AND VARIETIES

Fatsia japonica "Moseri" is more compact, with larger leaves.

F. japonica "Variegata" has leaves with creamy-white variegation, particularly along the edges.

➤➤ **Fern** see *Adiantum, Asplenium, Blechnum, Davallia, Dicksonia, Didymochlaena, Hemionitis, Nephrolepis, Pellaea, Phlebodium, Platycerium, Polystichum, Pteris*

CARING FOR YOUR PLANT

Watering and humidity: water your plant regularly so that the compost remains quite moist, but do not overwater. Water less often during the winter months, particularly at low temperatures. Spray the leaves in warm weather.

Light: enjoys quite bright conditions, otherwise the plant will become etiolated.

Feeding: feed every two to three weeks in spring and summer with food for foliage plants.

Repotting and growing medium: repot every year to begin with and then every two or three years in ordinary compost enriched with good yard soil. With larger specimens a top dressing will be sufficient.

Cultivation tip: to give your plant a bushy appearance, cut back the previous year's growth by half each spring. In winter, move it to a cool room, ideally 50° to 54° F (10° to 12° C).

TROUBLE SHOOTING

◆ The leaves become sticky and deformed: aphids are attacking the young shoots. Treat your plant with a suitable insecticide.

◄ *Fatsia japonica*

x *Fatshedera lizei*

Aralia ivy

Decorative interest

The aralia ivy is a shrub that can grow to 3 to 6½ feet (1 to 2 meters) in height. Its upright stems bear large, dark green, glossy leaves divided into five lobes. The stems usually require support as they have a tendency to droop as they get longer. "Variegata" is a variety with creamy-white variegation and is more demanding in terms of light and warmth.

Associates well with... for a more compact look, plant several specimens together in the same pot.

Ease of cultivation

The aralia ivy is a robust plant that is easy to grow but appreciates cool temperatures.

Propagation: take 3 to 4 inch (7 to 10 cm) terminal cuttings and insert them in a moist mixture of equal parts peat and sand. Grow on, under cover, at 68° F (20° C). Cuttings will root more quickly in spring.

Worth remembering

The aralia ivy is the result of hybridization of two different botanical genera. In 1910, the French horticulturalist Lizé produced a hybrid from an ivy (***Hedera helix***) and an aralia (***Fatsia japonica***)—hence the Latin name preceded by the letter "x."

CARING FOR YOUR PLANT

Watering and humidity: water moderately, allowing the surface of the compost to dry out between waterings. If the plant is kept in the cool in winter, only water sufficiently to prevent the compost drying out completely. In a heated room, spray the leaves from time to time.

Light: medium to bright conditions. The variety with variegated foliage requires more light but should be kept out of direct sunlight.

Feeding: feed every two to three weeks in spring and summer with food for foliage plants.

Repotting and growing medium: plants that have outgrown their pots can be potted on in spring, using ordinary compost.

Cultivation tip: avoid overwatering. The plain green aralia ivy will appreciate a period of winter rest at temperatures of 44° to 50° F (7° to 10° C). However, the variegated form requires a temperature of over 61° F (16° C).

TROUBLE SHOOTING

◆ The leaves become sticky and deformed: aphids are attacking the young shoots. Treat your plant with a suitable insecticide.

◆ The leaves become pale and dry: red spider mites thrive in warm, dry conditions. Increase the ambient humidity and spray the foliage more often. If necessary, treat the plant with an acaricide.

x *Fatshedera lizei* "Pia Bont" ▼

x *Fatshedera lizei* ▼

Ficus

F. benjamina   Weeping fig

Decorative interest

The weeping fig is one of the most common houseplants and is valued for its attractive appearance. It resembles a small tree with fine, trailing branches and slender, oval leaves. The leaves are slightly wavy and 2 to 4 inches (5 to 10 cm) long. At first pale green, they become darker green as they mature. The plant can grow to almost 6½ feet (2 meters) in height. The weeping fig is also suitable for cultivation as a bonsai. There are also many varieties with variegated foliage.

Ease of cultivation

The weeping fig is easy to cultivate in a large room with plenty of light. Try to avoid moving it: a sudden change of environment can cause the leaves to drop.
Propagation: take terminal cuttings in spring. Rinse the cut end in water to stop the sap flowing and dip it in hormone rooting powder. Keep your cuttings in a propagator at 70° to 75° F (21° to 24° C).

Worth remembering

Varieties with variegated foliage are trickier to look after.

TROUBLE SHOOTING

◆ Small brown lumps appear on the stems and leaf stalks and the leaves become sticky and are covered in a blackish deposit: scale bugs are this plant's main enemies. The blackish deposit is due to the fumagin fungus that develops on the honeydew deposited by these sap-sucking bugs. If there are relatively few scale bugs, remove them with a Q-tip dipped in alcohol. Use a systemic insecticide in the event of a major attack.

◆ The leaves drop: this is probably the result of overwatering. Leave the compost to dry out completely before watering again.

Ficus benjamina ▼

CARING FOR YOUR PLANT

Watering and humidity: water moderately during the growing period, allowing half the compost to dry out before watering again. Reduce watering in winter. Spray the foliage in warm weather or if the atmosphere is dry.
Light: enjoys bright conditions, but make sure you keep it out of direct sunlight.
Feeding: feed every two weeks in spring and summer with food for foliage plants.
Repotting and growing medium: repot in spring, if necessary, in ordinary compost with a good layer of drainage material in the bottom of the pot. For larger specimens an annual top dressing will suffice.
Cultivation tip: avoid waterlogged roots and cold drafts. In winter, do not allow the temperature to drop below 59° F (15° C).

Ficus benjamina ▶

● RELATED SPECIES AND VARIETIES

Some varieties of *Ficus benjamina* have plain green leaves; these include "**Danielle**" (very dark green), "**Monique**" (curly leaves), and "**Reginald**" (pale green, almost golden leaves). Others have leaves with creamy-white variegation, like "**Starlight**," "**Variegata**," and "**De Gantel**," or creamy-yellow leaves like "**Golden King**." *Ficus* "**Alii**" is another fig with a shrubby habit that can grow to 6½ to 10 feet (2 to 3 meters) tall and has long, narrow leaves. A robust plant that can cope with a medium light level, it has become extremely popular as a decorative species for offices and entrance halls.

Ficus benjamina "Naomi" ▶

Ficus benjamina "Golden King" ▲

Ficus benjamina "Reginald" ▼

Ficus benjamina "Curly" ▼

Ficus benjamina "Judi" ▶

Ficus benjamina "Danielle" ▼

Ficus benjamina "Starlight" ▼

Ficus benjamina "Wiandi" ▶

Ficus deltoidea
synonym: *Ficus diversifolia*

Ficus

Decorative interest
This slow-growing fig produces tough, obovate leaves 1½ to 3 inches (4 to 8 cm) long which are bright green on the upper surface and brownish-red on the underside. It is the only indoor fig to fruit abundantly, producing yellow or dull red berries ¼ to ¾ inch (0.5 to 1 cm) in diameter. The berries appear throughout the year, carried on short peduncles. Native to south-east Asia, this plant rarely exceeds 36 inches (90 cm) when pot-grown.

Ease of cultivation
Like most other *Ficus*, this species is a robust plant that can survive for many years indoors.
Propagation: between April and June, take 2 to 4 inch (5 to 10 cm) long cuttings from side shoots and root them in a mixture of equal parts peat and sand. Maintain a good level of humidity until they begin to grow.

Worth remembering
If ingested, the leaves of this plant are poisonous and its milky sap is a skin irritant.

CARING FOR YOUR PLANT

Watering and humidity: water moderately from spring to the end of summer, allowing the growing medium to dry out to a depth of an inch or so (a few centimeters) between waterings. Reduce watering in winter. Spray the leaves frequently in summer but also in winter if your home is very heated.
Light: bright conditions with some sunlight, but avoid exposure to hot sunlight in summer.
Feeding: feed every two to three weeks in spring and summer with food for foliage plants.
Repotting and growing medium: repot young plants every year, then every two or three years as they mature, using ordinary compost for foliage plants.
Cultivation tip: you can pinch out the tips of young stems in spring to encourage branching.

Ficus deltoidea ▶

TROUBLE SHOOTING

◆ White or brown scales appear on the underside of the leaves and along the branches and the plant becomes sticky: these are scale bugs. If they are few in number, remove them with a Q-tip dipped in alcohol. If the attack is more severe, treat the plant with a systemic insecticide.
◆ The leaves become pale and a lot of small, whitish spots appear on them: red spider mites thrive in warm, dry conditions. Increase the ambient humidity and spray the foliage. If necessary, treat the plant with an acaricide.

Ficus deltoidea ▼

Ficus elastica   Rubber plant

Decorative interest

Rubber plants were very fashionable in the 1970s and are still valued for their sturdiness and stature. This is an upright plant which branches very little, if at all. Its large, tough leaves are dark green and glossy on the upper surface but duller on the underside. There are several varieties, including some with variegated leaves. "Decora" is one of the most commonly cultivated varieties: the young leaves are protected by a reddish membrane and the central vein is reddish on the underside. When grown in a large pot, the rubber plant can reach a height of 6½ feet (2 meters).

Ease of cultivation

A sturdy plant that is easy to cultivate.

Propagation: between April and June, take 2 to 4 inch (5 to 10 cm) long cuttings from side shoots and root them in a mixture of equal parts peat and sand at normal room temperature. Air layering is also possible but requires a certain skill; it is mainly used to rejuvenate plants with bare stems.

Worth remembering

Rubber plants die more frequently from overwatering than underwatering.

CARING FOR YOUR PLANT

Watering and humidity: water moderately in summer, allowing the surface of the compost to dry out between waterings. Reduce watering in winter. Spray the leaves if the air is dry.

Light: bright light, but filtered by a thin curtain or blind.

Feeding: feed every two weeks in spring and summer with food for foliage plants.

Repotting and growing medium: repot in spring, every year to begin with, then every two or three years, using ordinary compost enriched with peat.

Cultivation tip: keep your plant out of cold drafts in winter and provide a minimum temperature of 61° F (16° C).

Ficus elastica ▼

Ficus elastica "Belize" ▶

TROUBLE SHOOTING

◆ Small brown lumps appear on the underside of the leaves along the central vein: these are scale bugs. Remove them with a Q-tip dipped in alcohol, or treat the plant with a systemic insecticide in cases of severe attack.

◆ White, cottony clusters appear on the leaves: mealy bugs can be difficult to eradicate. If there are only a few, remove them with a Q-tip dipped in alcohol. Otherwise, treat the plant with a systemic insecticide.

◆ The leaves turn pale and are covered in small, white spots: red spider mites thrive in warm, dry conditions. Increase the ambient humidity and spray the foliage. If necessary, treat the plant with an appropriate acaricide.

● RELATED SPECIES AND VARIETIES

Ficus elastica "Doescheri" has tough leaves with grayish-green, creamy-yellow, and white markings; the leaf stalks and central veins are pink.

F. elastica "Robusta" has larger, more rounded leaves.

F. elastica "Schijveriana" has pale green leaves with dark green markings.

◀ *Ficus elastica* "Melany"

Ficus elastica "Tineke" ▶

Ficus elastica "Abidjan" ▶

Ficus elastica "Robusta" ▼

Ficus lyrata

Fiddle leaf fig

Decorative interest

The leaves of this fig are 10 to 18 inches (25 to 45 cm) long and are shaped like the body of a violin; they are coarse, bright green, and glossy with prominent veins and wavy edges. Though slow growing, this plant can reach an impressive height. The main stem branches very little.

Ease of cultivation

The fiddle leaf fig is a robust plant and easy to cultivate.
Propagation: in spring, take 4 to 6 inch (10 to 15 cm) long stem cuttings and insert them in a mixture of equal parts peat and sand. Grow on under cover at a temperature of between 70° and 75° F (21° and 24° C).

Worth remembering

Clean the large leaves of this fig regularly with a damp sponge, while supporting them from beneath with your other hand.

Ficus lyrata "Bambino" ▼

CARING FOR YOUR PLANT

Watering and humidity: water moderately from spring to early fall, allowing the compost to dry out to a depth of about an inch (a few centimeters) between waterings. Reduce watering in winter. Spray the leaves from time to time.
Light: bright conditions, but keep it out of direct sunlight.
Feeding: feed every two weeks in spring and summer with food for foliage plants.
Repotting and growing medium: repot in spring, every year at first, then less often, using ordinary compost, and put a good layer of drainage in the bottom of the pot.
Cultivation tip: the fiddle leaf fig will not tolerate waterlogging. Avoid overwatering the plant.

TROUBLE SHOOTING

◆ The leaves become pale and dry: red spider mites thrive in warm, dry conditions. Increase the ambient humidity and spray the foliage more often. If necessary, treat the plant with an acaricide.
◆ Small brown lumps appear on the stems and leaves, which become sticky: these are scale bugs. Remove them with a Q-tip dipped in alcohol, or treat the plant with a systemic insecticide.
◆ The leaves turn yellow and drop: this is probably due to overwatering. Allow the compost to dry out before watering again.

Ficus lyrata ▼

Ficus pumila

Climbing fig, dwarf fig

synonym: *Ficus repens*

Decorative interest

This is a small fig with a climbing or trailing habit. It can also be trained to climb up a moss pole, clinging to it with its aerial roots. The small, dark green, heart-shaped leaves are ½ to 1¼ inches (1 to 3 cm) long. There are also variegated varieties.

Associates well with… you can grow a climbing fig at the foot of another upright fig or use it to cover the surface of a large planter.

Ease of cultivation

The climbing fig is happy in a quite shady room, but it is important to keep it well watered as its fine foliage dries out easily.

Propagation: in spring, take 4 to 6 inch (10 to 15 cm) long terminal cuttings and root them under cover in a mixture of equal parts peat and sand at 68° to 72° F (20° to 22° C).

Tip

Although the creeping fig is naturally branching, you can pinch out the tips of the stems to encourage the development of secondary branches.

CARING FOR YOUR PLANT

Watering and humidity: keep the compost moist throughout the year, allowing it to dry out only slightly between waterings. Spray the leaves regularly with soft water.

Light: medium to poor light. Varieties with variegated leaves will require more light.

Feeding: feed every two to three weeks in spring and summer with food for foliage plants.

Repotting and growing medium: repot the plant in spring if it has outgrown its pot, using ordinary compost with a little added peat.

Cultivation tip: avoid sudden changes of temperature, and water the plant very regularly to prevent the foliage from drying out. This species can tolerate temperatures of 41° to 45° F (5° to 7° C).

▼ *Ficus pumila* at the foot of a *Ficus benjamina*

TROUBLE SHOOTING

◆ The leaves turn pale and threads appear on the underside: red spider mites thrive in warm, dry conditions. Increase the ambient humidity and spray the foliage more often. If necessary, treat the plant with an appropriate acaricide.

◆ Small brown lumps appear on the stems and leaves, which become sticky: these are scale bugs. Try removing them with a Q-tip dipped in alcohol if there are only a few. If necessary, treat the plant with a systemic insecticide.

● **RELATED SPECIES AND VARIETIES**

Ficus pumila "Minima" has slender stems and small leaves less than ½ inch (1 cm) long.

F. pumila "Variegata" has leaves with creamy-white markings.

F. pumila "White Sunny" has leaves with white margins.

Ficus pumila
"White Sunny" ▶

Fittonia

Fittonia

Decorative interest

This genus includes two or three species of perennial creepers, native to the rainforests of South America, that are highly prized for their beautiful, variegated foliage. Their flowers are insignificant. *Fittonia verschaffeltii* produces quite large, dark green, oval leaves up to 4 inches (10 cm) long, with carmine veins. *F. verschaffeltii* var. *argyroneura* (synonym: *F. argyroneura*) has olive-green foliage with silvery highlights and striking white veins. *F. verschaffeltii* var. *argyroneura* "Nana" is a dwarf form with small leaves about an inch (2 to 3 cm) long and is valued as a terrarium plant. *F. verschaffeltii* "Pearcei" has small, pale green leaves with bright carmine red veins. *F. gigantea* is a species with an upright habit and large, oval, slightly pointed leaves that are green with dark pink veins.

Ease of cultivation

Fittonias require a high level of ambient humidity and a constant temperature.
Propagation: take terminal cuttings in spring and root them under cover in a mixture of equal parts peat and sand at 71° to 75° F (22° to 24° C). You can also remove root-bearing shoots.

CARING FOR YOUR PLANT

Watering and humidity: water moderately throughout the year with soft, tepid water, keeping the compost slightly moist. Stand the pot on a bed of damp gravel and spray the leaves regularly.
Light: medium to poor.
Feeding: feed every two to three weeks in spring and summer with half strength food for foliage plants.
Repotting and growing medium: repot every two to three years in spring, in compost enriched with peat and ericaceous compost. Use a shallow pot.
Cultivation tip: keep the fittonia out of drafts and bright light. Maintain as constant a temperature as possible (between 64° and 70° F/18° and 21° C), and keep the ambient humidity level high.

TROUBLE SHOOTING

◆ The leaves become dull and the edges curl: the air is too dry. Stand the pot on a bed of wet gravel and spray the foliage more often.

Worth remembering

Fittonias often begin to look less attractive after two or three years. It's best to replace them by taking cuttings.

▼ *Fittonia* hybrids

◄ *Fittonia verschaffeltii* var. *argyroneura*

➤ ***Fortunella*** see *Citrus*   ➤ ***Galanthus*** see *Crocus*

Gardenia

G. augusta   Gardenia, Cape jasmine
synonym: *Gardenia jasminoides*

Decorative interest

This small, bushy shrub is native to China. It has dark green, glossy, lanceolate leaves which provide the perfect backdrop to its blooms. The solitary flowers can be double or semi-double, are white and highly fragrant and between 1½ and 3 inches (4 and 8 cm) in diameter. They generally bloom between June and October. As a pot plant, the gardenia rarely exceeds 16 to 20 inches (40 to 50 cm) in height.

Ease of cultivation

Growing gardenias in a greenhouse is easy, but less so indoors.
Propagation: take 3 to 4 inch (8 to 10 cm) terminal cuttings in spring and root them under cover in a mixture of peat and sand at between 64° and 70° F (18° and 21° C). Hormone rooting powder will help to promote rooting.

Tip

In March, trim back long stems to maintain a compact appearance.

● RELATED SPECIES AND VARIETIES

Gardenia jasminoides "Veitchiana" blooms in winter (in fact, its flower buds are pinched out when they form in summer and early fall, to delay flowering).

TROUBLE SHOOTING

◆ White, cottony clusters appear on the leaves: mealy bugs can be difficult to eradicate. If there are only a few, remove them with a Q-tip dipped in alcohol. Otherwise, treat the plant with a suitable insecticide.
◆ The leaves become pale and dry: red spider mites thrive in warm, dry conditions. Increase the ambient humidity and spray the foliage (but not the flowers) more frequently. If necessary, treat the plant with an appropriate acaricide.

Gardenia augusta ▲

Gardenia augusta ▶

CARING FOR YOUR PLANT

Watering and humidity: water very regularly during the growing period to keep the compost slightly moist. Use soft water at room temperature. In fall and during the winter months, water less frequently. Spray the foliage frequently in warm weather but avoid wetting the flowers.
Light: bright conditions, but filter out summer sunlight during the hottest part of the day.
Feeding: feed every two to three weeks in spring and summer with food for flowering plants.
Repotting and growing medium: repot every two or three years in spring, in a mixture of ordinary compost and ericaceous compost.
Cultivation tip: give your plant good light and high humidity. In winter, gardenias are best kept in a conservatory at between 54° and 61° F (12° and 16° C).

➤ **Gibasis** see *Tradescantia*

Globba

G. winitii   Globba

Decorative interest

Native to Thailand, this rhizomatous perennial is a member of the ginger family (*Zingiber*) and produces extraordinary flowers that have earned it the name dancing ladies. The plant produces a clump of mid-green, lanceolate leaves that are heart-shaped at the base. At the end of summer and in the fall, each stem produces a terminal, pendant inflorescence composed of small, yellow flowers and violet-pink bracts. When pot-grown it reaches a height of about 24 inches (60 cm). This species has given rise to numerous hybrids with differently colored bracts.

Ease of cultivation

The globba is a tropical plant and requires good light and humidity. It is best grown in a heated conservatory or warm greenhouse.

Propagation: divide large clumps when repotting. It can be grown from seed in spring at 64° to 72° F (18° to 22° C).

CARING FOR YOUR PLANT

Watering and humidity: water your plant generously during the growing period so that the compost remains moist but not wet. Water less frequently in winter. Maintain a good level of humidity by standing the pot on a saucer filled with wet gravel. During warm weather, spray the leaves frequently.

Light: bright conditions, but keep it out of direct sunlight.

Feeding: feed every two to three weeks in spring and summer with food for flowering plants.

Repotting and growing medium: repot in spring, if necessary, in potting compost enriched with good yard soil and coarse sand to improve drainage.

Cultivation tip: give your plant a constant temperature of above 68° F (20° C). If possible, keep it in a heated conservatory or warm greenhouse.

Globba winitii ▶

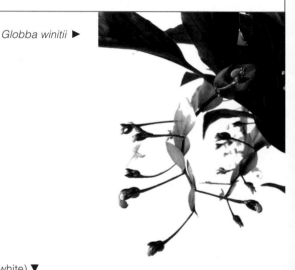

Globba (white) ▼

◀ *Globba winitii*

Gloriosa

G. superba "Rothschildiana"
synonym: *Gloriosa rothschildiana*

Gloriosa, Malabar lily, glory lily

Decorative interest
The Malabar lily is a tuberous plant with long, mid-green, glossy, lanceolate leaves that taper toward the tip to form a tendril 1 to 2 inches (3 to 5 cm) long. In summer, extraordinary flowers, 2 to 4 inches (5 to 10 cm) in diameter, appear in the axils of the upper leaves; they are composed of six wavy, reflexed petals, red with yellow margins, and with long, prominent, widely spread stamens. The gloriosa needs a support to cling to. As a pot plant it grows to a height of 3 to 6 feet (1 to 2 meters). In winter, the tubers must be kept cool and dry.

Ease of cultivation
Gloriosas need good light and a high level of humidity. Ideally they should be cultivated in a warm or temperate greenhouse.
Propagation: increase by dividing the tuber in early spring.

Worth remembering
This plant is very poisonous. Simply handling the tuber can lead to skin irritation.

Gloriosa superba "Rothschildiana" ▼ ▶

TROUBLE SHOOTING

◆ Deformed, sticky leaves reveal the presence of aphids: treat the plant with a suitable insecticide.

CARING FOR YOUR PLANT

Watering and humidity: after planting the tuber, water moderately until the first stems appear. Keep the compost moist in spring and summer. Gradually reduce watering until the parts of the plant above the soil disappear. Maintain an ambient humidity of over 50%.
Light: bright conditions with some sunlight, but keep it out of very hot sunlight.
Feeding: feed every two weeks in spring and summer with food for flowering plants.
Repotting and growing medium: at the end of winter, repot the tubers in fresh compost and increase the temperature gradually to encourage the tubers into growth.
Cultivation tip: keep the tubers dry during the winter, at between 52° and 58° F (11° and 14° C). The tubers are fragile, so handle them with care.

Gloxinia

G. sylvatica   Gloxinia
synonym: *Seemania sylvatica*

Decorative interest
This scaly-rhizomed perennial is native to South America and is cultivated for its striking, bright orangey-red flowers. The leaves are dark green and lanceolate with dentate edges. It is a "short day" plant, flowering between October and March. The small, tubular, velvety flowers bloom in the leaf axils and are orange-red with a yellow throat. This plant grows to 8 to 12 inches (20 to 30 cm) in height and width.

Ease of cultivation
The gloxinia is a demanding plant and unsuited to novice plant growers.
Propagation: the rhizomes are divided in spring when repotting, or basal shoots can be used for cuttings in June and grown on, under cover.

Worth remembering
This gloxinia should not be confused with the florists' gloxinia, which belongs to the genus *Sinningia*.

▼ *Gloxinia sylvatica*

CARING FOR YOUR PLANT

Watering and humidity: water your plant moderately during the growing period but do not leave water standing in the saucer. Reduce watering once the plant has finished flowering and gradually increase it again when growth begins in spring. To increase humidity levels, stand the pot on wet gravel.
Light: bright conditions, but keep it out of direct sunlight.
Feeding: feed every two to three weeks in spring and summer with food for flowering plants.
Repotting and growing medium: repot in spring, after the rest period, in a mixture of compost and peat, leaving the top of the rhizomes just level with the surface.
Cultivation tip: gloxinias must be protected from drafts and not overwatered.

● **RELATED SPECIES AND VARIETIES**
Gloxinia perennis produces a single, tall stem, bearing green, oval leaves, tinged with red on the underside. The violet-blue, bell-shaped, downy flowers appear in summer in the axils of the leaves on the upper part of the stem. The flower stem fades in the fall and the rhizomes must be kept dry during the winter.

◀ *Gloxinia perennis*

➤ **Gramineae** see *Bambusa, Pogonatherum*   ➤ **Graptopetalum** see *Echeveria*

Grevillea

G. robusta   Grevillea

Decorative interest

In its natural habitat in Australia, this grevillea is a tree that grows to 50 to 115 feet (15 to 35 meters) high! When pot-grown it grows no taller than 3 to 6 feet (1 to 2 meters), with a spread of 20 inches (50 cm). Its feathery, bipennate leaves are 6 to 12 inches (15 to 30 cm) long and resemble fern fronds. Dark green and tinged with brown when they open, they have silky hairs on the underside. As a houseplant the grevillea rarely flowers and only in very light situations, at which point it produces clusters of orange or red blooms.

Ease of cultivation

Grevilleas need a lot of light and a cool temperature in winter. The ideal situation is a cold greenhouse.

Propagation: grow from seed in spring at 55° to 64° F (13° to 18° C).

Worth remembering

Grevilleas can cause skin allergies.

CARING FOR YOUR PLANT

Watering and humidity: during the growing period water moderately but regularly so that the root ball remains slightly moist. In winter, allow half the compost to dry out between waterings. In temperatures above 64° F (18° C), increase the ambient humidity by standing the pot on wet gravel.

Light: enjoys bright conditions, with as much light as possible in winter.

Feeding: feed every two weeks in spring and summer with food for foliage plants.

Repotting and growing medium: repot in spring every year, in a mixture of ordinary compost and ericaceous compost.

Cultivation tip: in winter, keep your plant in a cool spot at 48° to 50° F (7° to 10° C), with plenty of light.

Grevillea robusta ▲

Grevillea robusta ▶

◀ *Grevillea* "banksii"

Grevillea "Fireworks" ▶

Guzmania

Guzmania

Decorative interest

Guzmanias are bromeliads that grow in the tropical rainforests of America. The genus includes almost 120 species and numerous hybrids, most of which are derived from *Guzmania lingulata*. This plant produces a rosette of green, strap-like leaves, 8 to 18 inches (20 to 45 cm) long from which a flower spike emerges toward the end of winter, bearing overlapping, bright red, orange, or pink bracts. The flowers themselves are in the center and are tubular and yellowish.

G. monostachya (synonym: *G. tricolor*) has green, glossy, strap-like leaves and a long flower spike bearing white flowers and green bracts, with purple stripes toward the lower part of the spike, and red and orange higher up.

G. dissitiflora has long, arching, leaves that are green with red stripes. The inflorescence has bright red bracts and yellow and white flowers.

G. wittmackii has slightly scaly, dark green leaves with a brown sheath. The inflorescence is composed of red bracts surrounding white, tubular flowers.

Guzmania lingulata ▲

Guzmania lingulata ▼

▲*Guzmania* "Omar Morobe"

▼*Guzmania lingulata* "Torch"

CARING FOR YOUR PLANT

Watering and humidity: during the growing period, water generously to keep the compost moist. In summer, regularly fill the rosette with soft water. Maintain a high level of humidity around the pot.

Light: bright conditions, but keep it out of direct sunlight as this will make the colors fade.

Feeding: feed every two to three weeks in spring and summer with half strength food for foliage plants.

Repotting and growing medium: plant offsets in compost for epiphyte bromeliads.

Cultivation tip: in winter, empty the water in the rosette and keep your plant at a temperature of above 64° F (18° C).

TROUBLE SHOOTING

◆ White, cottony clusters appear on the underside of the leaves: mealy bugs can be difficult to eradicate. If there are only a few, remove them with a Q-tip dipped in alcohol. In cases of severe attack, treat the plant with a suitable insecticide.

Ease of cultivation

Guzmanias must be protected from cold, humid conditions as this will cause their inflorescences to rot.

Propagation: in April, remove the basal offsets when they are approximately 3 inches (8 cm) long.

Worth remembering

The main rosette dies after flowering. However, the inflorescence remains decorative for many weeks and the plant can easily be reproduced from offsets.

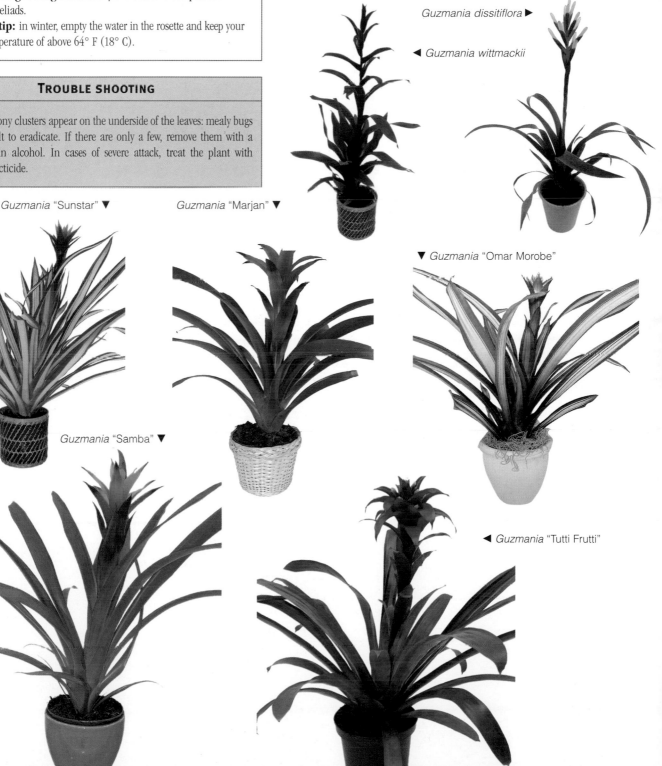

Guzmania dissitiflora ▶

◀ *Guzmania wittmackii*

Guzmania "Sunstar" ▼

Guzmania "Marjan" ▼

▼ *Guzmania* "Omar Morobe"

Guzmania "Samba" ▼

◀ *Guzmania* "Tutti Frutti"

Gymnocalycium

Gymnocalycium

Decorative interest

This genus comprises some fifty species of desert cactuses native to South America. These are small, rounded cactuses with prominent ribs and curved spines, the color of which often contrasts with the dark green stem. In early summer, quite large, funnel-shaped flowers appear in shades of red, pink, and white. One species, *Gymnocalycium mihanovichii*, has produced varieties with no chlorophyll in the stems in red, pink, yellow, violet, and white. They have to be grafted on to a green cactus in order to grow.

Ease of cultivation

These cactuses are easy to cultivate but require a very bright position.
Propagation: can be grown from fresh seed in spring at 68° F (20° C). Species that produce offsets can be propagated by removing the offsets in spring and planting them up.

Gymnocalycium zeggarea ▲

Gymnocalycium hybopleurum ▼

CARING FOR YOUR PLANT

Watering and humidity: water moderately during the growing period, allowing three-quarters of the growing medium to dry out between waterings. During the rest period, only water enough to prevent the compost drying out completely.
Light: enjoys bright conditions, but filter out the strong midday summer sun (these small cactuses live in the shade of bushes in their natural habitat).
Feeding: feed every two to three weeks in spring and summer with cactus fertilizer.
Repotting and growing medium: repot every two to three years in March or April in a free-draining compost for cactuses and succulents.
Cultivation tip: water sparingly. During the winter months, move your cactus to a cool, bright room at a temperature of 45° to 50° F (7° to 10° C).

TROUBLE SHOOTING

◆ White, cottony clusters appear in the hollows: mealy bugs can be difficult to eradicate. If there are only a few, remove them with a Q-tip dipped in alcohol. In cases of severe attack, treat the plant with a suitable insecticide.

Gymnocalycium mihanovichii (this is a small, rounded, colored cactus grafted on to a green cactus) ▼

Gynura

G. aurantiaca   Gynura

Decorative interest

This woody perennial, which starts life as an upright plant and then becomes a semi-creeper, has deeply dentate, dark green leaves, 4 to 8 inches (10 to 20 cm) long, covered in violet down. It produces small, yellowy-orange, insignificant flowers with an unpleasant odor; these are best removed when they appear, so as to encourage leaf growth. Gynuras can grow to 24 inches (60 cm) in height if trained on a support; if not, the stems will become trailing.

Ease of cultivation

The gynura is a robust plant but requires good light, warmth, and humidity.
Propagation: propagating from cuttings is easy. Take 4 inch (10 cm) terminal cuttings in early spring and root them in a mixture of equal parts peat and sand at 64° to 68° F (18° to 20° C).

Worth remembering

As young plants are more attractive, replace your gynura regularly by taking cuttings. Frequently pinch out the stems to encourage branching.

● RELATED SPECIES AND VARIETIES

Gynura aurantiaca "Purple Passion" (synonym: *G. sarmentosa*) is a creeping form with leaves covered in a thick, purple down on the underside, but less heavily on the upper surface.

CARING FOR YOUR PLANT

Watering and humidity: water moderately during the growing period, but less in winter. Never wet the foliage. Maintain a good level of humidity by standing the pot on damp gravel.
Light: bright conditions (but filter out the midday summer sun).
Feeding: feed every three weeks in spring and summer with food for foliage plants.
Repotting and growing medium: repot in spring, in ordinary compost with a little added peat.
Cultivation tip: give your plant conditions that are as constant as possible, avoiding any sudden changes in temperature. Gynuras need warmth but can tolerate temperatures as low as 55° F (13° C).

TROUBLE SHOOTING

◆ The leaves become sticky and deformed: aphids are attacking the young shoots. Remove them by hand if there are only a few. Otherwise, treat your plant with a systemic insecticide.

Gynura aurantiaca ▶

Gynura aurantiaca ▼

Hedera

H. helix   Ivy
synonym: *Hedera canariensis*

Decorative interest

In its juvenile form, the common ivy produces creeping stems bearing dark green leaves with 3 or 5 lobes. It has given rise to a number of highly decorative varieties. "**Cristata**" has bright green leaves with wavy, dentate edges. The leaves of the variety "**Glacier**" vary in size and have broad, irregular, white margins and a gray-green center. "**Goldheart**" has small, dark green leaves with long, pointed lobes. You can train the vigorous stems of these ivies or allow them to trail.

Associates well with... plant several varieties of different-colored ivies together in the same pot or combine them with other plants with decorative foliage.

Ease of cultivation

Ivies are easy to grow and are ideal for beginners.
Propagation: take 3 to 4 inch (8 to 10 cm) cuttings and root them in water or in cutting compost at ambient temperature.

Worth remembering

Most species send out short, adventitious roots which will cling to any damp surface.

CARING FOR YOUR PLANT

Watering and humidity: water moderately during the growing period but more sparingly in winter, particularly at low temperatures. In warm weather, spray the leaves regularly.

Light: ivy enjoys bright conditions. Variegated forms need two to three hours of sunlight each day but remember to keep other forms out of direct sunlight.

Feeding: feed every two to three weeks in spring and summer with food for foliage plants.

Repotting and growing medium: repot every year in spring, in ordinary compost.

Cultivation tip: do not hesitate to cut back long or bare stems. Replace old plants with cuttings. In winter, if you can, move your ivy to a cool room at around 50° F (10° C).

Hedera helix ▼

TROUBLE SHOOTING

◆ Deformed, sticky leaves reveal the presence of aphids: treat your plant with a suitable insecticide.

◆ The leaves become pale and dry: red spider mites thrive in warm, dry conditions. Increase the ambient humidity and spray the foliage. If necessary, treat the plant with an acaricide.

Hedera helix "Colibri" ▲

◄ *Hedera algeriensis* "Gloire de Marengo"

● RELATED SPECIES AND VARIETIES

Hedera canariensis is a large species with triangular, slightly lobed leaves. The variety "**Gloire de Marengo**" (synonyms: *H. canariensis* "Variegata," *H. algeriensis* "Gloire de Marengo") has variegated, gray-green leaves with creamy-yellow edges.

Hedera helix ▶

Hedera helix "Gold Kolibri" ▲

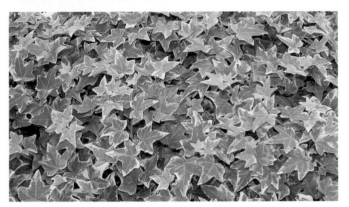

Hedera helix "Esther" ▲

Hedera helix "Elja" ▶

▲ *Hedera helix* "Evergreen"

Hedera helix "Goldchild" ▶

Hedera helix "Stricta" ▼

Hedera helix "Glacier" ▶

Heliconia

Heliconia, canna

Decorative interest

This genus comprises around a hundred species of short-rhizomed perennials that grow in the tropical forests of central and South America. These plants produce very large leaves, up to 5 feet (1.5 meters) long; these are spatulate, with long leaf stalks and have a certain resemblance to banana leaves. The flowers appear at different times of year, depending on the species. The spectacular, upright, or trailing inflorescences are composed of brightly colored bracts, often in shades of red, yellow, or orange. Arranged spirally, in two or three rows, they protect the real flowers, which are more modest. Heliconia inflorescences are much prized for flower arrangements.

Ease of cultivation

Heliconias are difficult to grow indoors; they need a lot of light and humidity, and are best grown in a warm greenhouse.

Propagation: you can divide the rhizomes when repotting in early spring; can also be grown from seed in early spring at 65° to 75° F (19° to 24° C).

CARING FOR YOUR PLANT

Watering and humidity: during the growing period, water your plant regularly to keep the growing medium slightly damp. Water less often in winter. Maintain a high level of humidity by spraying the foliage every day.

Light: very bright conditions, but with light shade during the hottest part of the day.

Feeding: feed every two weeks in spring and summer with food for flowering plants.

Repotting and growing medium: repot in spring, in a mixture of good yard soil and compost, enriched with well-rotted manure.

Cultivation tip: warmth and humidity are essential throughout the year, so keep your heliconia in a warm greenhouse, if possible. The minimum suitable temperature is 59° F (15° C).

Heliconia bihai ▼

TROUBLE SHOOTING

◆ Small brown lumps appear on the stems, the leaves become sticky: these are scale bugs. Remove them with a Q-tip dipped in alcohol, or treat the plant with a systemic insecticide.

◆ The leaves become pale and dry: red spider mites thrive in warm, dry conditions. Increase the ambient humidity and spray the foliage more frequently. If necessary, treat the plant with an acaricide.

Heliconia psittacorum ▲

Heliconia "Olympic Flame" ▲

Heliconia ▼

Hemigraphis

Hemigraphis

Decorative interest

This genus, native to tropical Asia, is composed of thin-stemmed plants with a carpeting habit. The cultivated species and varieties are valued for their colored leaves. The small, white flowers produced on terminal spikes are rare in cultivated plants.

Hemigraphis alternata (synonym: *H. colorata*) produces dentate, oval, heart-shaped leaves on violet-red stalks; the leaves are grayish-purple on the upper surface and reddish-purple on the underside. It will grow to 6 inches (15 cm) in height and 16 to 20 inches (40 to 50 cm) across.

H. "Exotica" has oval leaves that are more wrinkled and are purple-green on the upper surface and dark red on the underside.

H. "Crispy Red Flame" is a new form produced in Holland; it has a relatively upright habit but grows no higher than 12 inches (30 cm). It has crinkly, glossy leaves that are dark green with purple margins on the upper side and dark violet on the underside.

H. repanda is a species with a spreading habit and narrow, scalloped leaves, purple-red on the upper side and red on the underside.

Ease of cultivation

The hemigraphis prefers a warm, humid environment.

Propagation: in April, remove and plant up stems that have developed roots.

TROUBLE SHOOTING

◆ Small white bugs fly away when you touch the plant: whitefly are small, sap-sucking bugs that are difficult to eradicate. Treat the plant repeatedly with insecticide every eight to ten days.

CARING FOR YOUR PLANT

Watering and humidity: water your plant generously during the growing period but avoid overwatering. During the winter months, keep the compost just slightly moist. Stand the pot on damp gravel and spray the foliage daily when the temperature rises above 70° F (21° C).

Light: enjoys bright but filtered light. Keep it out of direct sunlight.

Feeding: feed every two to three weeks in spring and summer with food for foliage plants.

Repotting and growing medium: repot in spring, in a mixture of equal parts leaf mold and peat.

Cultivation tip: maintain a temperature of between 64° and 75° F (18° C and 24° C) throughout the year, and a good level of humidity.

Hemigraphis repanda ▶

◀ *Hemigraphis* "Crispy Red Flame"

Hemionitis

Hemionitis

Decorative interest

This genus includes seven species of fern with evergreen foliage that are native to damp, shady regions of tropical Asia and America. The broad, rounded fronds are borne on a dark leaf stalk but are not finely divided like so many other ferns. The fronds of *Hemionitis arifolia* are simple, cordiform to lanceolate, mid-green, and glossy. With *H. palmata* the limb is divided into five, rounded lobes with scalloped edges. The spores form a network of lines along the veins on the underside of the fertile fronds, which are narrower than the sterile ones. The leaf stalks of fertile fronds are long and rigid, while those of sterile fronds are shorter.

Ease of cultivation

These small ferns will thrive in the humid atmosphere of a terrarium. Otherwise, you can grow them in a temperate to warm greenhouse.

Propagation: spores can be sown when mature, at 66° to 75° F (19° to 24° C). In the case of *H. palmata*, you can remove the plantlets that form at the foot of the mother plant and at the base of the limb, and pot them up individually.

TROUBLE SHOOTING
◆ The edges of the fronds become brown and dry: it is probable that the humidity is too low. Stand the pot on a bed of damp gravel and spray the foliage frequently.

CARING FOR YOUR PLANT
Watering and humidity: during the growing period, water your plant sparingly, keeping the compost slightly moist but avoiding overwatering. Water less frequently in winter. Remember to maintain a good level of humidity at all times. **Light:** bright conditions, but keep it out of direct sunlight. **Feeding:** feed every two weeks in spring and summer with half strength food for foliage plants. **Repotting and growing medium:** repot in spring, if necessary, in a mixture of ericaceous compost and leaf mold, with added coarse sand to improve drainage. **Cultivation tip:** avoid overwatering the hemionitis as the roots are sensitive to damp, particularly during the winter. These ferns will be happy at average room temperature, with a minimum of 50° F (10° C).

◀ *Hemionitis arifolia* ▶

Hibiscus

Hibiscus

Decorative interest

This genus comprises almost 200 species of herbaceous plants, shrubs, and trees. The leaves can be deciduous or evergreen and are very varied in form. The varieties used for indoor cultivation are mainly derived from *Hibiscus rosa-sinensis* (China rose). Native to tropical Asia, this handsome shrub with bright green, evergreen foliage can grow to 6¹/₂ feet (2 meters) when grown in a pot. The leaves are 2³/₄ to 6 inches (7 to 15 cm) long, oval and pointed, with dentate edges. The solitary blooms are 4 to 5 inches (10 to 12 cm) in diameter and red in the species, with five petals surrounding a long cluster of stamens. They are short-lived but usually continue to appear at regular intervals. There are numerous varieties, not always named when sold commercially, in shades of white to red and yellow to orange, as well as some with double blooms.

Ease of cultivation

This very popular plant is quite easy to grow: it needs plenty of light and will benefit from a period of winter rest in a cool spot—a cool conservatory, for example. Be aware that over time your hibiscus will increasingly require a good deal of space.

Propagation: at the end of spring or in the summer, take 3 to 4 inch (7 to 10 cm) terminal cuttings and insert them in a damp mixture of equal parts peat and sand. Grow on, under cover, at 68° to 72° F (20° to 22° C).

Hibiscus rosa-sinensis ▶

CARING FOR YOUR PLANT

Watering and humidity: water your plant moderately but very regularly during the growing period. Reduce watering in winter, according to the temperature. During warm weather, increase the humidity around the plant.

Light: bright conditions with some sunlight (but avoid the midday summer sun).

Feeding: feed every eight to ten days in spring and summer with food for flowering plants.

Repotting and growing medium: repot in spring, every year to begin with, then every two years, in special geranium compost. When your plant has reached its optimum size a top dressing will suffice.

Cultivation tip: give your plant a period of winter rest in a bright spot at 53° to 59° F (12° to 15° C). In spring, cut the stems back by half to encourage branching and flowering.

Hibiscus rosa-sinensis ▲

Different color blooms of *Hibiscus rosa-sinensis*

Hippeastrum

Amaryllis

Decorative interest

Related to species of the genus *Amaryllis*, this large-bulbed plant grows well in a temperate room. There are numerous hybrids with plain or bicolor blooms in shades of white to red or even to orange. The bulb comes into growth at the end of fall or in winter. The thick flower-scape grows remarkably quickly, in advance of the bright green, strap-like leaves.

Ease of cultivation

The hippeastrum is not difficult to grow but certain rules must be observed if you want the bulb to flower again the following year.
Propagation: when repotting, remove the bulbils that have formed at the base of the bulb and plant them up in individual pots. They will need a few years to fatten up before they will flower.

Worth remembering

This genus is often confused with the genus *Amaryllis*, native to southern Africa, which flowers in the fall. The genus *Hippeastrum* comes from South America and its blooms appear in spring.
All parts of this plant can cause slight stomach problems if ingested.

TROUBLE SHOOTING

◆ Your bulb produces leaves but no flowers: it was not given the correct care the previous season. It is essential that the plant is exposed to bright light when the leaves are growing and that watering and feeding continue until early fall.

CARING FOR YOUR PLANT

Watering and humidity: water sparingly in the beginning, then increase the amount when the flower bud begins to form. Keep the compost moist while the plant is in flower. Stop watering when the leaves begin to turn yellow.
Light: requires bright conditions with some sunlight during the growing period.
Feeding: if you want to keep the plant, feed it with food for flowering plants every two weeks from the end of flowering until the end of summer.
Repotting and growing medium: after overwintering, pot up the bulb in ordinary compost, leaving the top half exposed, and move the pot to a warm, bright position. Gradually build up watering.
Cultivation tip: provide bright conditions when the leaves are developing and continue to water and feed. At the end of summer, reduce watering and feeding and allow the leaves to turn yellow. You can then remove them and keep the pot in a cool, dry place at 50° to 60° F (10° to 15° C) for three months.

Hippeastrum "Wonderland" ▶

Hippeastrum hybrid ▶

Howea

H. forsteriana
Kentia palm, howea
synonym: *Kentia forsteriana*

Decorative interest
Kentias are quite fast-growing palms. The main stem, which thickens over time, bears long, dark green, supple leaves divided into broad, tapering leaflets on long leaf stalks. Initially upright, the leaves gradually fall open to create a quite spreading plant. It therefore needs a good amount of space in which to develop fully.

Ease of cultivation
Kentias are easy plants to grow indoors.
Propagation: sow seed in trays at 80° F (27° C). Growing these seeds can be a slow process.

Worth remembering
Kentias can live for over twenty years when grown as houseplants.

CARING FOR YOUR PLANT

Watering and humidity: water generously during the growing period, so that the compost remains moist, but avoid overwatering. Reduce watering in winter, in accordance with the temperature. Spray the foliage from time to time in warm weather.
Light: bright conditions, but keep it out of direct sunlight.
Feeding: feed every two to three weeks in spring and summer with food for foliage plants.
Repotting and growing medium: repot in spring every two years. Young plants should be potted on in ordinary compost, but once mature, a top dressing will suffice.
Cultivation tip: don't leave water standing in the saucer. Average room temperature will suit kentias, but provide a minimum temperature of 54° F (12° C).

TROUBLE SHOOTING

◆ Small brown lumps appear on the stems and palms: kentias are susceptible to attack from scale bugs. Remove them with a Q-tip dipped in alcohol, or treat the plant with a systemic insecticide.
◆ The palms become pale and dry: red spider mites thrive in warm, dry conditions. Increase the ambient humidity and spray the foliage more often. If necessary, treat the plant with an acaricide.

◀▶ *Howea forsteriana*

Hoya

H. carnosa   Porcelain flower, wax flower

Decorative interest

Native to India, China, and Burma, the hoya is a vigorous, climbing perennial with thick, shiny, dark green, elliptical leaves, 1 to 3 inches (3 to 8 cm) long. In summer, it produces fragrant flowers which are white to pale pink with red centers, in umbel clusters of ten to thirty flowers. There is also a variegated form, "Variegata," which has leaves edged with cream and sometimes tinged with pink.

Ease of cultivation

This plant is easy to grow in a very bright room.
Propagation: in spring, take 3 to 4 inch (8 to 10 cm) stem cuttings and insert them in a slightly moist mixture of equal parts peat and sand. Grow on, under cover, at between 64° and 68° F (18° and 20° C).

Worth remembering

Don't cut the woody stalk that bore the first flowers: it will produce more flower buds.

● RELATED SPECIES AND VARIETIES

Hoya bella (synonym: *H. lanceolata* ssp. *bella*) is a less vigorous form with soft, downy stems, bearing small, fleshy leaves about an inch (2 to 3 cm) long that are oval, pointed, and mid-green. Its fragrant flowers, between ¼ and ¾ inch (0.5 and 2 cm) in diameter, are white with violet-red centers and grow in umbel clusters of seven to nine flowers.

H. linearis produces long, trailing stems with linear leaves 2 to 2½ inches (5 to 6 cm) long and ¼ inch (0.5 cm) wide. The umbels bear about a dozen creamy-white flowers with a light, lily fragrance.

H. longifolia is a vigorous species with long, trailing stems bearing thick, narrow, lanceolate leaves. There is a new variety called "**China Beans,**" with pendant leaves similar to haricot bean pods. This is very decorative when grown as a hanging plant.

Hoya longifolia
"China Beans" ▶

Hoya bella ▼

Hoya bella ▼

▲ *Hoya carnosa*
"Variegata"

TROUBLE SHOOTING

◆ The leaves become pale and dry: red spider mites thrive in warm, dry conditions. Increase the ambient humidity and spray the foliage. If necessary, treat the plant with an acaricide.

CARING FOR YOUR PLANT

Watering and humidity: water moderately during the growing period with soft water, keeping the compost slightly moist. Water sparingly in winter. In warm weather, spray the foliage (but not the flowers) with tepid, soft water.
Light: bright conditions with three to four hours of sunlight each day.
Feeding: feed every two to three weeks in spring and summer with food for flowering plants.
Repotting and growing medium: repot at the beginning of spring every two to three years, in ordinary compost lightened with added peat. Hoyas flower better when slightly constricted in their pot.
Cultivation tip: give your plant a period of winter rest in a cool, bright spot at 52° to 59° F (12° to 15° C). Once the flower buds have formed, don't move the plant.

Hyacinthus

H. orientalis **Hybrids**   Hyacinth

Decorative interest

Outside in the yard, hyacinths herald the arrival of spring, but they can also be used decoratively indoors, bringing a splash of bright color and filling the room with their powerful fragrance. Hyacinths are bulbous plants with bright green, linear leaves, from the middle of which emerges a dense cluster of small, bell-like, strongly scented flowers in a variety of colors. There are numerous varieties available.

To get hyacinths to flower indoors, choose "forced" bulbs. These have been specially prepared by growers to bring forward and promote flowering, usually in the middle of winter. Plant the bulbs between September and November in ordinary compost with added coarse sand, and keep the pots in a cool place at 41° to 50° F (5° to 10° C) in darkness (a basement or even the vegetable container of your ice-box). When the bulbs have formed shoots about 2 inches (5 to 6 cm) long—after about seven to twelve weeks in the dark, depending on the species—move the pots into a room with normal heating and light.

Ease of cultivation

Getting hyacinths to flower indoors is simply a matter of treating them correctly at the different stages of cultivation.

Propagation: not applicable.

Hyacinthus orientalis ▼

Hyacinthus orientalis ▶

CARING FOR YOUR PLANT

Watering and humidity: water moderately but regularly while the hyacinth is in flower, so that the compost remains slightly moist.

Light: very bright conditions. Turn the pot regularly so that the flower stem grows upright and straight.

Feeding: not applicable.

Repotting and growing medium: after flowering, plant the bulbs outside in the yard, where they will flower again next year.

Cultivation tip: to ensure flowering lasts as long as possible, keep your plant in a cool room, at temperatures of around 59° to 61° F (15° to 16° C).

Worth remembering

You can also grow hyacinths in water, in special wide-necked vases or jars. Follow the same method as for pot cultivation. Fill the hyacinth jar with water so that the water level is just below the base of the bulb, to avoid the risk of it rotting.

Tip

Start bulbs off at regular intervals, every two weeks, for example, so that you can enjoy staggered flowering over a longer period.

● RELATED GENERA

Other spring-flowering, bulbous plants are also suitable for indoor cultivation. **Narcissi** (*Narcissus*), for example, are much enjoyed for their bright colors. For preference choose early or miniature species and varieties such as Tête-à-Tête'—a *Cyclamineus* type narcissus that grows to only 6 to 8 inches (15 to 20 cm) in height. *Tazetta* type narcissi produce delicately fragranced flowers. **Tulips** (*Tulipa*) also make excellent spring pot plants. Choose early species and varieties, such as those of the *Forsteriana* and *Kaufmanniana* groups. By forcing the bulbs you can have tulips in bloom indoors by the end of December.

Hyacinthus orientalis ▲

Tulipa ▶

Narcissus "Tête-à-Tête" ▼

Narcissus tazetta "Paper White" ▼

Hydrangea

H. macrophylla   Hydrangea

Decorative interest

Given their cultivation requirements, hydrangeas are not strictly speaking houseplants. However, florists sell potted hydrangeas, most often in spring. These are plants that have been "forced" by growers to bring on early flowering. The large, rounded, pink, white, or blue inflorescences are set off by large, oval, dark green, dentate leaves. Flowering can last for six weeks if the temperature is quite cool (less than 61° F/16° C), but only three to four weeks when at normal room temperature.

CARING FOR YOUR PLANT

Watering and humidity: keep the compost very moist by watering generously. It should never be allowed to dry out.

Light: bright conditions, but keep it out of direct sunlight.

Feeding: feed every eight to ten days with food for flowering plants to promote flowering.

Repotting and growing medium: not applicable.

Cultivation tip: give your plant a cool temperature (55° to 64° F/13° to 18° C), and water regularly.

Hydrangea macrophylla "Fireworks White" ▼

Hydrangea macrophylla "Blaumeise" ▼

Hydrangea macrophylla ▼

Hydrangea macrophylla ▶

Ease of cultivation

Hydrangeas need frequent watering and a cool, bright position. After flowering you can either discard your hydrangea or plant it out in the yard in a semi-shaded position.

Propagation: difficult for non-professionals to achieve indoors.

Worth remembering

This species only produces really blue flowers on acid soil with a pH of less than 5.5. If grown in compost with a higher pH, the flowers will be plain pink. White flowers do not vary with the pH level.

➤ *Hymenocallis*
see *Eucharis*

Hypoestes

H. phyllostachya
Hypoestes, polka dot plant

synonym: *Hypoestes sanguinolenta*

Decorative interest

This small plant, native to Madagascar, is valued for its attractive, variegated foliage. It has simple, dark green, oval to lanceolate leaves 1 to 2 inches (3 to 5 cm) long, covered in pink markings of varying sizes. There are also varieties with white, pale pink to bright pink, and red variegation.

Associates well with… plant two or three different-colored varieties together in the same pot.

Ease of cultivation

This plant is relatively easy to grow in a room with plenty of light.

Propagation: in summer, take 3 to 4 inch (8 to 10 cm) terminal cuttings and root them in water or under cover in a mixture of sand and moist peat at between 64° and 70° F (18° and 21° C).

Worth remembering

Plants sold commercially are very compact. However, once at home they tend to spread and quickly become less attractive. Replace them by taking cuttings.

● RELATED SPECIES AND VARIETIES

Hypoestes phyllostachya "Carmina" has bright red leaves with green veins.
H. phyllostachya "Splash" has larger pink markings than the species form.
H. phyllostachya "Witana" has cream leaves with dark green veins.

TROUBLE SHOOTING

◆ Deformed, sticky leaves reveal the presence of aphids: treat your plant with a suitable insecticide.
◆ Small brown lumps appear on the stems and leaves: these are scale bugs. Remove them with a Q-tip dipped in alcohol or treat the plant with a systemic insecticide.

CARING FOR YOUR PLANT

Watering and humidity: water regularly during the growing period to keep the compost moist. Allow the surface of the compost to dry out between waterings. Reduce watering a little in winter.

Light: enjoys bright conditions, but keep it out of direct sunlight.

Feeding: feed every two weeks in spring and summer with food for foliage plants.

Repotting and growing medium: repot in spring, in ordinary compost. It is sometimes better to replace the plant each year by taking cuttings.

Cultivation tip: keep it in an averagely heated room in winter with a minimum temperature of 60° F (15° C). The higher the temperature, the more you must provide your plant with good humidity.

Hypoestes phyllostachya ▶

Hypoestes phyllostachya ▶

Impatiens

I. x novae-guinea
New Guinea impatiens

Impatiens
x novae-
guinea ▶

Decorative interest
With their bright blooms, New Guinea impatiens make excellent flowering pot plants. They are hybrids produced by crossing several species, including *Impatiens hawkerii* and *I. hookeriana*. These plants form a handsome clump of dark green, elliptical leaves, often with yellow or dark red variegation, and produce large flowers, over 2 inches (5 to 6 cm) across, in many shades of red, pink, and sometimes yellow.

Associates well with… combine different, strikingly colored varieties in the same container.

Ease of cultivation
Impatiens is an easy plant to cultivate indoors.

Propagation: at the end of spring or in summer, take 3 to 4 inch (8 to 10 cm) terminal cuttings and root them in water or in cutting compost.

Tip
When your plant becomes too large, cut back the longer branches. The stem tips will make excellent cuttings.

TROUBLE SHOOTING

◆ The leaves become sticky and deformed: aphids are attacking the shoots. Treat your plant with a suitable insecticide.

◆ Small white bugs fly away when you touch the plant: whitefly are small, sap-sucking bugs that are difficult to eradicate. Treat the plant repeatedly with insecticide every eight to ten days.

◆ The leaves become pale and dry: red spider mites thrive in warm, dry conditions. Increase the ambient humidity. If necessary, treat the plant with an acaricide.

Impatiens x *novae-guinea* ▶

CARING FOR YOUR PLANT

Watering and humidity: water regularly but not excessively during the growing season. Allow the surface of the compost to dry out between waterings. Reduce watering in winter.

Light: enjoys bright conditions, but keep it out of direct sunlight.

Feeding: feed every two weeks in spring and summer with food for flowering plants.

Repotting and growing medium: repot every year in early spring, in ordinary compost.

Cultivation tip: water carefully and keep a close eye on your plant in case of parasite attack. When it becomes less attractive, replace it by taking cuttings. The New Guinea impatiens requires a minimum temperature of 54° F (12° C).

Impatiens velvetea ▲

● RELATED SPECIES AND VARIETIES

The impatiens used as bedding in summer borders—which are derived from ***Impatiens walleriana***—also make ideal houseplants and can flower indoors continuously for many months. Their fleshy, branching stems carry pointed, oval, pale green leaves and plentiful flat flowers in a wide range of colors, depending on the variety. There are also bicolor forms, forms with double blooms, dwarf forms, and varieties with variegated foliage.

I. repens produces fleshy, red, creeping stems with small, rounded or kidney-shaped leaves, dark green on top and purple on the underside. The helmet-shaped, solitary flowers are bright yellow.

I. velvetea produces upright stems up to 36 inches (90 cm) long, with large, dark green, glossy leaves arranged spirally, and axillary flowers 1½ to 2¼ inches (4 to 6 cm) long in green, yellow, and red, with a white labellum.

Impatiens niamniamensis ▶

Impatiens repens ▲

Impatiens x novae-guinea ▼

Impatiens velvetea ▶

Ixora

I. coccinea

Ixora, flame of the woods

Decorative interest

This shrub, which is native to India and Sri Lanka, rarely grows taller than 24 inches (60 cm) when grown as a pot plant. Its branching stems bear dark green, glossy, oval leaves 2 to 4 inches (5 to 10 cm) long. The young leaves are tinged with bronze. Large, rounded inflorescences, 2 to 5 inches (5 to 12 cm) in diameter, appear from summer through to early fall. The flowers are tubular, terminating in a flattened opening in shades of red, orange, pink, and yellow.

Ease of cultivation

Ixoras are demanding in terms of light, warmth, and humidity, and can be difficult to cultivate successfully indoors. They are best grown in a heated conservatory or warm greenhouse.

Propagation: semi-woody cuttings can be taken in July to August and grown on, in a propagator with bottom heat, using hormone rooting powder. Rooting is not always successful.

Tip

After flowering, cut back the branches to half their length to maintain a compact appearance.

TROUBLE SHOOTING

◆ Small brown lumps appear on the stems and leaves: remove scale bugs with a Q-tip dipped in alcohol, or treat the plant with a systemic insecticide.

CARING FOR YOUR PLANT

Watering and humidity: water moderately but regularly throughout the year, allowing the compost to dry to a depth of about an inch (a few centimeters) between waterings. Use soft, tepid water. Maintain a high level of humidity.

Light: give your plant as much sunlight as possible all year round but filter it with a blind or curtain during the hottest part of the day in summer. During the winter months, artificial lighting can be used to compensate for the lack of light.

Feeding: feed every two weeks in spring and summer with food for flowering plants.

Repotting and growing medium: repot every year in spring, in a mixture of ordinary compost and peat, with a little added coarse sand.

Cultivation tip: the temperature should never be allowed to drop below 61° F (16° C).

◀ *Ixora* "Maui Geel"

Ixora coccinea ▶

◀ *Ixora* "Jacqueline"

Jasminum

J. polyanthum   Jasmine

Decorative interest

This climber is native to China. Its slender, green stems carry dark green leaves composed of five to seven leaflets, which are oval to elliptical. The flowers are tubular and highly fragrant; they grow in clusters and are white, tinged with pink. They bloom in spring. Provide a support, such as a hoop, around which the stems can twine and be supported.

Ease of cultivation

In order to flower again, jasmines need to overwinter in a cool place, such as a conservatory or temperate greenhouse.
Propagation: take herbaceous cuttings in April or semi-woody cuttings in summer, and root them under cover in a moist mixture of sand and peat.

Worth remembering

After flowering, you can cut back the long stems that have flowered.

TROUBLE SHOOTING

◆ The leaves become sticky and deformed: aphids are attacking the shoots. Treat your plant with a suitable insecticide.

CARING FOR YOUR PLANT

Watering and humidity: water generously with soft water at room temperature during the growing period. In winter, water less often, depending on the temperature. Maintain a good level of humidity around the plant, particularly in warm weather. Spray the foliage regularly, except during the flowering period.
Light: jasmines enjoy bright conditions, but filter out the midday sun in summer.
Feeding: feed every two weeks in spring and summer with food for flowering plants.
Repotting and growing medium: repot in early spring, if necessary, in ordinary compost.
Cultivation tip: during the winter, keep your jasmine in a conservatory or a cold but frost-free greenhouse. Make sure that it doesn't come into growth too quickly at the end of winter.

Jasminum polyanthum ▼

Jasminum officinale ▼

Jatropha

J. podagrica
Jatropha, bottle plant

Decorative interest
This shrubby, branching succulent has a short, gray trunk which is swollen at the base. Large, green, lobed, heart-shaped leaves emerge from the top and in summer and it produces small flowers ¼ inch (0.5 cm) across. These are scarlet to bright coral-red and are carried on long, green scapes, sometimes tinged with red. Native to central America and the West Indies, the bottle plant can grow to over 3 feet (1 meter) when grown in a pot.

Ease of cultivation
Relatively easy to cultivate in a room with plenty of light.
Propagation: can be grown from seed in spring or by taking stem cuttings from the tips of the lateral branches. Leave the cuttings to dry for a few days and insert them in a mixture of slightly moist peat and sand. Grow on at 78° F (25° C).

Worth remembering
Avoid contact with the sap of this plant as it can cause skin irritation.

TROUBLE SHOOTING
◆ Small brown lumps appear on the leaves: remove these scale bugs as soon as they appear with a Q-tip dipped in alcohol, or treat the plant with a systemic insecticide.

CARING FOR YOUR PLANT
Watering and humidity: water regularly during the growing period to keep the compost slightly moist but not wet. In the fall, reduce watering and stop watering altogether in winter.
Light: requires very bright conditions, but keep it out of direct sunlight on very hot days.
Feeding: feed every three to four weeks in spring and summer with fertilizer for cactuses and succulents.
Repotting and growing medium: repot in spring, if necessary, in a mixture of compost, peat, and coarse sand.
Cultivation tip: bottle plants need a definite period of winter rest at a temperature of around 59° F (15° C), during which they should not be watered.

Jatropha multifida ▼

Jatropha integerrima ▼

Jatropha podagrica ▶

Juncus

J. effusus "Spiralis"   Spiral rush

synonym: *J. effusus f. spiralis*

Decorative interest

This perennial rush forms a clump of cylindrical, aphyllous (leafless), dark green, glossy stems that twist into spirals. The intertwining stems can grow to 20 inches (50 cm) tall. In summer, the plant produces thin clusters of small, greenish-brown flowers. The spiral rush can be grown in a pot or in a shallow bowl of water, up to 4 inches (10 cm) deep. Plants often take a while to become established. In Japan, the type species is grown for its stems, which are used to make tatami rush mats.

Ease of cultivation

The spiral rush is used to a damp environment and requires sunlight. It will not tolerate dryness.

Propagation: divide large clumps in spring, when repotting.

Worth remembering

If a straight stem appears, remove the rhizome responsible to prevent the plant reverting to the type species.

CARING FOR YOUR PLANT

Watering and humidity: water your plant freely so that the compost remains very moist at all times. You can leave water standing in the saucer, particularly during warm weather. Spray your plant from time to time if the air is dry.

Light: requires bright and sunny conditions.

Feeding: feed every two weeks in spring and summer with food for foliage plants.

Repotting and growing medium: repot in early spring, if necessary, in ordinary compost enriched with good yard soil.

Cultivation tip: in summer, you can move your plant outside in the sun but make sure that it is never short of water. In winter, keep it in a conservatory or frost-free greenhouse.

● **RELATED SPECIES AND VARIETIES**

There are forms of *J. effusus* with variegated foliage, such as "**Vittatus**" and "**Zebrinus.**"

Juncus "**Pencil Grass**" produces a clump of dark green, straight stems with black markings at the tips. It grows to a height of 12 inches (30 cm).

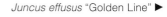
Juncus effusus "Golden Line" ▶

Juncus effusus "Spiralis" ▼

Juncus "Pencil Grass" ▲

Justicia

J. brandegeana
synonym: *Beloperone guttata*

Shrimp plant, beloperone

Decorative interest

This soft, shrubby, graceful little plant produces slender stems bearing mid-green, oval leaves that are glossy on the upper surface and downy on the underside. Almost all year long, small, short-lived, white flowers appear, emerging from overlapping, pinkish-brown to greenish-yellow bracts that resemble shrimps. The bracts remain on the plant for some time. As a pot plant, the beloperone will grow to 24 inches (60 cm) in height.

Ease of cultivation

It is not easy to maintain this plant in an attractive, compact shape.
Propagation: in spring, take 2 to 3 inch (5 to 8 cm) stem cuttings and plant them in a moist mixture of equal parts peat and sand. Grow on under cover at 68° to 72° F (20° to 22° C).

Worth remembering

At the end of winter, cut the stems back hard on plants that have spent the winter in the warm and which have become rather etiolated.

CARING FOR YOUR PLANT

Watering and humidity: water generously during the growing period but don't leave water standing in the saucer. Water less often in winter, depending on the temperature.
Light: enjoys bright conditions with a little direct sunlight.
Feeding: feed every two to three weeks in spring and summer with food for flowering plants.
Repotting and growing medium: repot every year in spring, in ordinary compost with added peat.
Cultivation tip: it is often best to replace this plant after two or three years. Regularly pinch out young plants to encourage branching. The shrimp plant enjoys a period of cool winter rest at a temperature of 59° F (15° C).

● RELATED SPECIES AND VARIETIES

Justicia brandegeana "Yellow Queen" is a less common form and has bright yellow bracts.

The jacobinia, *Justicia carnea* (synonyms: *Jacobinia pohliana*, *Justicia velutina*), is an upright, relatively unbranching shrub. Its large, dark green, heart-shaped leaves are elliptical and heavily veined. Conical, terminal inflorescences, composed of small, tubular, pink flowers, appear between June and October. When pot-grown, it can reach almost 4 feet (1.2 meters) in height.
J. rizzini (synonyms: *Jacobinia pauciflora*, *Justicia floribunda*) is a squat shrub with a rounded appearance; it has small, mid-green, oval leaves and tubular yellow and red flowers that grow in clusters on pendant flower spikes.

Justicia brandegeana ▶

Justicia rizzinii ▶

Justicia carnea ▶

Kalanchoe

K. blossfeldiana   Kalanchoe

Decorative interest

This small, bushy, succulent grows to only 12 to 16 inches (30 to 40 cm) in height and width. The bright green, fleshy, oval to rounded, scalloped leaves are dominated by dense clusters of small, tubular flowers in a range of colors from pink and red to orange and yellow. Kalanchoes need a period of short daylight hours before they will come into flower, so they generally bloom in winter. However, horticultural growers expose the plants to artificially short days, which is why they can be found in bloom almost all year round. They remain in flower for about three months.

Ease of cultivation

Kalanchoes are very easy plants to grow and are highly recommended for beginners.
Propagation: take terminal cuttings after flowering and plant them in a mixture of slightly moist peat and sand. Grow on at 70° to 73° F (21° to 23° C).

Worth remembering

It is difficult to get kalanchoes to flower again when grown indoors because of the artificial lighting. This is why most people discard them after flowering.

CARING FOR YOUR PLANT

Watering and humidity: water moderately once a week during the growing period, but less in winter.
Light: bright conditions with some sunlight, but filtered on very hot days.
Feeding: feed every two to three weeks during the flowering period with food for flowering plants.
Repotting and growing medium: repot in spring, in compost for cactuses and succulents.
Cultivation tip: water your plant by pouring water into the saucer as the leaves are very sensitive to damp. After ten to fifteen minutes, empty the saucer.

Kalanchoe blossfeldiana ▶

◀ *Kalanchoe blossfeldiana*

● **RELATED SPECIES AND VARIETIES**

Kalanchoe "Tessa" has a dwarf, spreading habit with trailing stems; the small, tubular, bell-like flowers are red and orange, and bloom in winter.

K. "Wendy" produces wide, bell-like flowers that are red with yellow tips.

K. pumila has pale green, oval leaves tinged with white, scalloped toward the tips, and small, pink, spring flowers with purple stripes.

Kalanchoe "Mirabella" ▼

Kalanchoe "Tessa" ▼

Kalanchoe "Wendy" ▼

▲ *Kalanchoe* "African"

Kalanchoe hybrid Bells ▶

Kalanchoe

Kalanchoes with decorative foliage

Decorative interest

Kalanchoes are succulents native to the semi-desert regions of Africa—with most originating in Madagascar. They have fleshy stems with thick leaves in a variety of shapes and sizes. Many are cultivated for the decorative quality of their foliage. Some species, such as *Kalanchoe daigremontiana* (synonym: *Bryophyllum daigremontianum*) produce young plantlets on the edges of the leaf limbs which drop and take root quite easily. *K. beharensis* is a bushy species with large, velvety, triangular leaves covered in short hairs. *K. tomentosa* is completely covered in a thick, white, felty down and its heavily dentate leaves often have brownish-red margins. *K. thyrsiflora* produces oval leaves which are flat on the upper surface and rounded on the underside; they are pale green with red toward the tips and are covered in a silvery bloom.

Ease of cultivation

Kalanchoes are easy plants to grow, providing you don't overwater them.
Propagation: take stem cuttings with one or two leaves and root them in a mixture of slightly moist peat and sand. You can also remove the young plantlets that, in certain species, form on the edges of the leaves, and plant these up.

Kalanchoe tomentosa ▼

Kalanchoe beharensis ▼

◄ *Kalanchoe thyrsiflora*

Kohleria

K. amabilis

synonym: *Isoloma amabile*

Kohleria

Decorative interest

Kohlerias are perennials that grow from scaly rhizomes and are native to the tropical forests of America. They are prized for their velvety flowers. The upright or creeping stems of *Kohleria amabilis* bear large, oval, dentate leaves tinged with purple along the veins. The bell-like, pendant flowers appear in summer in the axils of the leaves. They are dark pink with purple stripes on the lobes and throat, and about 1 inch (2 to 3 cm) long. This species is particularly attractive when grown as a hanging plant.

Ease of cultivation

Kohlerias are demanding plants.

Propagation: divide the rhizomes in spring when repotting.

● RELATED SPECIES AND VARIETIES

Kohleria eriantha produces red flowers with yellow markings; this species has given rise to numerous hybrids.

K. digitaliflora bears clusters of purple-pink, tubular flowers; the throat and lobes of these are white and the lobes are speckled with greenish-purple.

TROUBLE SHOOTING

◆ The leaves become pale and dry: red spider mites thrive in warm, dry conditions. Increase the ambient humidity and spray the foliage. If necessary, treat the plant with an acaricide.

CARING FOR YOUR PLANT

Watering and humidity: water moderately during the growing period. Reduce watering after flowering. In winter, water the dormant rhizomes just enough to stop the growing medium drying out completely. Maintain a good level of humidity around the plant by standing it on a bed of damp gravel.

Light: bright conditions, but keep it out of direct sunlight.

Feeding: feed every two weeks in spring and summer with food for flowering plants.

Repotting and growing medium: repot in February or March, in ordinary compost with a little added peat or perlite.

Cultivation tip: keep your plant at a constant temperature while in growth—between 68° and 75° F (20° and 24° C). Dormant rhizomes can be kept at 50° to 60° F (10° to 15° C).

Kohleria amabilis ▼

Kohleria lindeniana ▼

Lachenalia

Lachenalia, Cape cowslip

Decorative interest

This genus is composed of bulbous perennials that are native to South Africa. The basal leaves, which can be plain or patterned, are linear and thick. The inflorescences appear from fall to spring. They are carried on bare, sometimes patterned flower-scapes and consist of numerous, tubular flowers. *Lachenalia aloides* (synonym: *L. tricolor*), the most commonly cultivated species, grows to a height of 8 to 12 inches (20 to 30 cm) and produces yellow and red flowers; it has given rise to many hybrids. Lachenalias have a period of rest during the summer.

Ease of cultivation

These are demanding plants and not easy to cultivate.
Propagation: remove the bulbils that form at the base of the main bulb and pot them up individually.

Worth remembering

After planting, water sparingly until the first shoots appear.

CARING FOR YOUR PLANT

Watering and humidity: water moderately during the growing period—the bulb is susceptible to rotting. After flowering, reduce watering until the leaves fade, then keep the plant dry until new shoots begin to appear in the fall.
Light: full sunlight. Extra lighting is recommended in areas that are short of light in winter.
Feeding: feed every two weeks during the growing period with food for foliage plants.
Repotting and growing medium: repot the bulbs in September (grow several together in the same pot) in a light growing medium composed of compost, peat, and sand. Plant them at a depth equivalent to their height.
Cultivation tip: lachenalias do not like heat. Flowering will last longer at 59° to 64° F (15° to 18° C). Some people dispose of the plant once it has flowered.

TROUBLE SHOOTING

◆ The top of the bulb is beginning to rot: treat it with a fungicide in powder form.

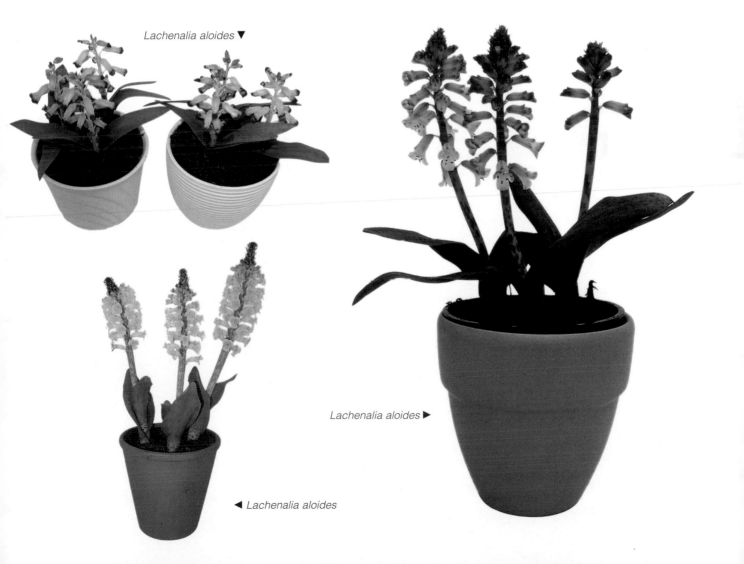

Lachenalia aloides ▼

Lachenalia aloides ▶

◀ *Lachenalia aloides*

Leea

L. guineensis "Burgundy"   Leea

Decorative interest

Leea guineensis is a branching shrub (in fact a small tree in its native habitat) with evergreen foliage; the leaves are composite and between 10 and 24 inches (25 and 60 cm) long. The dentate leaflets are obovate to elliptical, and slightly pointed. The young leaves are pale green in the species and bronze in the variety "Burgundy," creating an attractive contrast with the mature dark green, glossy foliage. The flowers appear in terminal clusters of small, pink, and scarlet buds, though leeas rarely flower when pot-grown. As a pot plant it can grow to 5 feet (1.5 meters) high. This genus is native to the tropics of Africa, Asia, and Australia.

Ease of cultivation

Not too difficult to grow, providing you give it the ambient humidity it needs.
Propagation: in summer, take semi-woody cuttings from the tips of the branches and put them in a propagator at about 78° F (25° C). Hormone rooting powder will encourage root formation.

● RELATED SPECIES AND VARIETIES

Leea rubra (synonym: *L. coccinea*) has bronze-green foliage. This species is sometimes called *L. guineensis* "Burgundy."

TROUBLE SHOOTING

◆ The leaves become pale and dry: red spider mites thrive in warm, dry conditions. Increase the ambient humidity and spray the foliage more often. If necessary, treat the plant with an acaricide.

Leea guineensis "Burgundy" ▼

➤ *Leptinella* see *Muehlenbeckia*

CARING FOR YOUR PLANT

Watering and humidity: water your plant regularly during the growing period to keep the compost moist, but not wet. During the winter months, allow the compost to dry out to a depth of nearly an inch (1 or 2 cm) between waterings. Maintain a good level of humidity by standing the pot on damp gravel.
Light: enjoys bright conditions, but make sure you keep it out of direct sunlight.
Feeding: feed every two to three weeks in spring and summer with food for foliage plants.
Repotting and growing medium: repot every year in spring, in ordinary compost with added coarse sand to improve drainage.
Cultivation tip: spray the foliage regularly, especially in winter if the plant is in a warm room. Avoid cold drafts. Don't expose your plant to temperatures below 61° F (16° C).

Leea rubra ▼

Licuala

L. grandis   Licuala, fan palm

Decorative interest

This palm produces handsome, rounded palms on long, bright green leaf stalks at the tip of a fine, slender trunk enclosed within the fibrous bases of the leaves. The connected segments that make up the palm give it a pleated appearance. Native to the New Hebrides, the licuala can grow to a height of 10 feet (3 meters) in its natural habitat.

Ease of cultivation

Licualas can be difficult to grow indoors as they need a lot of humidity. They will be happier in a greenhouse or heated conservatory with plenty of humidity.
Propagation: can be grown from seed in spring, in a propagator at 77° F (25° C).

Licuala grandis ▶

CARING FOR YOUR PLANT

Watering and humidity: water your palm generously once or twice a week during the growing period. Water less often in winter. Maintain a good level of humidity around your plant; in dry weather, spray the palms twice a day.
Light: enjoys bright conditions, but make sure you filter out the midday summer sun.
Feeding: feed every two weeks in spring and summer with food for foliage plants.
Repotting and growing medium: repot in spring, if necessary, in a mixture of compost and good yard soil, with a little added perlite to improve drainage.
Cultivation tip: maintain a constant temperature of 60° F (15° C) and avoid exposure to cold drafts.

TROUBLE SHOOTING

◆ Small brown, sticky lumps appear on the palms: these are scale bugs. Remove them with a Q-tip dipped in alcohol or treat the plant with a systemic insecticide.
◆ The leaves become pale and dry: red spider mites thrive in warm, dry conditions. Increase the ambient humidity and spray the foliage more often. If necessary, treat the plant with an acaricide.

Lithops and other pebble plants

Pebble plant, living stone

Decorative interest

These small succulents really do look like pebbles. There are a number of related species that look quite similar. Each plant is composed of two thick, fleshy, rounded leaves divided by a fissure where, in late summer or fall, a white or yellow flower similar to a daisy appears. The upper side of the leaves is often bluish-gray or brown, or has markings in these colors. In spring, young leaves develop to replace the old ones. Some species have a clumping habit.

Associates well with... you can grow several species of pebble plants together in the same pot.

Ease of cultivation

Lithops are easy to grow providing they have plenty of sunlight and a free-draining growing medium.

Propagation: can be grown from seed or by clump division in early summer.

● RELATED SPECIES AND VARIETIES

Plants of the genus *Conophytum* are also known as pebble plants. The body of the plant is composed in the same way—with two joined, fleshy leaves divided by a central fissure from which the flower emerges.

CARING FOR YOUR PLANT

Watering and humidity: water the compost thoroughly from summer to the end of the flowering period, allowing it to dry out before watering again. Then stop watering completely until the new leaves appear.
Light: full sunlight.
Feeding: not required.
Repotting and growing medium: repot every three years in spring, in compost for cactuses and succulents.
Cultivation tip: give your plant a period of dry rest after flowering. In winter, you can keep your pebble plant in a cool room at about 54° F (12° C).

TROUBLE SHOOTING

◆ White, cottony clusters appear at the base of the leaves: mealy bugs can be particularly difficult to eradicate. Remove them with a Q-tip dipped in alcohol.

Lithops ▼

Livistona

Livistona

Decorative interest

This genus comprises some thirty species of palms that grow in rainforests or near rivers in various tropical regions. They produce a single stem topped by palmate fronds borne on spiny stalks. As pot plants, their growth is limited and most often they have a rather squat, stipe-free appearance. Some livistonas, such as *L. australis*, are planted outdoors in areas like the south of France (they can tolerate temperatures as low as 18° F (−8° C), in well-drained soil. *L. rotundifolia* is a species native to Malaysia and is more sensitive to cold (minimum of 55° F/13° C), with rounded palms and segments divided along as much as two-thirds of their length.

Ease of cultivation

Livistonas will be happy in a well-lit room, or better still, a temperate greenhouse.
Propagation: grow from seed in a propagator with bottom heat.

CARING FOR YOUR PLANT

Watering and humidity: water twice a week during the growing period and allow the surface of the compost to dry out between waterings. Water less frequently in winter, in accordance with the temperature. Spray the foliage regularly in dry weather.
Light: full sunlight but filtered for young specimens of *L. rotundifolia*.
Feeding: feed every two weeks in spring and summer with food for foliage plants.
Repotting and growing medium: repot in spring, if necessary, in a mixture of good yard soil and compost.
Cultivation tip: when growing indoors, be sure to maintain a good level of humidity, especially in winter.

TROUBLE SHOOTING

◆ Small brown, sticky lumps appear on the palms: these are scale bugs. Remove them with a Q-tip dipped in alcohol, or treat the plant with a systemic insecticide.
◆ The palms become pale and dry: red spider mites thrive in warm, dry conditions. Increase the ambient humidity and spray the foliage more often. If necessary, treat the plant with an acaricide.

◄ *Livistona rotundifolia*

Livistona rotundifolia ▲

Ludisia

Ludisia

Decorative interest

Ludisias are terrestrial orchids native to China. Unlike most other orchids, they are cultivated mainly for their decorative foliage, which has earned them the name of jewel orchids. The most commonly cultivated species, *Ludisia discolor*, produces velvety, dark green leaves with silvery- to orangey-red striped markings, which grow in rosettes along the creeping rhizome. In fall and winter, an inflorescence of small, modest, white flowers with yellow labella appears at the end of the shoots.

Ludisia discolor var. dawsoniana ▶

CARING FOR YOUR PLANT

Watering and humidity: water regularly with soft water, sufficiently to keep the compost slightly moist but not wet. Water less frequently after flowering has finished.
Light: prefers shade.
Feeding: feed every three weeks in spring and summer with orchid fertilizer.
Repotting and growing medium: repot in spring, if necessary, in a coarse compost for terrestrial orchids. Pot up in shallow containers.
Cultivation tip: keep your ludisia at a temperature of between 61° and 68° F (16° and 20° C) and make sure the plant is not exposed to cold drafts.

TROUBLE SHOOTING

◆ The shoots are attacked by aphids: try dislodging them with a strong jet of water. The leaves of this plant can sometimes react badly to insecticide.

Ease of cultivation

This orchid is relatively easy to cultivate.
Propagation: take stem cuttings or divide the rhizome (though the plant is more attractive if allowed to form a large clump).

Ludisia ▼

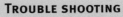

Mandevilla

Dipladenia

Decorative interest

These twining plants are prized for their abundant, colored flowers. The hybrids are most commonly cultivated, the majority of which are derived from *Mandevilla sanderi* (synonym: *Dipladenia sanderi*). These are vigorous plants with tough, dark green, glossy, elliptical, pointed leaves, 2 to 3 inches (5 to 8 cm) long. From spring to fall, clusters of flowers appear; these are usually pink or red, sometimes white, all with orange throats, and 1½ to 2¾ inches (4 to 7 cm) in diameter. *D. boliviensis* produces slender, very branching stems and white flowers with yellow centers. If cut back, dipladenias can be kept compact and shrubby, but you can also train them to climb on light supports or over a hoop.

Ease of cultivation

Dipladenias need a high level of humidity and are quite difficult to cultivate indoors.
Propagation: in spring, take terminal cuttings from young shoots and insert them in a mixture of moist peat and sand. Grow on, under cover, at 77° to 80° F (25° to 27° C).

Worth remembering

Dipladenias are poisonous. Their sap can cause irritation.

<table>
<tr><td>**TROUBLE SHOOTING**</td></tr>
<tr><td>◆ Small brown lumps appear on the stems and under the leaves, which become sticky: these are scale bugs. Remove them with a Q-tip dipped in alcohol, or treat the plant with a systemic insecticide.
◆ The leaves become pale and dry: red spider mites thrive in warm, dry conditions. Increase the ambient humidity and spray the foliage (not the flowers). If necessary, treat the plant with an acaricide.</td></tr>
</table>

◄ *Mandevilla sanderi* carmine

▲▼ *Mandevilla sanderi* pink

CARING FOR YOUR PLANT

Watering and humidity: during the growing period, water sufficiently to keep the compost quite moist. Reduce watering after flowering and water sparingly in winter. Maintain a high level of humidity around the plant.
Light: bright conditions, but filter sunlight during the hottest part of the day.
Feeding: feed every two weeks in spring and summer with food for flowering plants.
Repotting and growing medium: repot in spring, if necessary, in ordinary compost with added ericaceous compost.
Cultivation tip: a period of winter rest in the cool, at 55° to 60° F (13° to 15° C) will encourage flowering. In the fall, when flowering is over, cut the stems hard back.

Mandevilla sanderi ▶

Mandevilla dark red ▼

Mandevilla hybrid "Yellow" ▼

Mandevilla hybrid "Rubin" ▼

Mandevilla boliviensis ▶

Mandevilla boliviensis ▼

Maranta

Maranta, prayer plant

Decorative interest

This genus includes some twenty species of evergreen, rhizomatous perennials, native to the rainforests of tropical America, with the common feature that their leaves close at night. The main varieties cultivated are derived from *Maranta leuconeura*. The oblong leaves, borne on short leaf stalks, have superb, colored variegation. *M. leuconeura* "Erythroneura" has dark green leaves with yellowish-green variegation along the central vein, sometimes with bright red markings along the veins. *M. leuconeura* "Massangeana" has deep green leaves with silvery-gray variegation along the veins and purple on the underside. *M. leuconeura* "Kerchoveana" (synonym: *M. kerchoviana*) has very fine, mid-green, oval leaves with squarish, brown-green markings. *M. bicolor* is another handsome species with large, pale green leaves with dark green markings and purple on the underside.

Marantas form a low clump with stems that eventually trail over the sides of the pot. You can also train the stems up a moss pole to get a more upright shape.

Maranta leuconeura "Erythroneura" ▲

Ease of cultivation

A high level of humidity is absolutely essential for marantas.

Propagation: between May and September, take cuttings with one or two leaves from the side shoots. Root them under cover in a moist mixture of equal parts peat and sand at approximately 70° F (21° C).

CARING FOR YOUR PLANT

Watering and humidity: during the growing period, water your plant generously in order to keep the compost very moist. Reduce watering during the winter months. Increase the ambient humidity by standing the pot on damp gravel and spray the foliage frequently to maintain a high level of humidity.

Light: medium to bright conditions, but keep it out of direct sunlight.

Feeding: feed every two weeks in spring and summer with food for foliage plants.

Repotting and growing medium: repot every year in spring, in ordinary compost with added peat. It is best to use a wide, shallow pot as this suits the superficial root system of marantas best.

Cultivation tip: give your plant good humidity throughout the year and be sure to maintain a mild, constant temperature of not less than 60° F (15° C).

TROUBLE SHOOTING

◆ The leaves become pale and dry: red spider mites thrive in warm, dry conditions. Spray the foliage more often. If necessary, treat the plant with an acaricide.

Maranta leuconeura "Kerchoveana" ▲

Masdevallia

Masdevallia

Decorative interest

Masdevallias are orchids with evergreen foliage that grow in the cloud forests of central and South America. Small to medium plants, they do not have pseudo-bulbs but produce short, single-leaf stems from a creeping rhizome. The long, oval leaves are mid-green. The flower-scapes which emerge from the base bear one or two flowers. The forms and colors of these vary a great deal but they share the same triangular sepal shape, some with a long "tail."

Ease of cultivation

Masdevallias require a cool, constant temperature and a high level of humidity.
Propagation. you can try removing the offsets and potting them up individually, but masdevallias do not like being disturbed.

CARING FOR YOUR PLANT

Watering and humidity: water regularly throughout the year with soft water, but avoid overwatering, as the rhizome is susceptible to rotting. Maintain a high level of humidity.
Light: medium light conditions.
Feeding: feed every two weeks in spring and summer with orchid food.
Repotting and growing medium: these orchids don't like being disturbed. You can move the root ball and compost together into a slightly larger pot, if necessary, but take care not to break it. Use a fine orchid compost and wait for ten to fifteen days before starting to water again.
Cultivation tip: keep your plant at a temperature of 53° to 64° F (12° to 18° C).

TROUBLE SHOOTING

◆ Marks appear on the leaves: leaf rot can occur when the air is very humid and there is not sufficient ventilation. Do not expose the plant to airless, stale conditions.

Masdevallia x Aquarius ▼

Masdevallia coccinea ▼

Masdevallia x Aquarius ▼

Masdevallia coccinea ▼

Masdevallia coccinea ▼

Masdevallia coccinea ▼

Medinilla

M. magnifica   Medinilla

Decorative interest

This shrub, native to the Philippines, produces superb inflorescences of very exotic appearance. It produces branching stems bearing large, glossy leaves; these are dark green, broad, and tough, with paler, prominent veins. The pendant inflorescences form at the tips of the stems, usually between late winter and summer. They are composed of several layers of large, pink, translucent bracts enclosing clusters of small, coral-pink flowers. As pot plants, medinillas can grow to 3 to 5 feet (1 to 1.5 meters).

Ease of cultivation

Medinillas are really greenhouse plants and are difficult to cultivate indoors. They require heat, humidity, and light, and also a period of vegetative rest in the winter.
Propagation: can be propagated from terminal cuttings, but this can be difficult to achieve indoors.

Worth remembering

Don't move your plant once the flower buds have formed.

Medinilla magnifica ▼

CARING FOR YOUR PLANT

Watering and humidity: water your plant regularly during the growing period, sufficiently to keep the compost slightly moist. Use soft water at an ambient temperature. Reduce watering in winter. Wait for the flower-scapes to appear before increasing watering. Maintain a good level of humidity at all times by standing the pot on damp gravel, and water the foliage daily.
Light: enjoys bright conditions, but make sure you filter out sunlight in summer.
Feeding: feed every two weeks in spring and summer with food for flowering plants.
Repotting and growing medium: repot at the end of winter, if necessary, in ordinary compost enriched with peat, leaf mold, and sand.
Cultivation tip: in winter, keep your plant at between 59° and 64° F (15° and 18° C) with good light to encourage the formation of flower buds.

TROUBLE SHOOTING

◆ Scale bugs appear on the underside of the leaves: remove them with a Q-tip dipped in alcohol, or treat the plant with a systemic insecticide.
◆ The leaves become pale and dry:-red spider mites thrive in warm, dry conditions. Increase the ambient humidity. If necessary, treat the plant with an acaricide.

▲ *Medinilla magnifica*

➤➤ ***Megaskepasma*** see *Ruellia*
➤➤ ***Metrosideros*** see *Callistemon*

Mikania

Mikania

Decorative interest

The genus *Mikania* is a member of the family Compositae. It includes numerous species of climbing plants with woody or herbaceous stems growing in the tropical to temperate regions of the world. The species most commonly cultivated, *Mikania ternata*, produces long, trailing stems with composite leaves; these have five leaflets and are downy and deeply divided, green on the upper side, and purple on the underside. The flowerheads rarely appear on pot-grown plants.

Ease of cultivation

Mikanias are quite easy to cultivate but they need a cool temperature in winter.
Propagation: take cuttings in spring and root them under cover in a moist mixture of peat and sand at 72° to 77° F (22° to 25° C).

Tip

Pinch out the shoots when the plant comes into growth. If it becomes bare toward the base, cut back the stems or replace it by taking cuttings.

Mikania ternata ▼

TROUBLE SHOOTING

◆ The leaves become pale and dry: red spider mites thrive in warm, dry conditions. Increase the ambient humidity and stand the plant on a bed of wet gravel. If necessary, treat the plant with an acaricide.

CARING FOR YOUR PLANT

Watering and humidity: during the growing period, water regularly to keep the compost slightly moist. Water less often in winter, in accordance with the temperature. Maintain a good level of humidity around the pot.
Light: bright conditions, but filtered light in summer.
Feeding: feed every two weeks in spring and summer with food for foliage plants.
Repotting and growing medium: repot every year or two in spring, in a mixture of compost and good yard soil.
Cultivation tip: during the winter months, keep your mikania in a bright, cool spot at temperatures of between 53° and 60° F (12° and 15° C).

Miltoniopsis

Miltoniopsis

Decorative interest

Miltoniopsis are also known as pansy orchids because of their resemblance to this familiar garden flower. Their large, flat, often fragrant flowers have mask-like markings at the base of the labellum. The many hybrids available offer a wide range of colors, from pure white to deep red, as well as more pastel tones such as yellow and pink. Pansy orchids produce green pseudo-bulbs which bear narrow, oval, pale green leaves. Native to mountain areas, they thrive in a cool, humid environment.

Ease of cultivation

These orchids are not easy to cultivate indoors as they need cool conditions.

Propagation: divide large clumps when repotting. The pseudo-bulbs have a tendency to spill out of the pot.

CARING FOR YOUR PLANT

Watering and humidity: water regularly throughout the year with soft water so that the compost remains moist but not wet. Maintain a humid but well ventilated atmosphere around the plant. Spray in dry weather but avoid wetting the flowers or young shoots.

Light: enjoys quite bright conditions, but always be sure to keep it out of direct sunlight.

Feeding: feed with orchid food every two weeks in spring and summer, but only every three to four weeks during the rest of the year.

Repotting and growing medium: repot every year or two after flowering, in compost for epiphyte orchids. These plants are happiest when slightly cramped, so use small pots when repotting.

Cultivation tip: keep your plant at a daytime temperature of around 64° F (18° C), and 55° to 59° F (13° to 15° C) at night. In summer, the temperature should not exceed 72° to 75° F (22° to 24° C).

Miltoniopsis ▼

TROUBLE SHOOTING

◆ The leaves become pale and dry: red spider mites thrive in warm, dry conditions. Increase the ambient humidity and spray the foliage more often. If necessary, treat the plant with an acaricide.

➤ *Monstera* see *Philodendron*

Muehlenbeckia

Muehlenbeckia

Decorative interest

This genus contains around twenty species of shrubs and climbers growing among the rocks and forests of Oceania and South America. The pot-grown species, like *Muehlenbeckia complexa*, produces dark, intertwining stems covered in small, rounded, dark green leaves. Small, insignificant, greenish-white flowers appear in summer. Muehlenbeckias are quite resistant to cold and often form part of decorative plant arrangements in the fall. They are also used for topiary.

Ease of cultivation

It is easier to grow muehlenbeckias in a temperate greenhouse or conservatory. They grow rapidly and need regularly trimming.
Propagation: take herbaceous cuttings in spring and root them under cover in a moist mixture of peat and sand.

● RELATED GENUS

Leptinella are creeping perennials that can be clump-forming or carpeting, and come from the same regions of the southern hemisphere. Their divided or pennate leaves are often aromatic. In summer, they produce small flowerheads that resemble buttons.

CARING FOR YOUR PLANT

Watering and humidity: water moderately during the growing period but don't leave water standing in the saucer. In winter, water less frequently, depending on the temperature.
Light: bright conditions, but filtered light in summer.
Feeding: feed every two weeks in spring and summer with food for foliage plants.
Repotting and growing medium: repot every year or two in spring, in potting compost lightened with coarse sand.
Cultivation tip: during the winter months, keep your plant in a cool, bright place such as a conservatory or temperate greenhouse. Muehlenbeckias do not respond well to severe cold but can be grown outside in mild climates.

TROUBLE SHOOTING

◆ The leaves become sticky and deformed: aphids are attacking the shoots. Treat your plant with a suitable insecticide.

Muehlenbeckia complexa ▼

Leptinella dioica ▲

Murraya

Chinese box, orange jasmine

Decorative interest

This genus includes a few species of non-spiny trees and shrubs with composite leaves. Some are suitable for bonsai cultivation. One of these is *Murraya paniculata* (synonym: *M. exotica*), a tree that can grow to 10 feet (3 meters) tall in its natural habitat in south-east Asia. It has dark green, glossy, evergreen leaves composed of nine to eleven oval leaflets. In spring, it produces small, white, scented flowers that are followed by red berries.

Ease of cultivation

Chinese box is a tropical plant which needs warmth and protection from cold drafts.

Propagation: take 3 to 4 inch (8 to 10 cm) semi-woody cuttings and root them under cover in a moist mixture of peat and sand, with bottom heat. Rooting is not always successful.

● RELATED SPECIES AND VARIETIES

Murraya koenigii is a related species grown on the island of Reunion under the name "caloupilé" and is known in English as the curry leaf tree. Its leaves are pointed and divided into lanceolate leaflets, which are strongly aromatic. They are used as a spice or condiment in Indian and Creole cooking.

▼ *Murraya paniculata*

▲ *Murraya paniculata*

CARING FOR YOUR PLANT

Watering and humidity: water your plant regularly with soft water during the growing season, keeping the compost moist. During the winter months, water less frequently, in accordance with the temperature. Spray the foliage every day with soft water at ambient temperature.

Light: very bright conditions, but filter out the summer sun during the hottest part of the day.

Feeding: feed every two to three weeks in spring and summer with food for foliage plants.

Repotting and growing medium: repot every two years in spring, in potting compost with added peat and sand.

Cultivation tip: in winter, keep your plant in a bright spot with a minimum temperature of 59° F (15° C).

TROUBLE SHOOTING

◆ Small white bugs fly away when you touch the plant: whitefly are small, sap-sucking bugs that are difficult to eradicate. Treat the plant repeatedly with insecticide every eight to ten days.

Musa

Banana tree

Decorative interest

Banana trees are sucker-producing perennials native to various tropical regions of the world. As well as their economic interest, they are also cultivated for their large, paddle-shaped leaves, the sheathed base of which forms a false trunk. Some species can grow to over 16 feet (5 meters) tall in their native habitat. *Musa acuminata* is an Asian species which has given rise to numerous varieties cultivated mainly for their fruit. "**Dwarf Cavendish**" is a compact, dwarf form particularly well suited to indoor cultivation. As a pot plant it can grow to 3 to 6.5 feet (1 to 2 meters) in height. The elliptical, mid-green leaves are 24 to 36 inches (60 to 90 cm) long and 12 inches (30 cm) wide. The flower-scape is composed of trailing inflorescences with tough, purple bracts. The 2 inch (5 cm) flowers appear in June to July and are followed by edible, pipless fruit.

Ease of cultivation

Banana trees need warmth and humidity. They can be kept outdoors in summer if sheltered from the wind.
Propagation: remove offsets in April and pot them up individually.

Worth remembering

The banana tree is a monocarpic plant, which means that it dies after flowering. Remove any fruiting stems and offsets will appear at the foot of the plant.

Musa acuminata ▼

➤ *Muscari* see *Crocus*

➤ *Narcissus* see *Hyacinthus*

CARING FOR YOUR PLANT

Watering and humidity: water abundantly from April to September, but reduce watering in fall and winter. Maintain a good level of humidity around the plant.
Light: bright but filtered light.
Feeding: feed every two weeks in spring and summer with food for foliage plants.
Repotting and growing medium: every year in spring, repot young specimens in ordinary compost enriched with peat.
Cultivation tip: banana trees like a warm, damp environment and are best suited to greenhouse cultivation.

TROUBLE SHOOTING

◆ The leaves become pale and dry: red spider mites thrive in warm, dry conditions. Increase the ambient humidity and spray the foliage. If necessary, treat the plant with an acaricide.

Musa "Laterita" ▼

Musa uranoscopos ▼

Musa "Tropicana" ▶

Nematanthus

N. gregarius
synonym: *Hypocyrta radicans*

Hypocyrta

Decorative interest

This plant, from the tropical forests of Brazil, can grow to 16 inches (40 cm) high. Its creeping, sometimes climbing stems bear bright green, glossy, fleshy, elliptical leaves, ¾ to 1½ inches (2 to 4 cm) long. In summer, it is covered in small, orange, elongated flowers with swollen corollas.

Ease of cultivation

Hypocyrta are quite easy to cultivate, providing they are given a definite period of winter rest with a temperature of between 55° and 59° F (13° and 15° C).
Propagation: in spring, take 3 to 4 inch (8 to 10 cm) terminal cuttings and plant them in a mixture of equal parts peat and sand. Grow on, under cover, at between 68° and 72° F (20° and 22° C).

CARING FOR YOUR PLANT

Watering and humidity: water moderately during the growing period to keep the growing medium moist but not wet. Reduce watering in winter in accordance with the temperature.
Light: bright conditions, but keep it out of direct sunlight.
Feeding: feed every two weeks in spring and summer with food for flowering plants.
Repotting and growing medium: repot in spring every two to three years, in ordinary compost lightened by the addition of peat.
Cultivation tip: at the end of winter, cut long stems back by half to encourage branching. This is an excellent plant to grow in hanging containers.

▲ *Nematanthus gregarius*

TROUBLE SHOOTING

◆ The leaves become sticky and deformed: aphids are attacking the young shoots and flowers. Treat your plant with a suitable insecticide.

Nematanthus gregarius ▶

Neoregelia

N. carolinae "Tricolor"   Neoregelia

Decorative interest

This bromeliad, native to the tropical forests of South America, produces a spreading rosette composed of twelve to twenty strap-like leaves, 12 to 20 inches (30 to 50 cm) long; they are dentate with green and ivory-white, longitudinal stripes. The central leaves turn bright red prior to flowering, which can occur at any time of year. The coloring persists for several months. The flowers themselves are white or bluish and insignificant, and appear in the hollow of the rosette.

Ease of cultivation

Neoregelias are accommodating plants and relatively easy to cultivate.
Propagation: remove the offsets that form around the plant when they have reached at least half its height, and pot them up in bromeliad compost.

Neoregelia concentrica ▼   *Neoregelia carolinae* "Tricolor" ▼   *Neoregelia* "Flandria" ▼

Neoregelia carolinae "Tricolor" ▼

Nepenthes

Nepenthes

Decorative interest

This genus includes seventy species of carnivorous climbers that grow in marshy rainforest areas. Some are epiphytes and grow on trees. The leaves, which are 2 to 2¾ inches (5 to 7 cm) long, are mid-green and lanceolate to strappy, terminating in a tendril, the tip of which may carry a large urn protected by an operculum. The thickened, striped edge of the urn secretes a liquid that attracts bugs and even larger prey, such as small amphibians and birds. They fall into the trap, drown, and are digested. The size of this vigorous plant varies according to the growing conditions. Nepenthes can be cut back in spring to restrict their growth. There are also numerous hybrids.

Ease of cultivation

Nepenthes are very difficult to cultivate indoors as, among other things, they require a very high level of humidity.

Propagation: nepenthes can be propagated from seed, stem cuttings, or by layering, but this can be difficult for amateurs.

Nepenthes rafflesiana ▼▶

TROUBLE SHOOTING
◆ Your plant is not producing any more urns: the atmosphere is probably too dry. Spray the plant several times a day.

CARING FOR YOUR PLANT

Watering and humidity: during the growing period, water every two days so that the compost remains moist at all times, but don't leave water standing in the saucer. Use water that is completely free of lime and always at room temperature. In winter, water once or twice a week. Maintain a very high level of humidity—up to 90%—by using a humidifier, for example.

Light: bright conditions, but keep it out of direct sunlight.

Feeding: feed with orchid food every ten days in spring and summer. Continue feeding in winter, but only once a month.

Repotting and growing medium: repot every two years in spring, in an openwork basket in a light growing medium composed of 40% pine bark, 40% perlite, and 20% peat.

Cultivation tip: the growing medium must not be constantly saturated, nor must it be allowed to dry out. The temperature will depend on where the plant originates: 75° F (24° C) during the day and 59° to 70° F (15° to 21° C) at night for species from areas situated at an altitude of less than 3280 feet (1000 meters); 64° F (18° C) in the daytime and 50° F (10° C) at night for high altitude species.

Nepenthes tobaicca ▼

Nepenthes dicksoniana ▶

Nepenthes alata ▼

Nepenthes madagascariensis ▼

Nephrolepis

N. exaltata   Nephrolepis

Decorative interest

The rhizome of this fern produces dense clumps of fronds. Long and arching, they are divided into narrow, bright green pinnules with wavy edges. They can grow to over 3 feet (1 meter) long in some specimens. There are dozens of varieties with a range of fronds: finely serrated, divided, fringed, and feathery. There are also dwarf forms.

Ease of cultivation

The nephrolepis is a relatively accommodating fern but it will perform better in an environment with a high level of humidity.

Propagation: divide the clump in spring when repotting. Growing from spores is difficult for amateurs.

● RELATED SPECIES AND VARIETIES

The Boston fern, *Nephrolepis exaltata* "Bostoniensis," has larger fronds, initially upright, then arching.

N. exaltata "Elegantissima" has bipennate fronds.

N. exaltata "Gracillima" has very fine, tripennate fronds.

N. exaltata "Hilii" is a very vigorous variety with bipennate fronds with lobed or ruffled pinnules.

N. exaltata "Mini Ruffle" is a very compact variety.

N. exaltata "Verona" produces trailing fronds which are very decorative, making it an excellent plant for a hanging container.

N. cordifolia is a less vigorous species with a more upright habit and shorter, narrower fronds than those of *Nephrolepis exaltata*.

Nephrolepis exaltata ▼

CARING FOR YOUR PLANT

Watering and humidity: water generously during the growing period to keep the compost very moist. Reduce watering in winter in accordance with the temperature. Spray the foliage every day to stop the tips of the fronds drying out.

Light: requires medium to bright conditions, but keep it out of direct sunlight.

Feeding: feed every two to three weeks in spring and summer with half strength food for foliage plants.

Repotting and growing medium: repot in spring every year, in ordinary compost with added peat and sand.

Cultivation tip: give your plant plenty of space and a high level of humidity. Room temperature is fine but it can tolerate temperatures as low as 59° F (15° C).

TROUBLE SHOOTING

◆ Small brown lumps appear on the fronds: these are scale bugs. If there are only a few, remove them with a Q-tip dipped in alcohol. In cases of severe attack, treat the plant with a systemic insecticide. It is best to use insecticide sticks that you insert into the compost, as nephrolepis can react badly to aerosol-based products.

Nephrolepis exaltata "Bostoniensis" ▼

Nephrolepis cordifolia ▼

Nertera

N. granadensis   Nertera, coral bead, bead plant
synonym: *Nertera depressa*

Decorative interest
This small, carpeting plant has fine, creeping, trailing stems covered in small, oval, green leaves. However, it is mainly cultivated for its small, pearl-like, orange berries which are very decorative and last for several months, usually from summer to winter. The berries follow small, insignificant, greenish flowers. This species is native to cool, humid regions of South America.

Ease of cultivation
Nerteras are usually discarded when fruiting is over, but it is possible to keep the plant for longer if the appropriate care is given.
Propagation: nerteras can be propagated by dividing the root ball in spring or from seed in March.

Worth remembering
To encourage fruit formation, it may be necessary to pollinate your plant manually, by transferring pollen from flower to flower using a fine brush.

CARING FOR YOUR PLANT

Watering and humidity: keep the compost moist at all times, but not wet. Reduce watering slightly from the end of the fruiting period until the plant comes into flower again. It is best to water from underneath, as the leaves can easily succumb to rotting. In warm weather, stand the pot on damp gravel.
Light: bright conditions, but keep it out of direct sunlight.
Feeding: feed once a month with heavily diluted plant food, from flowering until the berries form.
Repotting and growing medium: repot in spring, in ordinary compost with added coarse sand or perlite. Compost for cactuses and succulents is also suitable.
Cultivation tip: during the fruiting period, keep your plant in a cool room at 61° to 64° F (16° to 18° C) with good ventilation. In winter, keep it in a conservatory at between 50° and 53° F (10° and 12° C).

TROUBLE SHOOTING

◆ The leaves turn black: during the winter period this plant is sensitive to overwatering, which can cause the roots to rot.

Nertera granadensis ▶

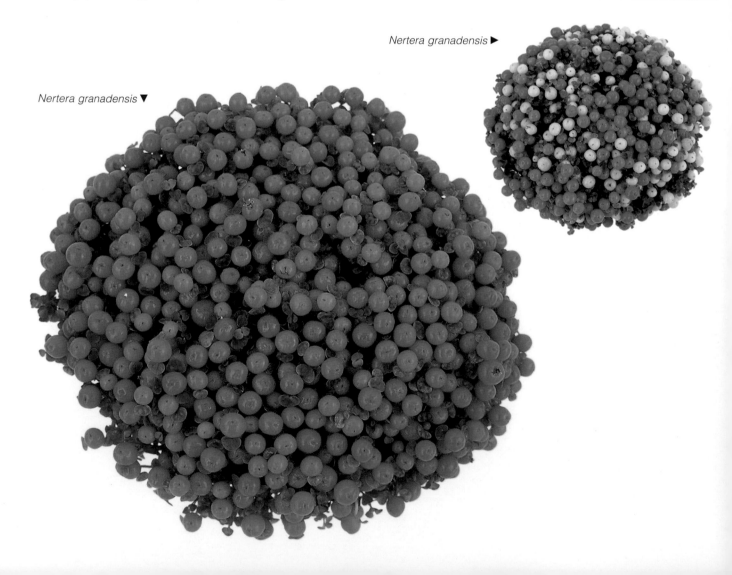

Nertera granadensis ▼

Nidularium

N. billbergioides
synonym: *Canistropsis billbergioides*

Nidularium

Decorative interest

Native to the rainforests of Brazil, this epiphyte bromeliad produces an open rosette of bright green, strap-like, pointed leaves with dentate edges. The inflorescence appears from the heart of the rosette and rises well above the leaves; it consists of white, tubular flowers surrounded by long-lived, orange bracts. Flowering can occur at any time of year. The variety "**Citrinum**" produces a smaller rosette and a star-like inflorescence of lemon-yellow bracts.

Ease of cultivation

Nidulariums are relatively easy plants to grow but will benefit from a high level of ambient humidity.
Propagation: remove and pot up basal offsets when they have grown to about 4 inches (10 cm) high. They will flower in two or three years.

Worth remembering

Like all bromeliads, nidulariums die after flowering, but they can be easily replaced from basal offsets.

CARING FOR YOUR PLANT

Watering and humidity: during the growing period, water the compost regularly. Make sure there is always some water in the hollow of the rosette, but change it every two weeks. In winter, empty the rosette and water the plant less often. Remember to use soft water. Maintain a high level of ambient humidity by standing the pot on wet gravel and spraying the foliage frequently.
Light: bright conditions, but keep it out of direct sunlight.
Feeding: feed every two to three weeks in spring and summer with half strength food for foliage plants.
Repotting and growing medium: repot offsets in a bromeliad compost. Nidulariums are happy in small pots with a diameter of 3 to 4 inches (8 to 10 cm).
Cultivation tip: keep your plant out of direct sunlight as this can burn the leaves. Do not expose it to temperatures below 55° F (13° C).

● **RELATED SPECIES AND VARIETIES**

Nidularium fulgens and its varieties are widely cultivated. The species produces pale green, strap-like leaves with dark green markings and brilliant red, lanceolate bracts.
N. innocentii produces dark green leaves that are very glossy on the underside, and a rosette of reddish-brown bracts surrounding greenish-white flowers. "**Lineatum**" is a variety with white-striped leaves. "**Nana**" has shorter leaves that are purple on the underside.
N. regelioides produces bright green leaves tinged with darker green, and a rosette of bright red bracts surrounding red and white flowers.

Nidularium billbergioides "Citrinum" ▼

Odontoglossum

Odontoglossum

Decorative interest

This genus includes a hundred species of epiphyte orchids that grow on the edges of high altitude forests (between 6,500 and 10,000 feet/2,000 and 3,000 meters) in central and South America. These orchids have given rise to thousands of hybrids, including many intergeneric hybrids (crosses between two or more different genera). Odontoglossums produce green pseudo-bulbs which, from their tips, produce between one and three narrow, mid-green, oval leaves. The flower-scapes emerge from the base of the pseudo-bulbs at different times of year, depending on the hybrid. Upright or arching, they bear numerous flowers in a very varied range of shapes and colors.

Ease of cultivation

Odontoglossums prefer cooler temperatures and so are not easy to cultivate indoors. However, there are intergeneric hybrids that are more heat tolerant.

Propagation: you can divide large clumps when repotting, but to ensure a successful result you should make sure that you pot up at least three pseudo-bulbs and a new shoot in a single pot.

Worth remembering

The well known hybrid *Vuylstekeara Cambria*, with its very popular varieties "**Edna**" and "**Plush**," belongs to this vast group of plants. The name *Cambria* is now used by horticulturalists to describe hybrids of complex descent selected, among other things, for their relative ease of cultivation.

CARING FOR YOUR PLANT

Watering and humidity: water very regularly with soft water during the period when pseudo-bulbs are forming and do not allow the growing medium to dry out completely. Water less often at cooler temperatures. Maintain a good level of humidity throughout the year.

Light: bright conditions, but filter out the midday summer sun.

Feeding: feed every two weeks during the growing period with orchid fertilizer.

Repotting and growing medium: repot, if necessary, when the new shoots are well developed and new roots have appeared. Use compost for epiphyte orchids and wait for ten to fifteen days before starting to water again.

Cultivation tip: in summer, find a cool spot for your odontoglossum. Keep an eye on the temperature and if it rises above 75° F (24° C), shade your plant and spray the foliage frequently. A temperature difference of 14° to 18° F (8° to 10° C) between day and night is recommended.

Rossioglossum grande ▶

▼ *Odontoglossum* Burkhard "Holm Gera"

TROUBLE SHOOTING

◆ White, cottony clusters appear at the base of the leaves: mealy bugs can be difficult to eradicate. If there are only a few, remove them with a Q-tip dipped in alcohol. In cases of severe attack, treat the plant with a suitable insecticide.

● RELATED SPECIES AND VARIETIES

The following intergeneric hybrids—obtained by crossing two or three genera—have similar growing requirements: ***Odontocidium*** (*Odontoglossum* x *Oncidium*); ***Odontioda*** (*Odontoglossum* x *Cochlioda*); ***Vuylstekeara*** (*Odontoglossum* x *Cochlioda* x *Miltonia*); and ***Wilsonara*** (*Odontoglossum* x *Cochlioda* x *Oncidium*).

◀ x *Vuylstekeara Cambria* "Plush"

Odontoglossum cordatum ▲

▼ *Odontoglossum rossii*

Oncidium

Oncidium

Decorative interest

This genus includes some 400 species of evergreen orchids in a wide variety of shapes and sizes. Oncidiums have given rise to a wide range of hybrids, many of which are the result of crossing them with other genera, such as *Odontoglossum*. Oncidiums come from very varied natural habitats and do not all share the same cultivation requirements, particularly where temperature is concerned. Generally speaking, the flowers are mainly yellow with a prominent labellum, but hybrids with species like *O. ornithorynchum* in their ancestry produce blooms in shades of red and pink.

Ease of cultivation

This group includes a wide range of orchids which vary as to how easy they are to cultivate. Generally speaking, the hybrids are easier to grow.
Propagation: divide large clumps when repotting.

Oncidium boissiense ▼

CARING FOR YOUR PLANT

Watering and humidity: water freely with soft water while the pseudo-bulbs are forming, allowing the growing medium to become dry between waterings. After this, water less often or replace watering with light spraying of the surface of the compost. Maintain a good level of humidity. Avoid wetting the leaves of thick-leaved oncidiums.
Light: thick-leaved oncidiums require very bright conditions. Those with soft leaves need less light.
Feeding: feed every two weeks during the active growing period with orchid fertilizer.
Repotting and growing medium: repot every two years when the plant puts out a new shoot, in compost for epiphyte orchids. Use small pots.
Cultivation tip: remember to find out about your oncidium's specific requirements when purchasing it. However, in general most of these orchids will be comfortable at temperate conditions of between 64° and 77° F (18° and 25° C) during the day and 55° to 61° F (13° to 16° C) at night.

TROUBLE SHOOTING

◆ The leaves become pale and yellow: red spider mites thrive in warm, dry conditions. Increase the ambient humidity and spray the foliage more frequently. If it becomes necessary, treat the plant with an appropriate acaricide.

▼ *Oncidium kramerianum*

Pachira

P. aquatica
Pachira, Guyana chestnut

Decorative interest
This interestingly shaped plant is often sold with a "braided trunk." In the wild, the pachira is a tree that grows in the wetlands of central America. As a pot plant it can grow to over 6 feet (2 meters). It has a smooth trunk or several woody stems, and large, evergreen leaves consisting of between five and nine bright green, glossy, oval leaflets. It rarely flowers when grown indoors.

Ease of cultivation
Pachiras need warmth and humidity during the growing period. They are best when cultivated in a warm greenhouse.
Propagation: heeled stem cuttings can be taken at the end of summer and grown on under cover with heat, but this can be difficult for amateurs.

Worth remembering
The pachira belongs to the same family as the baobab and, like the latter, also stores water in its trunk.

Pachira aquatica ▼

◄ *Pachira aquatica*

CARING FOR YOUR PLANT

Watering and humidity: during the growing period, water regularly to keep the compost moist at all times, but don't leave water standing in the saucer. In winter, allow the surface of the compost to dry between waterings. Maintain a high level of humidity throughout the year.
Light: bright conditions, but keep it out of direct sunlight in summer during the hottest part of the day.
Feeding: feed every two to three weeks in spring and summer with food for foliage plants.
Repotting and growing medium: repot young plants in spring every year, and then every two or three years, using ordinary compost. An annual top dressing will be sufficient for specimens in large pots.
Cultivation tip: position your plant in a warm, bright spot with a minimum temperature of 60° F (15° C), but make sure you keep it protected from strong sunlight.

TROUBLE SHOOTING

◆ The leaves become pale and dry: red spider mites thrive in warm, dry conditions. Increase the ambient humidity and spray the foliage more often. If necessary, treat the plant with an acaricide.

Pachypodium

P. lamerei   Pachypodium

Decorative interest

Pachypodiums are perennial succulents native to the arid regions of South Africa
and Madagascar. Some species develop a swollen caudex. *Pachypodium lamerei*
has a thick, very spiny trunk, branching toward the top and crowned by clusters
of large, dark green, glossy, linear leaves. In its native habitat the plant can grow
to 16 to 20 feet (5 to 6 meters) tall. As pot plants, pachypodiums rarely exceed
3 to 5 feet (1 to 1.5 meters). Flat, creamy-white flowers with yellow hearts may
appear on mature plants.

Ease of cultivation

Pachypodiums are susceptible to rotting and must not be exposed to too much
humidity. It is important to give them a period of dry winter rest.
Propagation: can be grown from seed at 68° to 75° F (20° to 24° C). You can
also take cuttings from the branches at the end of spring and root them in a
mixture of slightly moist peat and sand.

Pachypodium bispinosum ▲

▲ *Pachypodium
bispinosum*

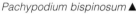

Pachypodium lamerei ▼

● **RELATED SPECIES AND VARIETIES**

Pachypodium bispinosum produces a coarse, partially buried caudex. The
slender branches bear pale green, downy, lanceolate leaves.

CARING FOR YOUR PLANT

Watering and humidity: water sparingly during the growing period.
Keep your plant dry during the winter.
Light: full sunlight.
Feeding: feed once a month in spring and summer with food for cactuses
and succulents.
Repotting and growing medium: repot every three or four years in
spring, in a free-draining compost such as cactus compost.
Cultivation tip: in winter, keep your plant in a bright, cool room at 55°
to 59° F (13° to 15° C) and do not water. Some of the leaves may drop
during this period.

TROUBLE SHOOTING

◆ Small brown lumps appear on the leaves: these are scale bugs. Remove
them with a Q-tip dipped in alcohol, or treat the plant with a systemic
insecticide.

Pachystachys

P. lutea   Pachystachys

Decorative interest
This attractive plant, which came back into cultivation in the 1960s, is native to Peru and is mainly valued for its inflorescences, which last all summer. It produces dark green, oval, pointed, slightly textured leaves. The terminal inflorescences, which are 2 to 4 inches (5 to 10 cm) long, are composed of golden-yellow bracts, from which a succession of white, double-lipped flowers about 2 inches (4 to 5 cm) long emerge. Each flower lasts only a few days, but the colored bracts last much longer.

Ease of cultivation
Pachystachys is quite an easy plant to cultivate for those who already have some experience.
Propagation: take 3 to 4 inch (8 to 10 cm) stem cuttings in spring and root them under cover in a moist mixture of equal parts peat and sand at between 64° and 68° F (18° and 20° C).

TROUBLE SHOOTING

◆ The ends of the leaves turn brown: the air is too dry. Spray the leaves more often.

Pachystachys lutea ▼

Pachystachys lutea ▲

CARING FOR YOUR PLANT

Watering and humidity: water your plant moderately but regularly during the growing period to keep the compost moist but not wet. In winter, allow the compost to dry out to a depth of an inch or so (a few centimeters) between waterings. Maintain a good level of ambient humidity by standing the pot on damp gravel. Spray the foliage (not the flowers) during periods of warm weather.
Light: bright but filtered light.
Feeding: feed every two to three weeks in spring and summer with food for flowering plants.
Repotting and growing medium: repot every year in spring, in ordinary compost with added peat and with a good layer of drainage material in the bottom of the pot.
Cultivation tip: in spring, cut back the stems to 6 inches (15 cm) from the base. This plant does not enjoy high temperatures: the maximum summer temperature should be 70° F (21° C).

Palisota

Palisota

Decorative interest

This genus, native to tropical Africa, belongs to the spiderwort family. Palisotas are herbaceous, clump-forming perennials, usually with very short stems. The sheathed leaves are narrow and lanceolate, edged with reddish or brownish hairs, and have a paler median vein. The terminal clusters of small flowers are sometimes followed by violet-red berries. The leaves of *Palisota pynaertii* are grayish on the underside; its variety "**Elizabethae**" has a white band along the median vein.

Ease of cultivation

Unlike other spiderworts, palisotas are quite tricky to grow.
Propagation: divide large clumps when repotting, making sure that each section has several leaves and well-developed roots.

TROUBLE SHOOTING

◆ The leaves become pale and dry: red spider mites thrive in warm, dry conditions. Increase the ambient humidity and spray the foliage frequently. If necessary, treat the plant with an acaricide.

CARING FOR YOUR PLANT

Watering and humidity: water generously during the growing period with water at room temperature, but don't leave water standing in the saucer. Water less often in winter and allow the surface of the compost to dry out between waterings. Maintain a good level of humidity around the pot.
Light: bright conditions, but keep it out of direct sunlight.
Feeding: feed every two weeks in spring and summer with food for foliage plants.
Repotting and growing medium: repot in spring, if necessary, in ordinary compost with added peat and a good layer of drainage material in the bottom of the pot.
Cultivation tip: palisotas are happiest when cultivated in a warm greenhouse, as this provides them with the warmth and humidity they need. The temperature must not be allowed to drop below 61° F (16° C).

▲ *Palisota* "Westlandia"

Cochliostema odoratissimum,
a species related to the *Palisota*
▶

➤➤ *Palm* see *Caryota, Chamaedorea, Chrysalidocarpus, Cocos, Cycas, Euterpe, Howea, Licuala, Livistona, Phoenix, Rhapis*

Pandanus

P. veitchii

Pandanus, screw pine

Decorative interest

This pandanus is native to Polynesia and is cultivated for its decorative foliage, which is similar to that of a pineapple plant. A clump of long, tough, strap-like leaves, edged with fine spines, grows from its short, woody trunk; the leaves have green and cream stripes. As it matures, the plant develops thick, aerial roots which support it. As a houseplant, the leaves can grow up to 24 to 36 inches (60 to 90 cm) in length.

Ease of cultivation

The pandanus is easy to grow providing it is given good humidity.
Propagation: remove the basal offsets in early spring and pot them up in a mixture of peat and sand. Grow on, under cover, at between 68° and 75° F (20° and 24° C).

● RELATED SPECIES AND VARIETIES

Pandanus veitchii "Compacta" is a more compact variety with leaves 16 to 24 inches (40 to 60 cm) long, with more marked stripes.

CARING FOR YOUR PLANT

Watering and humidity: during the growing period, water moderately with soft water at room temperature. In winter, water less frequently. Maintain a humid atmosphere around your plant.
Light: bright conditions with some direct sunlight, but keep it out of very hot sunlight.
Feeding: feed every three to four weeks in spring and summer with food for foliage plants.
Repotting and growing medium: repot in spring every two years in ordinary compost with added peat and sand. Be careful when handling this plant as the edges of the leaves are sharp.
Cultivation tip: the pandanus will not tolerate air that is too dry—maintain a good level of humidity.

TROUBLE SHOOTING

◆ The leaves become pale and dry: red spider mites thrive in warm, dry conditions. Increase the ambient humidity and spray the foliage more often. If necessary, treat the plant with an acaricide.

◄ *Pandanus veitchii*

▼ *Pandanus veitchii*

Paphiopedilum

Venus' slipper

Decorative interest

The Venus' slippers that are sold commercially as houseplants are usually hybrids and more robust than the botanical species. The plant produces quite short, strap-like leaves, interwoven at the base. They are plain green in Venus' slippers that grow in cool areas and mottled in those from warm areas. Each clump of leaves produces a flower spike bearing one or more waxy flowers with a slipper-shaped labellum, often in a color that contrasts with the other petals. Various hybrids are available in shades of white, yellow, green, brown, pink, and purple, and are often spotted or striped.

Ease of cultivation

It is important to give these plants the correct growing conditions. Hybrids with mottled foliage are best as houseplants, as they don't require such a large temperature difference between day and night.

Propagation: you can divide the clumps, but only if they have become too bulky, as Venus slippers grow best when in a tight clump.

◄ *Paphiopedilum* hybrid

◄ *Paphiopedilum* hybrid

➤➤ *Parthenocissus* see *Cissus*

CARING FOR YOUR PLANT

Watering and humidity: water moderately, allowing the compost to dry to a depth of an inch (2 cm) before watering again. Avoid wetting the leaf sheath as it can easily rot. In winter, water very little but don't allow the compost to dry out completely. Stand the pot on a bed of damp gravel.

Light: medium light conditions in summer, brighter in winter, but keep it out of direct sunlight.

Feeding: feed every three to four weeks in spring and summer with orchid food.

Repotting and growing medium: repot, if necessary, after flowering using a special orchid compost. After repotting, leave watering for about two weeks (during this time you can spray the surface of the compost lightly every day).

Cultivation tip: in the fall, to encourage flowering, keep your orchid in the cool during the night; hybrids with mottled foliage need a temperature difference of 9° to 12° F (5° to 7° C) between day and night, and those with plain, green foliage require a 14° to 18° F (8° to 10° C) difference.

▲ *Paphiopedilum armeniacum*

Paphiopedilum "Anja Beverly Hills" ▼

▲ *Paphiopedilum* "Gina Short"

Paphiopedilum ▼

Paphiopedilum "Van Dyck" ▼

Pavonia

P. multiflora   Pavonia
synonym: *Triplochlamys multiflora*

Decorative interest
This Brazilian shrub is a member of the mallow family and is cultivated for its bright red flowers, which have earned it the name "Brazilian Candles." In its native habitat it grows to 6 to 10 feet (2 to 3 meters) in height. Its upright stems bear green, oval to lanceolate, dentate leaves. From September to March, curious purple-red, cup-shaped flowers appear. The red segments in fact form the calycle—a second calyx which encloses the first. The true flowers, which are small and violet, are gathered in a dense cluster in the center. In plants cultivated indoors, the inflorescence usually remains closed.

Ease of cultivation
This is a sensitive plant which requires plenty of light and a high level of humidity. Cultivation in a warm greenhouse is ideal.
Propagation: take semi-woody cuttings and root them in a propagator with bottom heat. They can be difficult to root successfully.

TROUBLE SHOOTING

◆ Small brown lumps appear on the stems and the leaves become sticky: these are scale bugs. Remove them with a Q-tip dipped in alcohol, or treat the plant with a systemic insecticide.
◆ The leaves become pale and dry: red spider mites thrive in warm, dry conditions. Increase the ambient humidity and spray the foliage more often. If necessary, treat the plant with an acaricide.

CARING FOR YOUR PLANT

Watering and humidity: during the growing period, water regularly with tepid water so that the growing medium remains moist but not wet. Water less often during the winter period. Maintain a good level of humidity around the pot.
Light: bright conditions, but keep it out of direct sunlight.
Feeding: feed every two weeks in spring and summer with food for flowering plants.
Repotting and growing medium: repot in spring, if necessary, in ordinary compost lightened by the addition of some peat or perlite.
Cultivation tip: avoid cold drafts and give your plant careful, regular care. In winter. the temperature should not be allowed to drop below 61° F (16° C).

Pavonia multiflora ▶

Pellaea

Pellea

Decorative interest

This genus includes around eighty species of terrestrial ferns, with either deciduous or evergreen foliage, mainly native to warm regions of America. The species most commonly cultivated as a houseplant is *Pellaea rotundifolia*. This small, open fern has arching fronds 8 to 12 inches (20 to 30 cm) long, composed of a tough, brown, central vein with small, round, glossy, dark green, alternating leaflets about ¾ inch (2 cm) across. *P. falcata* produces longer fronds with a very scaly central vein and lanceolate leaflets ¾ to 2 inches (2 to 5 cm) long.

Associates well with... these ferns grow well with other plants and are suitable for cultivation in a terrarium.

TROUBLE SHOOTING

◆ Small brown lumps appear on the fronds: scale bugs are difficult to eradicate. Treat the plant with a systemic insecticide.

CARING FOR YOUR PLANT

Watering and humidity: water regularly to keep the compost slightly moist at all times, but don't leave water standing in the saucer. In winter, water less frequently if your plant is in a cool place.

Light: enjoys medium to bright conditions, but keep the plant out of direct sunlight.

Feeding: feed every two to three weeks in spring and summer with food for foliage plants.

Repotting and growing medium: repot young plants every year in spring and then every two to three years. Use ordinary compost with added peat and shallow pots as pelleas have a superficial root system.

Cultivation tip: during spells of warm weather, spray the foliage from time to time. Pelleas can tolerate winter temperatures as low as 50° F (10° C).

Ease of cultivation

Pelleas are easy to grow indoors as they tolerate dry air better than other ferns.

Propagation: divide the clump in spring. Pot up sections of rhizomes with fronds and roots into individual pots.

Pellaea falcata ▲

▲ *Pellaea rotundifolia*

Pellionia

P. repens
Pellionia

synonyms: *Elatostema repens, Pellionia daveauana*

Decorative interest
Pellionias belong to the same family as nettles. These creepers are valued for their variegated foliage. *Pellionia repens* produces greenish-pink stems that can grow to 24 inches (60 cm) long and are covered in leaves of varying shape—from elliptical to oval—and of varying color. The dark, bluish-green upper surface of the leaves has gray and pale green markings often tinged with bronze, while the underside is pink with a purple margin.

Ease of cultivation
Pellionias require a very high level of humidity and will often suffer if kept in a warm room in winter.

Propagation: stem cuttings can be taken all year round and rooted in a propagator at 72° to 74° F (22° to 23° C).

Worth remembering
Pellionias will be happy growing in a hanging basket.

● RELATED SPECIES AND VARIETIES
Pellionia pulchra (synonym: *Elatostema pulchra*) has distinct mauve stems and oval leaves that are dark green on the upper surface and pale purple on the underside. The leaves have broad, very dark veins.

CARING FOR YOUR PLANT

Watering and humidity: during the growing period, water generously but not excessively. Water less frequently in winter. Maintain a high level of ambient humidity.

Light: bright conditions, but keep it out of direct sunlight.

Feeding: feed every two weeks in spring and summer with food for foliage plants.

Repotting and growing medium: repot in spring, but only if the plant is pot-bound. Pot up in ordinary compost with added peat.

Cultivation tip: in winter, stand your plant in a container of wet gravel and keep it away from radiators as pellionias cannot tolerate too much heat during the winter months.

Pellionia repens ▲

TROUBLE SHOOTING

◆ White, cottony clusters appear at the base of the leaves: mealy bugs can be difficult to eradicate. If there are only a few, remove them with a Q-tip dipped in alcohol. In cases of severe attack, treat the plant with a systemic insecticide.

Pentas

P. lanceolata   Pentas

Decorative interest

When grown in a pot, this small, tropical shrub will rarely grow taller than 20 inches (50 cm). The upright stems bear large, dark green, opposed, downy, lanceolate leaves. It is grown mainly for its decorative terminal clusters of small, star-like flowers. Their color varies from white to magenta and from pink to lavender-blue, depending on the variety. Pentas flower from summer to fall, but flowers can appear intermittently at almost any time of year.

Ease of cultivation

Pentas can be difficult to get to flower again and require a period of rest after flowering.

Propagation: take 2 to 2¾ inch (5 to 7 cm) cuttings and root them under cover in a moist mixture of equal parts peat and sand at 72° to 75° F (22° to 24° C).

Worth remembering

After two or three years, your pentas will become less attractive and is best replaced.

CARING FOR YOUR PLANT

Watering and humidity: water moderately, just enough to keep the compost slightly moist, not wet. During the period of vegetative rest following flowering, water only sufficiently to stop the compost drying out.
Light: very bright conditions, with at least four hours of sunlight each day.
Feeding: feed every two weeks in spring and summer with food for flowering plants.
Repotting and growing medium: repot young plants every year in spring, in ordinary compost.
Cultivation tip: give your plant a period of about two months' rest after flowering. In winter, keep it in the cool at around 59° F (15° C) in a greenhouse or bright conservatory.

Pentas lanceolata ▶

Pentas lanceolata ▼

TROUBLE SHOOTING

◆ The leaves turn yellow and wilt: your plant is probably suffering from overwatering.
◆ The leaves become pale and dry: red spider mites thrive in warm, dry conditions. Increase the ambient humidity and spray the foliage. If necessary, treat the plant with an acaricide.

Peperomia

P. obtusifolia   Peperomia
synonym: *Peperomia magnoliifolia*

Decorative interest

This 6 to 12 inch (15 to 30 cm) high peperomia produces upright then trailing stems bearing tough, elliptical, glossy, mid-green leaves, 2 to 3 inch (5 to 8 cm) long. In spring or summer, 4 to 5 inch (10 to 12 cm) white flower spikes appear. This species, native to Santo Domingo, is not commonly cultivated but numerous, often variegated, horticultural varieties are available.

Associates well with... peperomias are often grown with other small, flowering plants.

Ease of cultivation

This peperomia is a robust plant and is mainly at risk from overwatering.

Propagation: take 4 inch (10 cm) stem cuttings. These will root easily in a mixture of slightly moist sand and peat.

Worth remembering

In spring, cut back leggy stems that have become bare during the winter. Pinch out the ends of shoots to encourage branching.

Peperomia caperata "Schumi" ▼

TROUBLE SHOOTING

◆ The leaves become pale and dry: red spider mites thrive in warm, dry conditions. Increase the ambient humidity and spray the foliage. If necessary, treat the plant with an acaricide.

Peperomia obtusifolia ▶

▼ *Peperomia rotundifolia*

◀ *Peperomia caperata* "Helios"

CARING FOR YOUR PLANT

Watering and humidity: during the growing period, water moderately but allow the compost to dry out to a depth of about an inch (a few centimeters) between waterings. In winter, water only sufficiently to stop the compost drying out completely. In warm weather, spray the leaves with soft water at room temperature.

Light: bright conditions with some direct sunlight for varieties with variegated foliage, but not during the hottest part of the day.

Feeding: feed every three weeks in spring and summer with half strength food for foliage plants.

Repotting and growing medium: repot in spring, but only if necessary, in a mixture of equal parts compost and peat. Use shallow pots.

Cultivation tip: water your plant quite sparingly but maintain a humid environment. Do not allow the temperature to drop below 59° F (15° C).

● RELATED SPECIES AND VARIETIES

Peperomia argyreia forms a clump of thick leaves, 2 to 4 inches (5 to 10 cm) long; they are rounded, and pointed at the tips. The dark green limb has broad, silvery-gray stripes and is supported on a red leaf stalk. Creamy-white flower spikes appear throughout the year. *P. scandens* "Variegata" also has variegated foliage. Its creeping or trailing stems bear fleshy, oval to elliptical leaves which are pale green with broad, creamy-yellow edges.

P. caperata is a very popular species, as are its many varieties. This plant forms a clump of leaves about an inch (2 to 3 cm) long borne on pinkish-red stems. The heart-shaped limb is heavily textured and dark green with almost black highlights in the furrows. White flower spikes emerge from the foliage on pink stalks from summer to fall. "Emerald Ripple" has dark green leaves; "Little Fantasy" is a dwarf variety growing no higher than 3 inches (8 cm); "Luna Red" has dark, purple-red leaves and stems; those of "Tricolor" are pale green with cream edges and slightly pink in the center.

Peperomia caperata "Pink Lady" ▼

Peperomia caperata "Alesi" ▼

Peperomia "Pixie" ▼

Peperomia verticillata ▼

Peperomia pereskiifolia ▶

Peperomia caperata "Lilian" ▶

◀ *Peperomia scandens*

Phalaenopsis

Phalaenopsis, butterfly orchid

Decorative interest

Phalaenopsis are epiphyte orchids without pseudo-bulbs, producing fleshy roots and overlapping, basal leaves; these are dark green, largely oval, and thick. The tall, arching flower-scapes appear at any time of year, carrying several (sometimes twenty or more) quite large flowers which, with their outspread petals, bear a certain resemblance to a butterfly. The labellum is divided into three lobes. Hybrids are available in a wide range of colors, most often in shades of white, pink, purple, and sometimes yellow. The flowers are often slightly dappled or striped. Flowering lasts for a long time, several months sometimes. The smaller-flowered hybrids do not flower for as long.

Ease of cultivation

Phalaenopsis are among the orchids that are relatively easy for amateurs to grow.

Propagation: if basal offsets form you can remove them and pot them up carefully. Keep them in a warm greenhouse and water sparingly.

CARING FOR YOUR PLANT

Watering and humidity: water moderately throughout the year with soft water at room temperature. Allow the growing medium to dry to a depth of an inch (a few centimeters) between waterings. Take care not to pour water into the heart of the plant. Stand the pot on damp gravel and water the foliage (but not the flowers) frequently.

Light: bright condition, but keep it out of direct sunlight. The sun will make the leaves turn reddish and this is followed by deeper burns if the plant is not moved into the shade.

Feeding: when new leaves are developing, feed your plant every two weeks with food for foliage plants at half or a third the normal strength. Then continue feeding with food for flowering plants, again heavily diluted, until the flowers begin to open.

Repotting and growing medium: repot every two years in spring or early fall, in a light, free-draining orchid compost. Don't repot your plant while it is in flower. Wait until the new leaves are an inch or two (a few centimeters) long.

Cultivation tip: water your phalaenopsis sparingly and keep it at a warm temperature throughout the year (between 68° and 72° F/20° and 22° C).

Phalaenopsis ▶

◀ *Phalaenopsis*

◀ *Phalaenopsis pallens*

Phalaenopsis luoddomanniana ▲

Phalaenopsis "Mivac" ▶

x *Doritaenopsis* ▼

Worth remembering

When the scape has finished flowering, don't cut it back to the base. Leave two or three eyes (small swellings) on the stem: you will soon see a new stem form from one of the remaining eyes.

● RELATED SPECIES AND VARIETIES

The botanical species available from specialist producers are more difficult to cultivate as houseplants.

Phalaenopsis amabilis produces large, white flowers 4 inches (10 cm) in diameter with a yellow-edged labellum and red markings in the throat.

P. schilleriana produces dark green leaves with silver-gray markings on top and purple on the underside. It is a prolific flower producer, with pink blooms and a white or yellow labellum with reddish-purple markings.

P. stuartiana also has leaves with silver speckles, white flowers with purple markings, and a yellow and pink labellum.

● RELATED GENERA

Doritaenopsis are intergeneric hybrids produced by crossing *Phalaenopsis* and *Doritis*. Although rather more demanding in terms of warmth, they are cultivated in much the same way as phalaenopsis. The leaves are usually thick and more tolerant of light and dryness. The flowering period is often longer, but they don't provide a second flowering. The main species used in these crossings is **Doritis pulcherrima**, an Asiatic orchid producing an upright infloresence with dark, purple-mauve flowers and a dark purple labellum with white stripes. The hybrids generally have smaller flowers than the phalaenopsis itself.

There are also other hybrid genera, including **Asconopsis** (*Ascocentrum* x *Phalaenopsis*) and **Renanthopsis** (*Renanthera* x *Phalaenopsis*).

Philodendron

Philodendron

Decorative interest

This genus comprises several hundred species of shrubs, small trees, and climbers that put out aerial roots and are native to the tropical rainforests of America. The cultivated species are grown for their tough leaves, which come in a wide variety of shapes and colors. The limbs will often vary in appearance, depending on the age of the plant.

The red philodendron, *Philodendron erubescens*, is a climbing species native to Colombia, with purple stems and oval leaves, heart-shaped toward the base. The limb is dark green and glossy on the upper surface and coppery-red on the underside, and is borne on a purple-red leaf stalk 8 to 12 inches (20 to 30 cm) long. Aerial roots appear at each node. When trained up a support, this plant can grow to over 6 feet (2 meters) tall. Its varieties "**Imperial Red**" and "**Red Emerald**" are particularly attractive. *P. Burgundy* is a more slow-

Philodendron scandens ▶

Philodendron "Lemon" ▼

CARING FOR YOUR PLANT

Watering and humidity: water moderately during the growing period, but don't leave your plant standing in water. In winter, water less frequently in accordance with the temperature. In warm weather, spray the leaves from time to time.

Light: bright conditions, but keep it out of direct sunlight.

Feeding: feed every two weeks in spring and summer with food for foliage plants.

Repotting and growing medium: repot young plants every year in spring, in a mixture of equal parts ordinary compost and peat or perlite. A top dressing will be sufficient for larger plants.

Cultivation tip: avoid very cool temperatures and waterlogging around the roots. Keep the temperature quite warm—not less than 60° to 62° F (15° to 16° C). Remove dust from the leaves regularly with a damp sponge.

TROUBLE SHOOTING

◆ The leaves at the base turn yellow and drop: this is due to overwatering. Stop watering and allow the plant to recover. When it has done this, water less often.

Philodendron melanochrysum ▼

◀ *Philodendron* "Imperial Red"

Philodendron "Mondaianeru" ▼

Philodendron "Red Emerald" ▼

▼ *Philodendron melinonii*

Philodendron "Silver King" ▼

Philodendron "Cobra" ▶

Philodendron "Fun Bun" ▼

growing hybrid with lanceolate leaves that are bright red when young, becoming olive-green on the upper surface and purplish-red on the underside.

The **climbing philodendron**, *P. scandens*, is a common houseplant. It grows rapidly, producing long, spindly, non-branching stems with small, pointed, heart-shaped leaves that are bronze-green when young, later becoming glossy and dark green. You can grow this plant in a hanging container, allowing its stems to trail, or you can train it to grow up a support.

P. selloum (synonym: *P. bipinnatifidum*) produces a short, upright, woody stem from the top of which emerges a rosette of very large, bright green leaves divided into numerous narrow lobes with wavy edges. The leaf stalks measure 16 to 24 inches (40 to 60 cm) long and the limbs are 12 inches (30 cm) across. This plant can grow quite large and requires a lot of space.

Ease of cultivation

Philodendrons are easy to cultivate in a large room with plenty of light, particularly the creeping philodendron.

Propagation: terminal cuttings will root easily under cover in a slightly moist mixture of peat and sand at between 70° and 75° F (21° and 24° C). Non-climbing species are grown from seed.

Tip

The best kind of support is a moss-covered pole. If kept damp, it will encourage the development and anchorage of aerial roots.

● RELATED GENUS

Monstera deliciosa (monster fruit, ceriman) is a species related to the philodendron. Along with rubber plants, it is one of the most popular houseplants. Its thick, non-branching stems put out numerous aerial roots. The young, shiny, heart-shaped leaves are bright green and resemble those of philodendrons. They gradually divide to take on their characteristic split-leaf appearance. Borne on 12-inch (30-cm) leaf stalks, the limbs can grow to 16 to 20 inches (40 to 50 cm) across. The infloresence, which is rare in plants grown indoors, is a creamy-white spath surrounding a fleshy spadix, followed by an edible white fruit. Bright conditions and a high level of humidity will allow this plant to thrive. *M. deliciosa* "Variegata" is a much less common variety, with leaves with cream variegation.

Monstera deliciosa "Variegata" ▼

Monstera deliciosa ▶

Phlebodium

P. aureum
Golden polypody, rabbit's foot fern

synonym: *Polypodium aureum*

Decorative interest

This fern, native to central and South America, takes its common name from its branching, creeping rhizomes, which grow along the surface of the soil. They are covered in long, brownish-yellow hairs. The large fronds, 3 feet (1 meter) long, have a triangular to oval limb, deeply divided into around twenty leaflets and bluish-green on both sides. The long, smooth leaf stalks are brown, as is the median vein.

Ease of cultivation

This is an undemanding fern but appreciates a certain degree of humidity.

Propagation: divide the rhizomes in spring, taking segments of 2 to 3 inches (5 to 8 cm). Root them under cover at 64° to 68° F (18° to 20° C). It is also possible to grow these plants from fresh spores, but the process is a long one.

TROUBLE SHOOTING

◆ Small brown lumps appear under the fronds: these are scale bugs. Remove them with a Q-tip dipped in alcohol. You can also try treating the plant with a systemic insecticide, though ferns are not always tolerant of plant treatment products.

CARING FOR YOUR PLANT

Watering and humidity: during the growing period, water generously, keeping the growing medium moist. In winter, water less frequently, according to the temperature. Maintain a good level of humidity around the pot.

Light: medium light conditions, but always keep it out of direct sunlight.

Feeding: feed every two weeks in spring and summer with half strength food for foliage plants.

Repotting and growing medium: repot in spring when the rhizomes are covering the entire surface of the pot. Use potting compost with added fibrous peat and perlite.

Cultivation tip: you can keep the golden polypody fern at room temperature all year round, but it can tolerate temperatures as low as 50° F (10° C).

Phlebodium aureum ▼

Phlebodium aureum ▼

Phoenix

P. canariensis   Canary Island palm

Decorative interest

The Canary Island palm is valued for its decorative shape. When grown in a pot it can reach a height of 6½ feet (2 meters), or even more. It produces a short, stocky stipe from which emerge large, pennate palms composed of numerous, dark green, stiff, linear leaflets. The yellow clusters of pendant flowers are rarely seen on specimens cultivated indoors.

Ease of cultivation

This is quite an easy palm to grow indoors. However, it will benefit from a period of winter rest at 50° to 55° F (10° to 13° C).

Propagation: this palm can be grown from seed but the process is slow and best left to the experts. *Phoenix roebelenii* sometimes produces offsets which can be used for propagation.

Worth remembering

The Canary Island palm is related to the date palm, *Phoenix dactylifera*, which grows faster but has a less attractive shape.

● RELATED SPECIES AND VARIETIES

Phoenix roebelenii is a smaller palm—generally less than 3 feet (1 meter) tall—with a graceful habit. It produces a crown of arching palms composed of numerous, dark green, slender, supple leaflets. It will grow happily in bright, filtered light conditions.

Phoenix canariensis ▶

CARING FOR YOUR PLANT

Watering and humidity: during the growing period, water generously and regularly so that the compost remains quite moist. In winter, water less frequently, according to the temperature. In warm weather, spray the foliage often, with soft water.

Light: enjoys bright conditions, so give your plant as much sunlight as possible throughout the year.

Feeding: feed every two to three weeks in spring and summer with food for foliage plants.

Repotting and growing medium: repot young plants every year in spring, then every two or three years, using a mixture of two parts ordinary compost to one part good yard soil and one part sand. For large specimens growing in big containers, a top dressing will suffice.

Cultivation tip: move your palm out on to a terrace or into the yard during the summer.

TROUBLE SHOOTING

◆ Small brown lumps appear on the palms, which become sticky: these are scale bugs. Remove them with a Q-tip dipped in alcohol, or treat the plant with a systemic insecticide.

Phoenix roebelenii ▼

Pilea

P. cadierei   Pilea, aluminum plant

Decorative interest

This thick, bushy plant has an upright habit and can grow to 16 inches (40 cm) high, but will benefit from regular pinching out to maintain a more compact shape. The dark green leaves are textured, oval and dentate with striking silvery markings. The flowers are insignificant and resemble those of nettles, which belong to the same family.

Associates well with... the attractive, variegated foliage of pileas means that they work well in arrangements with other foliage and flowering plants. They can also be used to provide ground cover in large containers.

Ease of cultivation

This pilea is very easy to grow.

Propagation: cuttings will root easily in a slightly moist mixture of peat and sand, or in water.

◀ *Pilea cadierei*

● RELATED SPECIES AND VARIETIES

Pilea involucrata has thick, heavily textured leaves that grow in tight rosettes at the tip of the stems; they are coppery-green on the upper side and dark purple on the underside.

P. involucrata "Norfolk" has leaves with bronze and silver variegation. Its creeping stems take root easily in the compost.

Pilea involucrata "Norfolk" ▼

Pilea glaucophylla "Greyzy" ▼

Pilea depressa "Sao Paulo" ▲

Pilea "Moon Valley" ▲

Pilea involucrata "Silver Tree" ▲

Pinguicula

Butterwort

Decorative interest

Butterworts are insectivorous perennials that catch prey with their sticky leaves. They grow in wetland areas of the northern hemisphere and also in South America. Unlike the species that come from temperate regions, those from warm regions do not require a period of dormancy and, because of this, are easier to cultivate as houseplants. Butterworts form rosettes of yellowy-green, fleshy leaves. They have a shiny appearance because of the mucilaginous secretions that attract and trap bugs. Once a bug has been caught, the edges of the leaves slowly roll up to facilitate digestion. Butterworts produce attractive flowers, in a variety of colors, carried on slender stems and usually appearing in spring.

Ease of cultivation

These carnivorous plants require a level of humidity in excess of 75%, which is difficult to achieve indoors.

Propagation: at the end of summer, remove the young plants that may have formed around the main plant and pot them up.

CARING FOR YOUR PLANT

Watering and humidity: during the growing period, leave the bottom of the pot standing in a little water (soft water). In winter, water once or twice a week, depending on the temperature. Maintain a good level of humidity around the pot, but don't wet the leaves.
Light: bright but filtered conditions; sunlight will burn the leaves.
Feeding: feed once a month in spring and summer with quarter strength orchid food.
Repotting and growing medium: repot in spring every two to four years, depending on the state of the plant. Use a mixture of blond peat, perlite, and sphagnum moss.
Cultivation tip: in winter, keep your plant at between 50° and 59° F (10° and 15° C). These compact species are ideal for growing in a terrarium, providing it is regularly ventilated to avoid the air becoming stale meaning the consequent risk of fungal diseases.

TROUBLE SHOOTING

◆ Butterworts respond badly to plant treatment products. If your plant is attacked by bugs, isolate it by putting it in an airtight, transparent plastic bag. The bugs will die of suffocation in about ten days.

▲ *Pinguicula* x *weser*

➤➤ *Carnivorous plants* see *Dionaea, Drosera, Nepenthes, Sarracenia, Utricularia.*

➤➤ *Succulent* see *Adenium, Aeonium, Agave, Aglaonema, Aloe, Ananas, Beaucarnea, Callisia, Ceropegia, Crassula, Echeveria, Echinocactus, Euphorbia, Gymnocalycium, Hoya, Kalanchoe, Lithops, Opuntia, Pachypodium, Peperomia, Portulacaria, Rhipsalidopsis, Rhipsalis, Sansevieria, Schlumbergera, Sedum, Senecio*

Platycerium

Staghorn fern, elkhorn fern

Decorative interest

This genus includes around fifteen species of epiphyte ferns with evergreen foliage and short rhizomes, growing in tropical forests in various parts of the world. The species most commonly cultivated indoors is *Platycerium bifurcatum*. This fern produces two types of fronds. The fertile, upright then trailing fronds, which resemble a stag's antlers; these are pale green, covered in a fine down, and measure 20 to 24 inches (50 to 60 cm). The sterile, brownish fronds grow one above the other in the center of the plant. This plant is often seen under the name *Platycerium alcicorne*.

P. superbum (synonym: *P. grande*) has sterile fronds with deeply lobed edges, 20 inches to 3 feet (50 cm to 1 meter) long, forming an impressive crown.

Ease of cultivation

The staghorn fern is relatively easy to grow and can last several years indoors when given the correct care.

Propagation: best left to the experts.

▼ *Platycerium superbum*

Platycerium bifurcatum ▼

CARING FOR YOUR PLANT

Watering and humidity: water once a week on average, a little more often in summer and a little less in winter. Immerse the pot in water for fifteen minutes, then drain it. In warm weather spray the foliage frequently with soft, tepid water.

Light: enjoys bright conditions, but make sure you keep it out of direct sunlight.

Feeding: feed once a month in summer with a weak solution of plant food added to the water in which it is soaking.

Repotting and growing medium: if necessary, repot pot-grown specimens in a fibrous, free-draining compost. The staghorn fern can also be grown on a piece of bark or in a hanging basket.

Cultivation tip: avoid waterlogging around the roots. In winter, the staghorn fern will tolerate some coolness of temperature, but not less than 59° F (15° C).

TROUBLE SHOOTING

◆ Small brown lumps appear on the fronds: these are scale bugs. Rub them off carefully with a Q-tip dipped in alcohol. Do not use an insecticide, or the fronds will turn black.

Plectranthus

Plectranthus

Decorative interest

This genus includes between 200 and 300 species of annuals, perennials, and shrubs native to various warm regions of the world. The cultivated species are valued for their trailing habit, their foliage, which is variegated in some varieties, and their flowers, particularly among the hybrids.

Plectranthus forsteri (synonym: *P. coleoides*) produces long stems, initially upright then trailing, covered in pale green, oval leaves, 2 to 4 inches (6 to 10 cm) long with jagged edges; the variety "**Marginatus**" has leaves with creamy-white margins.

P. oertendahlii is a vigorous species with rounded, pale green, scalloped leaves 1¼ to 1½ inches (3 to 4 cm) long that are reddish on the underside, particularly in a bright light. This plectranthus is very suitable for growing as a hanging plant.

In winter, the flowering hybrids produce upright inflorescences composed of small, tubular, bilabial flowers in shades of pink, mauve, and white.

Ease of cultivation

The plectranthus is a quite demanding and fast-growing plant.

Propagation: in spring and summer, take 2 to 3 inch (5 to 8 cm) terminal cuttings. Root them in water or in a moist mixture of equal parts peat and sand.

Worth remembering

Pinch out the tips of the stems regularly to encourage branching. This will help the plant to maintain a more compact shape.

TROUBLE SHOOTING

◆ The leaves become pale and dry: red spider mites thrive in warm, dry conditions. Increase the ambient humidity and spray the foliage. If necessary, treat the plant with an acaricide.

Plectranthus forsteri "Marginatus" ▼

CARING FOR YOUR PLANT

Watering and humidity: water quite generously during the growing period, but don't leave water standing in the saucer. In winter, water less often, depending on the temperature.

Light: bright conditions with a little sunlight.

Feeding: feed every two weeks in spring and summer with food for foliage plants.

Repotting and growing medium: these plants rarely need repotting. As they become less attractive with age, replace them every two or three years by taking cuttings. Use ordinary compost.

Cultivation tip: during the winter months, you can keep your plectranthus in a cool room at temperatures of between 55° and 59° F (13° and 15° C).

Plectranthus hybrid ▶

Plectranthus oertendahlii ▼

Pogonatherum

P. paniceum Dwarf bamboo grass

Decorative interest

Native to China, eastern Asia, and Australia, this grass forms a compact clump of upright stems that can grow to 12 to 16 inches (30 to 40 cm) high; at first upright, as they mature they have a tendency to trail. This plant puts out numerous shoots and develops quickly in size. It is heavily branching with fine, yellow-green, linear leaves similar to those of bamboo. Pot-grown plants don't flower.

Ease of cultivation

This can be a tricky plant to cultivate as it requires warmth and humidity.
Propagation: by clump division in spring.

Worth remembering

When your plant becomes untidy you can renew it by division.

CARING FOR YOUR PLANT

Watering and humidity: water regularly so that the compost remains moist at all times. Maintain a high level of humidity by standing the pot on a bed of damp gravel. Spray the foliage frequently.
Light: enjoys bright conditions, but make sure you keep it out of direct sunlight in summer.
Feeding: feed every two to three weeks in spring and summer with food for foliage plants.
Repotting and growing medium: repot every year in spring, in a mixture of good yard soil and compost with added peat.
Cultivation tip: dwarf bamboo grass enjoys heat and humidity. During the winter, the temperature should not be allowed to fall below 61° F (16° C).

TROUBLE SHOOTING

◆ The leaves curl up and turn yellow: the air is too dry. Increase the ambient humidity and spray the foliage more often.

Pogonatherum paniceum ▼

Polyscias

Polyscias

Decorative interest

This genus contains around a hundred small, evergreen trees that grow in the tropical regions of Africa, Asia, and the Pacific. They are cultivated for their shrubby appearance and attractive foliage.

Polyscias scutellaria "Balfourii" (also found with the name *P. balfouriana* "Marginata") produces branching stems with glossy, dark green leaves, often edged with white, which change form as they mature. At first simple and rounded, they later divide into three larger, round leaflets.

P. guilfoylei is an upright shrub (or even a small tree in its natural habitat), which has a non-branching habit and large, almost round, pennate leaves growing at the ends of the branches. These consist of five to nine mid-green leaflets of varying form, divided or serrated, and edged with irregular, spiny teeth. The variety "**Victoriae**" is smaller and less bushy, and has leaves with creamy-white margins.

P. fruticosa (aralia ming) is a species with heavily divided leaves composed of three to seven dark green, shiny, narrowly oval to lanceolate leaflets with dentate edges.

P. filicifolia produces arching leaves composed of numerous, narrow, bright green leaflets with plain or finely dentate edges.

Ease of cultivation

Polyscias are rather delicate plants which need warmth and humidity in order to produce luxuriant foliage.

Propagation: in spring, take 3 to 4 inch (8 to 10 cm) long terminal cuttings and root them under cover in a moist mixture of equal parts peat and sand at 70° to 75° F (21° to 24° C).

CARING FOR YOUR PLANT

Watering and humidity: during the growing period, water moderately but regularly so as to keep the compost quite moist. Water less often in winter. Spray the foliage every day.

Light: enjoys bright conditions, but make sure you keep it out of direct sunlight.

Feeding: feed every two weeks in spring and summer with food for foliage plants.

Repotting and growing medium: repot in spring every two years in ordinary compost with added peat and sand.

Cultivation tip: polyscias don't really have a period of rest. In winter, keep your plant at a temperature of at least 64° F (18° C), and always provide good ambient humidity.

TROUBLE SHOOTING

◆ The leaves drop: the air is too dry. Stand the pot in a large dish filled with damp gravel.

◆ The leaves become pale and dry: red spider mites thrive in warm, dry conditions. Increase the ambient humidity and spray the foliage more often. If necessary, treat the plant with an acaricide.

Worth remembering

Polyscias don't like being moved. However, they respond well to pruning and make good plants for bonsai treatment.

Polyscias guilfoylei ▶

Polyscias scutellaria "Balfourii" ▼

▼ *Polyscias* "Fabian"

Polyscias fruticosa ▼

Polystichum

P. falcatum   Holly fern
synonyms: *Cyrtomium falcatum, Phanerophlebia falcata*

Decorative interest

Native to China and Japan, this robust and very common fern is usually sold
under the name *Cyrtomium falcatum*. Open, dark green, glossy fronds, 8 to
24 inches (20 to 60 cm) long and divided into tapering, dentate leaflets, emerge
from the rhizome situated at the base of the plant. The holly fern owes its name
to its leaflets which are more like holly leaves than traditional fern fronds. The
spore cases, which are green and later brown, are found on the underside of
the leaflets. There are a number of different varieties.

Ease of cultivation

This is one of the easiest ferns to cultivate indoors. It does, however, appreciate a
certain coolness.

Propagation: propagate by clump division in early spring, taking care that
each fragment has at least three or four fronds.

TROUBLE SHOOTING

◆ Small brown lumps appear on the stems and pinnules: these are scale
bugs. Remove them with a Q-tip dipped in alcohol, or treat the plant with a
systemic insecticide.

● RELATED SPECIES AND VARIETIES

Native to Asia, *Polystichum tsus-simense* produces a rhizome covered in
blackish scales which sends out tufts of triangular, bipennate fronds, 8 to 12
inches (20 to 30 cm) long, composed of dark green, lanceolate leaflets which are
in turn divided into ½ to ¾ inch (1 to 2 cm) long pinnules. When the
young fronds are still closed, they are covered in silvery scales.

P. setiferum is a hardy species with silky, dark green,
bipennate fronds.

Polystichum falcatum ▶

CARING FOR YOUR PLANT

Watering and humidity: water very regularly during the growing
period so that the compost remains slightly moist. In winter, water less
frequently, particularly at low temperatures. Spray the foliage often when
the temperature rises above 72° F (22° C).

Light: medium to quite bright conditions, but keep it out of direct
sunlight.

Feeding: feed every two weeks in spring and summer with food for foliage
plants.

Repotting and growing medium: repot in early spring if the plant is
pot-bound. Use ordinary compost lightened by the addition of peat. Once
your plant is in a 6 to 8 inch (15 to 18 cm) pot, a top dressing will suffice.

Cultivation tip: this fern enjoys a cool temperature in winter. If possible,
keep it in a cool conservatory.

Polystichum setiferum ▼

Portulacaria

P. afra Elephant plant, small leaf jade

Decorative interest

The elephant plant, also known as the small leaf jade, is a succulent shrub or small tree native to southern Africa. Although it can grow to 10 to 13 feet (3 to 4 meters) in its natural habitat, it rarely exceeds 3 feet (1 meter) when grown in a pot. Slow growing and very branching, it is an excellent plant for bonsai treatment. Its thick stems carry bright green, opposed, stalkless, rounded leaves. The pale pink flowers are insignificant.

Ease of cultivation

This plant is a sun lover and can be easily grown in a conservatory or temperate greenhouse.
Propagation: take stem cuttings in spring and summer, and root them in a slightly moist mixture of peat and sand.

Worth remembering

In some African nature reserves, the elephant plant is a source of food for elephants, hence the name by which it is sometimes known.

Portulacaria afra "Variegata" ▼

Portulacaria afra ▲

CARING FOR YOUR PLANT

Watering and humidity: during the growing period, water sparingly, allowing the compost to become quite dry between waterings. In winter, keep your plant almost dry.
Light: full sunlight.
Feeding: feed once a month in spring and summer with food for cactuses and succulents.
Repotting and growing medium: repot in spring, if necessary, in compost for cactuses and succulents.
Cultivation tip: in winter, keep your plant in a cool, bright spot at a temperature of between 50° and 59° F (10° and 15° C).

TROUBLE SHOOTING

◆ White, cottony clusters appear at the base of the leaves: mealy bugs can be difficult to eradicate. If there are only a few, remove them with a Q-tip dipped in alcohol. If you are unsuccessful, treat the plant with a suitable insecticide.

Primula

P. obconica   Primula, primrose

Decorative interest

This perennial, usually cultivated as an annual, produces a rosette of large, quite tough, oval to rounded leaves, with scalloped edges and mid-green, hairy leaf stalks. During winter and spring, clusters of flowers in shades of pink, red, violet-blue, and white appear on long stems.

Associates well with… you can put several varieties of primulas together or combine them with other winter-flowering plants such as hyacinths.

Ease of cultivation

This primula is usually discarded after flowering. However, you can get it to flower again (but generally only once) if you give it the correct care. Flowering will last longer in a cool room at 54° to 59° F (12° to 15° C).

Propagation: grown from seed in plant nurseries at a cool temperature, between February and June.

Worth remembering

Some primulas, notably *Primula obconica*, contain an irritant (primine) which can cause allergic reactions in some people.

Primula obconica ▶

TROUBLE SHOOTING

◆ The leaves turn yellow: the position is too warm and dry. As hard water can also cause leaf chlorosis, make sure you water your plant with soft water.

● **RELATED SPECIES AND VARIETIES**

The fairy primrose, *Primula malacoides*, is a related species with pale green, oval, hairy, dentate leaves, 2 to 4 inches (5 to 10 cm) long. The star-like flowers, ¼ to ¾ inch (1 to 2 cm) in diameter, grow in clusters one above the other on slender flower stalks 12 to 16 inches (30 to 40 cm) tall. The flowers can be white, pink, or red, and often have a yellow eye. This primula is discarded after flowering and grown afresh from seed each year.

The hybrids of *Primula vulgaris* are better for outdoor decoration but can also be used in colorful indoor plant arrangements, although they are short-lived at warm temperatures. After flowering, these primulas can be planted out in the yard.

Primula vulgaris

Primula malacoides ▼

Primula malacoides ▼

Primula malacoides ▼

Primula vulgaris ▼ *Primula vulgaris* ▼ *Primula vulgaris* ▼

Pseuderanthemum

Pseuderanthemum

Decorative interest

This genus includes around sixty species of perennials, shrubs, and sub-shrubs that grow in tropical forests. The main variety cultivated as a houseplant is *Pseuderanthemum atropurpureum* "Variegatum," an upright shrub with non-branching stems which carry long, oval, purplish-bronze leaves with creamy-yellow and pink markings, and are 4 to 6 inches (10 to 15 cm) long. In summer, mature specimens cultivated in greenhouses will produce compact, terminal spikes of small, tubular, white flowers tinged with pink.

Ease of cultivation

This is a delicate plant which requires heat and humidity.
Propagation: take semi-woody cuttings in summer and root them under cover with bottom heat at 72° to 77° F (22° to 25° C). Hormone rooting powder will encourage successful rooting.

CARING FOR YOUR PLANT

Watering and humidity: water moderately throughout the year with water at room temperature. Maintain a high level of humidity by standing the pot on a bed of damp gravel. Spray the foliage frequently in dry weather.
Light: full but filtered sunlight.
Feeding: feed every two weeks in spring and summer with food for foliage plants.
Repotting and growing medium: repot in spring when the roots are beginning to poke out through the drainage holes. Use a mixture of compost and good yard soil.
Cultivation tip: avoid cold drafts and keep the temperature above 61° F (16° C) in the winter. A warm greenhouse is an ideal place to grow this plant.

TROUBLE SHOOTING

◆ The leaves become pale and dry: red spider mites thrive in warm, dry conditions. Increase the ambient humidity and spray the foliage. If necessary, treat the plant with an acaricide.

● RELATED GENERA

Other plants from the same family (Acanthacea) also have handsome, decorative foliage.
Strobilanthes dyerianus is an upright, shrubby, branching plant. The hairy stems bear oval, pointed, dark green leaves with metallic-blue highlights on the upper surface and dark purple undersides.
Sanchezia nobilis is also an upright, branching shrub. Its red-tinted branches have lanceolate, dentate leaves that are dark green with yellow markings along the veins. This plant has a tendency to become leggy at the base and will need to be replaced periodically.

◀ *Strobilanthes dyerianus*

Pteris

Pteris

Decorative interest

This vast genus includes numerous species of ferns with deciduous or evergreen foliage that are native to tropical forests. The underground rhizomes produce a clump of fronds, divided to varying degrees. The **Cretan brake**, *Pteris cretica*, grows to only 8 to 12 inches (20 to 30 cm) high and has fronds carried on stiff, blackish stalks; these fronds are composed of fine, linear leaflets with wavy, pale green edges. *P. cretica* "Albolineata" has leaflets with white variegation along the median vein. *P. cretica* "Wimsettii" is a variety with very finely divided, curly leaves.

P. ensiformis has two types of fronds: the fertile ones, which are large with narrow leaflets, and the sterile ones, which are more open and have broader leaflets. *P. ensiformis* "Victoriae" produces fronds in which the leaflets themselves are divided into pinnules with silvery-white markings along the median vein. The variegation is more marked in a shady situation.

Associates well with... these plants work well with other ferns and with plants with decorative foliage and flowering plants.

Ease of cultivation

Pteris are robust ferns and are relatively easy to cultivate indoors.

CARING FOR YOUR PLANT

Watering and humidity: water regularly with soft water so that the compost stays moist at all times, but don't overwater. Water less often in winter, according to the temperature. Increase the level of humidity by standing the pot on damp gravel and spray the foliage frequently, particularly at high temperatures.

Light: enjoys medium to bright conditions, but keep it out of direct sunlight.

Feeding: feed every two to three weeks in spring and summer with half strength food for foliage plants.

Repotting and growing medium: repot in spring every two to three years, in ordinary compost with added peat.

Cultivation tip: avoid cold drafts and sudden changes of temperature. The minimum growing temperature is 55° F (13° C).

Propagation: divide the clump in spring and pot up sections of the rhizome.

Pteris ensiformis ▶

▲ *Pteris cretica* "Albolineata"

TROUBLE SHOOTING

◆ Small brown lumps appear on the fronds, which become sticky: these are scale bugs. Remove them with a Q-tip dipped in alcohol, or treat the plant with a systemic insecticide.

▲ *Pteris cretica* "Roweri"

Pteris cretica "Parkeri" ▲

Pteris straminea ▶

◀ *Pteris fauriei*

▼ *Pteris quadriaurita* "Tricolor"

◀ *Pteris tremula*

Radermachera

R. sinica   Radermachera
synonym: *Stereospermum sinicum*

Decorative interest
This upright, bushy shrub, which is a small tree in its native habitat, rarely grows to over 3 feet (1 meter) tall as a houseplant. Its stems bear large leaves composed of oval, pointed leaflets, which are an attractive glossy green. The tiering effect of the branches gives the plant a graceful appearance.

Ease of cultivation
This is a robust, undemanding plant, but it does appreciate a cool temperature in winter.

Propagation: in late spring, take 3 to 4 inch (8 to 10 cm) stem cuttings and root them under cover in a moist mixture of equal parts peat and sand at 68° to 72° F (20° to 22° C).

● RELATED SPECIES AND VARIETIES
There is also a variegated variety but it is not commonly available.

CARING FOR YOUR PLANT

Watering and humidity: during the growing period, water moderately but regularly so that the compost remains slightly moist. In winter, water less frequently, depending on the temperature. In warm weather, spray the foliage with soft water at room temperature.

Light: bright conditions, but keep it out of direct sunlight in summer.

Feeding: feed every two to three weeks in spring and summer with food for foliage plants.

Repotting and growing medium: repot every year in spring to begin with, in ordinary houseplant compost.

Cultivation tip: keep your radermachera in a cool room, at around 61° F (16° C) in winter. This plant responds badly to exposure to cigarette smoke.

Radermachera sinica ▶

TROUBLE SHOOTING

◆ The leaves drop: this could be due to waterlogging around the roots. Allow the compost to dry out and gradually start watering again.

Rhapis

Rhapis, lady palm

Decorative interest

This genus includes around a dozen species of small palms with clumping stems that grow in the tropical and subtropical forests of China and south-east Asia. The most commonly cultivated species, *Rhapis excelsa*, is a very elegant palm forming a clump of upright, fibrous stems. The palmate leaves are composed of five to eight segments that taper at the trunk end and are dark green and glossy. As a pot plant, it is slow growing but can reach 5 feet (1.5 meters) in height. As it matures, the lower leaves have a tendency to turn brown and drop.

CARING FOR YOUR PLANT

Watering and humidity: water moderately during the growing period, allowing the compost to dry out to a depth of an inch or so (a few centimeters) between waterings. In winter, water less often, according to the temperature. Keep the humidity by standing the pot on damp gravel.
Light: bright conditions, with filtered sunlight and a little direct sunlight in winter.
Feeding: feed every two to three weeks in spring and summer with food for foliage plants.
Repotting and growing medium: repot in spring every two or three years, if necessary, in ordinary compost with added peat. With larger plants, a top dressing will suffice.
Cultivation tip: in winter, keep this palm in a cool, bright room at about 59° F (15° C). It will tolerate temperatures as low as 41° F (7° C).

R. excelsa "Zuikonishiki" is a variety that grows no more than 24 inches (60 cm) high and has leaves with creamy-yellow variegation.
   R. humilis has a slenderer appearance; it has fine stems and more rounded leaves composed of ten to twenty segments with pointed tips.

Ease of cultivation

The rhapis is an undemanding plant and will thrive providing it gets sufficient light and humidity.
   Propagation: in spring, remove basal shoots that have roots and pot them up in potting compost. Keep them in a warm place and water only sparingly until they begin to grow.

◀ *Rhapis excelsa*

TROUBLE SHOOTING

◆ Small brown lumps appear on the leaves, which become sticky: these are scale bugs. Remove them with a Q-tip dipped in alcohol, or treat the plant with a systemic insecticide.

Rhipsalidopsis

R. gaertneri
synonym: *Hatiora gaertneri*

Easter cactus, rhipsalidopsis

Decorative interest

This epiphyte cactus with flat, trailing, crenate stems is very similar to the Christmas cactus (**Schlumbergera**), but is known for its abundant spring flowering. Each stem is composed of mid-green, flattened, sometimes angular segments, 1½ inches (4 cm) long. The bell-like flowers are about 1 to 1½ inches (3 to 4 cm) long, scarlet, and bloom in March to April.

Ease of cultivation

The Easter cactus is easy to grow but to flower well, it needs a period of rest in the cool at about 53° to 59° F (12° to 15° C) during the winter.
Propagation: take cuttings comprising two segments after flowering. Leave them to dry for one or two days and plant them in a mixture of equal parts peat and sand, and keep these slightly moist at 68° to 72° F (20° to 22° C).

Rhipsalidopsis ▼

CARING FOR YOUR PLANT

Watering and humidity: water moderately during the growing period to keep the compost slightly moist but not wet. Water less often in winter, and also during the two or three weeks after flowering. In a warm situation, spray the foliage frequently.
Light: bright conditions, but filter sunlight during the hottest part of the day.
Feeding: feed every two to three weeks in spring and summer with food for cactuses and succulents.
Repotting and growing medium: repot after the rest period that follows flowering, but only if necessary, in a light, fibrous growing medium of the type used for epiphyte bromeliads.
Cultivation tip: avoid cold drafts and water this plant with soft, tepid water.

Tip

Once the flower buds have formed, avoid variations of temperature, humidity, and light, or the buds may drop.

● RELATED SPECIES AND VARIETIES

Rhipsalidopsis rosea (synonym: *Hatiora rosea*) has smaller segments, about ¾ inch (2 cm) long, and pale pink flowers that have a more star-like form. There are also numerous hybrids that have been produced from these two species.

TROUBLE SHOOTING

◆ White, cottony clusters appear on the leaves: mealy bugs can be difficult to eradicate. If there are only a few, remove them with a Q-tip dipped in alcohol. If you are unsuccessful, treat the plant with a suitable insecticide.

Rhipsalis

Rhipsalis, mistletoe cactus

Decorative interest

These epiphyte cactuses, native to equatorial forests, vary in appearance. Their heavily branching, creeping stems can be thin and rounded, or flattened, or angular. Their trailing habit makes them ideal for cultivation in hanging containers. In winter, they produce clusters of small, starry flowers which are followed by round, translucent, white fruit. The fruit and appearance of the plant are similar to those of mistletoe, hence the name mistletoe cactus by which the plant is also known.

Rhipsalis baccifera produces long, cylindrical, trailing green stems bare of leaves and spines but which bear white flowers.

R. capilliformis produces very fine, trailing, heavily branching stems in pale green, with silky areoles. The small flowers are greenish-white.

R. cassutha also has slender, cylindrical stems, and cream flowers.

R. pilocarpa has dark green stems covered in silky, white hairs and longitudinal ribs. Small, creamy-white, heavily scented flowers appear at the ends of the stems in late winter.

Ease of cultivation

The rhipsalis is a sturdy plant that appreciates good ambient humidity in warm weather.

Propagation: in spring and summer, take 2 to 3 inch (5 to 8 cm) cuttings. Leave them to dry for a few hours then plant several cuttings together in a pot filled with compost.

Rhipsalis cassutha ▼

CARING FOR YOUR PLANT

Watering and humidity: during the growing period, water your plant regularly with soft water so that the compost remains moist but not wet. Reduce watering in winter. During periods of warm weather, spray the plant every day.

Light: enjoys medium to bright conditions, but be sure to keep it out of direct sunlight.

Feeding: feed once a month in spring and summer with food for cactuses and succulents.

Repotting and growing medium: repot in spring every two years in a peat-based compost with added coarse sand, or in a compost for epiphyte cactuses.

Cultivation tip: move your plant outside in summer to a shady spot. In winter, you can keep it in a cool room at around 59° F (15° C).

TROUBLE SHOOTING

◆ White, cottony clusters appear on the stems: mealy bugs can be difficult to eradicate. If there are only a few, remove them with a Q-tip dipped in alcohol. In cases of severe attack, treat the plant with a suitable insecticide.

Rhipsalis baccifera ▼

Rhododendron

Azalea

Decorative interest

Pot-cultivated azaleas are, for the most part, hybrids originating in China and Japan, and derived mainly from two species, *Rhododendron simmsii* and *R.* x *obtusum* (which is, in fact, a natural hybrid of *R. kaempferi* and *R. kiusianum*). Generally sold in flower between early winter and late spring, they have small, very dark green, glossy, oval leaves which are often hairy. The flowers are quite large—2 to 2¾ inches (5 to 7 cm) in diameter—and can be single or double. They are produced in terminal clusters of two to five blooms. The colors are very varied, coming in shades of red, pink, orange, magenta, salmon, and white. Hybrids are often found under the name *Azalea indica*. They vary in height between 8 and 20 inches (20 and 50 cm), depending on the variety.

Rhododendron hybrid ▶

TROUBLE SHOOTING

◆ The leaves become dry and fall: your plant is suffering from too much heat and dryness. Move it to a cooler spot. Spray with soft water, and water it more regularly.
◆ The leaves become pale and dry: red spider mites thrive in warm, dry conditions. Increase the ambient humidity and spray the foliage more often. If necessary, treat the plant with an acaricide.

Ease of cultivation

It can be difficult to keep these plants indoors for more than a few weeks at a temperature of 68° F (20° C). They are better suited to cultivation in a temperate conservatory.

Propagation: professionals propagate azaleas from stem cuttings.

Worth remembering

Pinch out the tips of the shoots regularly to maintain a compact appearance, and deadhead your plant frequently.

▼ *Rhododendron* hybrid

CARING FOR YOUR PLANT

Watering and humidity: water every two to three days during the flowering period. Keep the compost slightly moist the rest of the time. Use soft water and increase the ambient humidity around the plant if the temperature rises above 61° F (16° C).

Light: enjoys a bright position while in flower, but keep it out of direct sunlight. When it is not in flower, give your plant medium light conditions.

Feeding: feed every two to three weeks in summer, but only if you are keeping your plant from one year to the next. Use food for ericaceous plants.

Repotting and growing medium: if necessary, repot after flowering, in ericaceous compost.

Cultivation tip: when it is indoors, keep your azalea at a temperature of between 59° and 64° F (15° and 18° C) to ensure a longer flowering period. When flowering is over, move your plant to a very cool spot and water moderately. If you can, put it outside in the shade during the mild weather. Water with soft water to keep the compost moist and spray the foliage in warm weather. Bring it back indoors before the first frosts and keep it in a cool room at 44° to 55° F (7° to 13° C) while the flower buds are developing.

▼ *Rhododendron* hybrid

▼ *Rhododendron* x *obtusum*

Rhododendron x *obtusum* ▼

Rhododendron x *obtusum* ▼

Rhododendron hybrid ▼

Rosa

Rose

Decorative interest

Roses cultivated as houseplants are miniature forms deriving mostly from species that have adapted to living at relatively high temperatures. These roses most often come in the form of small, branching bushes, with five to seven dark green, glossy, dentate leaflets. The flowers are small and can be single or double. They come in a range of colors, predominantly yellow, red, and pink. The plants are generally between 8 and 12 inches (20 and 30 cm) tall.

Ease of cultivation

Indoor roses are short-lived plants and are usually discarded after flowering. However, it is possible to keep them, providing they are overwintered in a greenhouse or cold conservatory.

Propagation: professionals propagate these plants from cuttings.

CARING FOR YOUR PLANT

Watering and humidity: during the flowering period, water your rose regularly to keep the root ball moist. Water less frequently during the period of vegetative rest if you are keeping your plant in a cold greenhouse.

Light: full sunlight.

Feeding: feed every two to three weeks in spring and summer with rose fertilizer.

Repotting and growing medium: if you are disposing of your plant after flowering, there is no point in repotting it. If keeping it, repot it every year in early spring, in special rose compost or good yard soil enriched with an organic fertilizer, such as dehydrated manure.

Cultivation tip: deadhead regularly and cut back lightly after flowering. Move your rose to a frost-free greenhouse or conservatory for the winter. Some roses that come from species that are not very hardy may not survive if left outside in the yard.

TROUBLE SHOOTING

◆ The leaves become sticky and deformed: aphids are attacking the shoots. Treat your plant with a suitable insecticide.

◆ The leaves become pale and dry: red spider mites thrive in warm, dry conditions. Increase the ambient humidity and spray the foliage. If necessary, treat the plant with an acaricide.

Rosa ▶

Ruellia

Ruellia

Decorative interest

The genus *Ruellia* (synonym: *Dipteracanthus*) consists of around 200 very diverse species of perennials, shrubs, and sub-shrubs. Native to warm regions of the world, they have opposed, entire leaves which can be stalkless or borne on leaf stalks, and are usually downy. Some have decorative foliage, like *Ruellia makoyana*, which produces leaves veined with silver and purple on the underside and solitary, funnel-shaped, carmine-pink flowers. *R. colorata* has terminal inflorescences with long-lasting, bright, reddish-pink bracts.

Ease of cultivation

Ruellias are quite easy plants to grow; they appreciate good ambient humidity and moderate heat.
Propagation: take terminal cuttings in spring and root them under cover in a mixture of peat and sand at 70° to 75° F (21° to 24° C).

TROUBLE SHOOTING

◆ The leaves become sticky and deformed: aphids are attacking the young shoots. Treat your plant with a suitable insecticide.
◆ The leaves become pale and dry: red spider mites thrive in warm, dry conditions. Increase the ambient humidity. If necessary, treat the plant with an acaricide.

CARING FOR YOUR PLANT

Watering and humidity: during the growing period, water regularly so that the growing medium remains moist, but don't leave water standing in the saucer. In winter, water less frequently, depending on the temperature. Maintain a good level of humidity by standing the pot on a bed of damp gravel. Avoid wetting the downy foliage.
Light: enjoys bright conditions, but keep it out of direct sunlight.
Feeding: feed every two weeks in spring and summer with food for foliage plants.
Repotting and growing medium: repot every year or two in spring, in ordinary compost with a little added peat.
Cultivation tip: most importantly, avoid sudden changes of temperature and cold drafts. Pinch out young shoots in order to encourage branching.

Ruellia hybrid ▲

Ruellia hybrid ▲

Ruellia colorata ▼

● **RELATED GENUS**
Megaskepasma   erythrochlamys belongs to the same family as ruellias. This shrub, native to tropical America, has opposed, oval leaves growing on flattened stems. It produces terminal infloresences of small, white flowers surrounded by red bracts.

◄ *Megaskepasma erythrochlamys* "Zomerster"

Saintpaulia

Saintpaulia, African violet

Decorative interest

The many hybrids and varieties of African violets are derived from different species. The plant forms rosettes of dark to mid-green, velvety, rounded, fleshy leaves, the size of which depends on the variety. The flower stems appear at different times of year. They carry clusters of white, pink, violet, bicolor, and multicolored flowers. These can be single or double and some have wavy or fringed petals. The largest varieties grow no taller than 8 to 10 inches (20 to 25 cm) high, but they can reach 16 inches (40 cm) in diameter. In recent years, miniature varieties have also become available.

Associates well with... you can group several different-colored varieties together in a wide container.

Ease of cultivation

The ease with which they can be grown has been a major factor in the popularity of African violets.

Propagation: propagate from leaf cuttings with the stalk attached. Push the stalk up to the start of the limb into moist cutting compost. Grow on, under cover, at between 68° and 75° F (20° and 24° C).

Worth remembering

Water saintpaulias from below, as they are very susceptible to neck rot.

Saintpaulia hybrids ▶

TROUBLE SHOOTING

◆ White, cottony clusters appear on the leaves: mealy bugs can be particularly difficult to eradicate. Remove them as soon as possible with a Q-tip dipped in alcohol. The leaves of saintpaulias react badly to insecticide sprays.

CARING FOR YOUR PLANT

Watering and humidity: water moderately throughout the year. Saintpaulias are very susceptible to waterlogging around the roots. Don't wet the foliage as it marks very easily.

Light: enjoys bright conditions, but make sure you keep it out of direct sunlight in summer.

Feeding: feed throughout the year with food for flowering plants: every two weeks from spring to fall; every three to four weeks in winter.

Repotting and growing medium: repot after flowering if the roots are coming out of the pot. Use a geranium compost lightened with some peat or perlite.

Cultivation tip: be especially careful to water correctly. The ideal temperature for saintpaulias is between 64° and 75° F (18° and 24° C).

Saintpaulia hybrids with bicolor flowers ▶

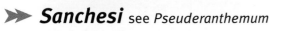

➤ *Sanchesi* see *Pseuderanthemum*

Sansevieria

Sansevieria, mother-in-law's tongue, snake plant

Decorative interest

Sansevierias are some of the easiest plants to grow. Native to arid regions of southern Africa and Asia, these rhizomatous plants produce thick, upright leaves either in clumps or in fairly open rosettes. *Sansevieria trifasciata* "Laurentii" is a very popular plant with long, upright, fleshy, pointed leaves that have pale green and dark green horizontal markings, and creamy-yellow edges. They can grow to over 3 feet (1 meter) tall. Their flowers, which are rare in pot-grown specimens, are produced in spikes on upright stems. *S. trifasciata* "Bantel's Sensation" produces leaves with markings similar to the species but with irregular, vertical, cream stripes at the top of the large leaves. *S. trifasciata* "Hahnii" is a dwarf variety which grows no taller than 6 inches (15 cm), producing a rosette of green leaves with yellow and gray markings. *S. trifasciata* "Golden Hahnii" has leaves with wide, yellow margins. *S. trifasciata* "Silver Hahnii" has silvery-green leaves with dark green markings.
S. cylindrica is a rare species with stiff, dark green, cylindrical leaves with gray-green stripes.

Ease of cultivation

Sansevierias are robust plants and perfect for beginners. They will withstand most things, except overwatering.
Propagation: they can be propagated when repotting. Divide the clump; pieces of root that have leaves can then be individually potted up in compost. You can

Sansevieria trifasciata "Laurentii" ▶

CARING FOR YOUR PLANT

Watering and humidity: water your plant very moderately during the growing period and allow the compost to become quite dry between waterings. In winter, water very little. Sansevierias have a good tolerance of dry air.
Light: bright conditions, but keep it out of very hot sunlight. Sansevierias can tolerate some shade, but the leaves will have less coloring.
Feeding: feed every three to four weeks in spring and summer with heavily diluted food for foliage plants or a fertilizer for succulents.
Repotting and growing medium: repot every two to three years in spring, in a light, free-draining, compost for cactuses and succulents. This plant enjoys being slightly cramped in its pot.
Cultivation tip: adjust watering carefully, particularly in winter. Your plant will be happy at room temperature, with a minimum temperature of 55° F (13° C).

TROUBLE SHOOTING

◆ The leaves become soft and brown: this is probably due to overwatering. To prevent this problem, avoid getting water around the neck of the plant when watering and remember to allow the compost to dry between each watering.

Sansevieria trifasciata "Hahnii" ▼

also remove the offsets that form at the base of the plant. Pot these up in compost if they have developed sufficient roots, or root them in a mixture of peat and sand if the roots are still small. Sansevierias can also be propagated from leaf cuttings, but this technique is not suitable for varieties with yellow margins, as it will produce plants with plain green leaves.

Worth remembering

Be careful not to break the pointed tips of the leaves, as this will stop them growing.

Sansevieria trifasciata ▼

Sansevieria trifasciata "Golden Hahnii" ▲

▼ *Sansevieria cylindrica*

Sarracenia

Sarracenia

Decorative interest

This genus includes eight species of carnivorous, evergreen, and deciduous perennials. Their pitcher-shaped traps are highly decorative. *Sarracenia purpurea* grows naturally in the peatlands and acid wetlands of America, from the Canadian arctic as far south as New Jersey. These plants have short, thick rhizomes which produce leaves modified into nectariferous pitchers arranged in rosettes. Bugs are attracted by the nectar, enter the pitchers, become trapped, and are digested by the various enzymes the plant secretes. The pitchers, which are narrow at the base and open out toward the top, have an upright operculum and are green with purple veins. Purple flowers, 2¼ to 3¼ inches (3 to 8 cm) in diameter, appear in spring. The plant will grow to a height of 4 to 6 inches (10 to 15 cm), but can have a diameter of as much as 3 feet (1 meter). *S. rubra* produces leaves 4 to 28 inches (10 to 70 cm) long, which are green, tinged with red, with a purple-veined operculum and dark purple flowers on long stems. There are also numerous natural and artificial hybrids.

Ease of cultivation

These carnivorous plants are very difficult to cultivate indoors and are best suited to a cold greenhouse.

Propagation: can be grown from fresh seed sown on the surface of wet peat moss, or by division in spring.

Tip

Don't divide the clump every year. This is a plant that becomes more attractive with age.

CARING FOR YOUR PLANT

Watering and humidity: between May and September, keep the growing medium moist at all times. Stand the pot in a saucer filled with rainwater. During the rest of the year, remove the saucer and keep the compost just slightly moist.
Light: full sunlight throughout the year.
Feeding: not applicable.
Repotting and growing medium: use deep, wide pots, at least 8 inches (20 cm) in diameter. Repot in spring, if necessary, in a light, acid mixture of blond peat, lime-free sand, and perlite or polystyrene.
Cultivation tip: sarracenias can tolerate large differences of temperature. During the winter months, keep the plants in the cool at between 46° and 53° F (8° and 12° C), with a minimum temperature of 41° F (5° C).

TROUBLE SHOOTING

◆ The leaves become soft and turn brown: this is probably due to overwatering. To prevent this problem, avoid wetting the neck of the plant when watering and allow the compost to dry between one watering and the next.

Sarracenia rubra ▲

Sarracenia purpurea ▶

Saxifraga

S. stolonifera   Saxifrage, mother of thousands

Decorative interest

The genus *Saxifraga* includes numerous garden plants, but the species *Saxifraga stolonifera*, native to China and Japan, is cultivated indoors, where it makes a highly original hanging plant. It is a carpeting plant, forming loose rosettes of rounded, dark green leaves with veins that are silvery on the upper surface and purple on the underside. It puts out numerous, reddish, filiform stolons that produce plantlets at their tip. *S. stolonifera* "Tricolor" is a highly decorative variety, though less vigorous, and has leaves with creamy-white edges that are tinged with pink when brightly lit.

Ease of cultivation

This saxifrage is easy to grow, providing it is given a period of winter rest. However, regular replacement is advised in order to maintain it as an attractive houseplant.

Propagation: in spring, remove and plant up the young plantlets that have formed at the tips of the stolons. You can also leave them attached to the mother plant and separate them once they are well rooted.

Saxifraga stolonifera "Tricolor" ▶

Schefflera

S. arboricola
Schefflera, umbrella tree

synonym: *Heptapleurum arboricola*

Decorative interest

The attractive, decorative appearance of the schefflera and its ease of cultivation have made it a very popular plant. It produces a single stem which can grow to 6½ feet (2 meters) tall, with long-stemmed leaves composed of seven to ten green, radiating leaflets 2¾ to 4 inches (7 to 10 cm) long. Unless you grow several scheffleras together in the same pot, this plant will only require a quite narrow space.

Ease of cultivation

This schefflera is easy to cultivate as a houseplant.

Propagation: take terminal cuttings 2 to 3 inches (5 to 8 cm) long and root them in water or in a moist mixture of peat and sand at 68° to 75° F (20° to 24° C).

CARING FOR YOUR PLANT

Watering and humidity: during the growing period, water moderately, allowing the compost to dry out slightly before watering again. In winter, water less often, in accordance with the temperature.

Light: bright conditions, but keep it out of direct sunlight. The variegated forms require more light.

Feeding: feed every two to three weeks in spring and summer with food for foliage plants.

Repotting and growing medium: repot every year in spring to begin with, using ordinary compost. When the plant has reached its full size an annual top dressing will suffice.

Cultivation tip: at high temperatures, increase the ambient humidity by standing the pot on a bed of damp gravel. The minimum winter temperature is 53° to 59° F (12° to 15° C), and 61° to 64° F (16° to 18° C) for variegated forms.

Tip

Support the main stem with a stake so that it remains vertical.

◀▼ *Schefflera arboricola*

TROUBLE SHOOTING

◆ Small brown lumps appear on the stems and leaves: these are scale bugs. Remove them with a Q-tip dipped in alcohol, or treat the plant with a systemic insecticide.

◆ The leaves become pale and dry: red spider mites thrive in warm, dry conditions. Increase the ambient humidity and spray the foliage. If necessary, treat the plant with an acaricide.

◆ The leaves drop: this is probably due to overwatering or exposure to cold drafts.

● RELATED SPECIES AND VARIETIES

Schefflera arboricola "Geisha Girl" has a more compact habit and green leaves with more rounded leaflets.

S. arboricola "Variegata" has leaves with yellow and green variegation.

S. actinophylla (synonym: *Brassaia actinophylla*) has leaves divided into five to seven leaflets, 3 to 10 inches (8 to 25 cm) long, glossy and bright green. This species has a spreading habit and requires a lot of space.

Schefflera actinophylla ▼

Schefflera arboricola ▼

Schefflera

S. elegantissima
Dizygotheca, false aralia

synonym: *Dizygotheca elegantissima*

Decorative interest

Valued for its fine, light foliage, the dizygotheca can grow to over 3 feet (1 meter) as a houseplant but is slow growing. The main stem branches very little and has leaves composed of narrow, finely divided leaflets. These are initially coppery-red and later become a dark bronze-green.

Associates well with... the slender foliage of dizygothecas contrasts well with plants with broader leaved, variegated foliage.

Ease of cultivation

This plant is quite tolerant of indoor conditions, providing the air is not too dry.

Propagation: scheffleras are generally grown from seed, but this can be difficult.

● RELATED SPECIES AND VARIETIES

Schefflera elegantissima "Castor" has broader, denser leaves.

CARING FOR YOUR PLANT

Watering and humidity: water moderately with soft, tepid water so that the compost remains slightly moist during the growing period. In winter, water a little less often if kept in a cool room. Spray the foliage daily and stand the pot on a bed of damp gravel.

Light: bright conditions, but keep it out of direct sunlight.

Feeding: feed every two to three weeks in spring and summer with food for foliage plants.

Repotting and growing medium: repot in spring if the roots are filling the pot, using compost with a little added sand.

Cultivation tip: avoid exposure to cold drafts, which can cause the leaves to drop, and maintain a temperature of at least 61° F (16° C) in winter.

TROUBLE SHOOTING

◆ The leaves become pale and dry: red spider mites thrive in warm, dry conditions. Increase the ambient humidity and spray the foliage more often. If necessary, treat the plant with an acaricide.

◆ White, cottony clusters appear on the leaves: mealy bugs can be difficult to eradicate. Remove them with a Q-tip dipped in alcohol or treat the plant with a systemic insecticide.

▼ *Schefflera elegantissima*

Schefflera venulosa ▼

◄ *Schefflera elegantissima* "Castor"

Schlumbergera

Christmas cactus, schlumbergera

Decorative interest

The Christmas cactuses grown as houseplants are usually hybrids of botanical species such as **Schlumbergera truncata** (synonym: *Zygocactus truncatus*). They produce trailing stems, sometimes as much as 24 inches (60 cm) long, composed of mid-green, flat segments with pointed edges. The tubular flowers, consisting of several layers of star-like petals, reach a length of 2 to 3 inches (5 to 8 cm) and are about 1 inch (2 to 3 cm) in diameter. They can be pink, red, or white, sometimes yellow, and bloom in late fall or winter.

Ease of cultivation

With a little experience, these plants are easy to grow indoors.
Propagation: in spring or summer, take stem cuttings with two or three segments. Allow them to dry for a few hours and plant them in a mixture of peat and sand.

Worth remembering

Once formed, the flower buds are likely to drop if the plant is moved or exposed to sudden changes of temperature or cold drafts.

Tip

In summer, move your plant outdoors to a sheltered, semi-shaded position to strengthen the young shoots.

CARING FOR YOUR PLANT

Watering and humidity: during the flowering period and from spring to early fall, water regularly to keep the compost moist, but don't leave water standing in the saucer. Reduce watering during the two to four weeks following flowering and again in the fall before flowering begins.
Light: bright to slightly shaded conditions, but keep it out of direct sunlight in summer.
Feeding: feed every two weeks in spring and summer with food for cactuses and succulents.
Repotting and growing medium: repot after flowering, if necessary, in compost for cactuses and succulents.
Cultivation tip: in the fall, give your plant a quite cool temperature of about 59° to 64° F (15° to 18° C) and reduce watering, as this will encourage abundant flowering.

TROUBLE SHOOTING

◆ White, cottony clusters appear on the leaves: mealy bugs can be difficult to eradicate. If there are only a few, remove them with a Q-tip dipped in alcohol. If you are unsuccessful, treat the plant with a systemic insecticide.

Schlumbergera ▼

Schlumbergera ▼

Schlumbergera ▼

➤ *Scindapsus* see *Epipremnum*

Scirpus

S. cernuus
Fiber optic grass

synonym: *Scirpoides cernuus*

Decorative interest
This small, herbaceous, semi-aquatic plant produces a dense tuft of soft green, filiform leaves, 8 to 12 inches (20 to 30 cm) long, directly from the rhizome. Initially upright, they gradually arch and trail, covering the pot. A small, white or cream flower develops at the tip of each leaf; the flowers can appear at any time of year.

Ease of cultivation
This is not a difficult plant to grow. If kept at 55° F (13° C), it will continue growing without interruption.

Propagation: divide the clump in spring when repotting.

Tip
This plant is often sold in a cardboard tube with a fountain of trailing leaves springing from the top. Remove the tube on purchase as it is not needed and will reduce the life of your plant.

Scirpus cernuus ▶

CARING FOR YOUR PLANT

Watering and humidity: during the growing period, water your plant generously in order to keep the compost very moist. You can leave water standing in the saucer. Water less frequently at cooler temperatures.
Light: medium light conditions.
Feeding: feed once a month during the growing period—at temperatures above 55° F (13° C)—with food for foliage plants.
Repotting and growing medium: repot when the plant has completely filled its pot, using a mixture of equal parts ordinary compost, peat, and good yard soil.
Cultivation tip: as it matures, this plant becomes less attractive; don't hesitate to divide it. It makes a good hanging plant but take care that the compost does not dry out too quickly.

➤ **Spiderworts**
see *Callisia, Dichorisandra, Gibasis, Palisota, Siderasis, Tradescantia*

Scutellaria

S. costaricana	Scutellaria

Decorative interest

The genus *Scutellaria* includes numerous species of annuals, herbaceous and rhizomatous perennials, and sub-shrubs. Scutellarias are very cosmopolitan plants, growing mainly in temperate regions and mountainous tropical areas of the world. Those grown as houseplants are species such as *Scutellaria costaricana*, native to Costa Rica. This plant, which is 12 inches (30 cm) tall, produces upright, purple stems with dark green, slightly textured, oval to elliptical leaves, 4 to 6 inches (10 to 15 cm) long. In summer, it produces superb terminal clusters of long, bright red, tubular flowers with yellow hearts. There are hybrids in various colors, including red, pink, and purple.

Ease of cultivation

Scutellarias can be difficult to grow indoors. They are best suited to a warm greenhouse.

Propagation: take herbaceous cuttings in spring and root them under cover in a moist mixture of peat and sand, with bottom heat. Rooting can be difficult.

CARING FOR YOUR PLANT

Watering and humidity: during the growing period, water regularly with water at room temperature, sufficiently to keep the compost moist. Water less frequently in winter. Maintain a good level of humidity around the pot. Spray the foliage daily in warm, dry weather.

Light: bright conditions, but keep it out of direct sunlight.

Feeding: feed every two weeks in spring and summer with food for flowering plants.

Repotting and growing medium: repot in spring, if necessary, in a mixture of good humus-rich soil and compost, lightened by the addition of a little coarse sand.

Cultivation tip: this scutellaria requires warm conditions, with a minimum temperature of 59° F (15° C), a high level of humidity, and good light.

TROUBLE SHOOTING

◆ The leaves become pale and dry: red spider mites thrive in warm, dry conditions. Increase the ambient humidity and spray the foliage. If the attack is particularly severe, treat the plant with an appropriate acaricide.

◆ Small white bugs fly away when you touch the plant: whitefly are small, sap-sucking bugs that are difficult to eradicate. Treat the plant repeatedly with insecticide every eight to ten days.

Scutellaria costaricana ▼

Scutellaria costaricana "Red Fountain" ▼

Sedum

Stonecrop

Decorative interest

The genus *Sedum* contains several hundred species of very varied appearance, though most are succulents. Native to the northern hemisphere, Madagascar, and mountainous areas of Africa and South America, many of them are hardy. The majority of stonecrops grown as houseplants are originally from Mexico. They are valued for their attractive foliage. The fleshy, heavily branching stems are covered in stalkless leaves that are also fleshy. The donkey's tail stonecrop, *Sedum morganianum*, produces trailing stems covered in small, cylindrical, whitish leaves; it is especially decorative when grown in a hanging container. The green leaves of *S. burrito* are lightly tinged with purple on the young shoots. The leaves of *S. rubrotinctum* turn reddish when the atmosphere is warm and dry.

Ease of cultivation

Stonecrops are not difficult to grow but they require a lot of light and a period of winter rest in the cool.
Propagation: in spring or summer, take 2 to 3 inch (5 to 8 cm) stem cuttings. Remove some of the bottom leaves and allow the cuttings to dry for one or two days. Root them in a slightly moist mixture of peat and sand or directly in the growing medium recommended for the adult plants.

TROUBLE SHOOTING

◆ White, cottony clusters appear at the base of the leaves: mealy bugs can be difficult to eradicate. If there are only a few, remove them with a Q-tip dipped in alcohol. If you are unsuccessful, treat the plant with a suitable insecticide.

CARING FOR YOUR PLANT

Watering and humidity: during the growing period, water moderately, allowing the surface of the compost to dry between waterings. In winter, water less often, depending on the temperature.
Light: full sunlight throughout the year.
Feeding: feed every two weeks in spring and summer with food for foliage plants.
Repotting and growing medium: repot in spring, in compost for cactuses and succulents. It is best to use shallow pots.
Cultivation tip: in winter, keep your plant in a conservatory or temperate greenhouse at around 50° F (10° C).

Sedum morganianum ▼

Sedum burrito ▼

Selaginella

Selaginella

Decorative interest

This genus includes several hundred species of evergreen perennials that grow mainly in the tropical rainforests of the world. The cultivated species are valued for their fine foliage which resembles that of ferns. *Selaginella martensii* produces branching stems, first upright, then trailing, covered in fleshy, mid-green, glossy leaves, ½ to ¾ inch (1 to 2 cm) long. It grows to about 6 inches (15 cm) tall with a spread of 8 to 10 inches (20 to 25 cm). *S. martensii* "Variegata" has leaves with silvery-white variegation at the tips.

S. kraussiana is a fast-growing, creeping species that forms a mat of bright green leaves. *S. kraussiana* "Aurea" has golden-green foliage.

S. apoda produces soft, delicate, spreading stems covered in tiny, pale green leaves.

S. lepidophylla, the rose of Jericho, has the unusual quality of surviving several months without water. The plant rolls itself up into a tight ball and unfurls again when it is watered. The dry plants are sold as curiosities.

Associates well with... you can grow selaginellas with ferns in a large container or in a terrarium with other moisture-loving plants.

Ease of cultivation

Selaginellas are delicate plants and enjoy a warm, humid atmosphere.

Propagation: in spring, take 2 to 3 inch (5 to 8 cm) cuttings and root them in some moist compost. You can also divide the rhizomes when repotting.

CARING FOR YOUR PLANT

Watering and humidity: water your plant generously throughout the year to keep the compost moist, but don't leave water standing in the saucer. Spray the foliage frequently with soft water if the plant is not being kept in a terrarium.

Light: medium light conditions, but no sunlight.

Feeding: feed every two to three weeks with a weak solution of foliage plant food.

Repotting and growing medium: repot in spring, if necessary, in a mixture of peat, sand, and ericaceous compost.

Cultivation tip: throughout the year, maintain a temperature of between 64° and 75° F (18° and 24° C), with a high level of ambient humidity. Avoid drafts of dry or cold air.

Selaginella apoda ▼

Selaginella kraussiana ▼

Selaginella martensii "Jori" ▶

Senecio

Groundsel

Decorative interest

There are over 1,000 species of these woody or herbaceous plants. They are varied in appearance—some upright, some climbers—and produce leaves of various kinds, including succulent ones. Most of the species cultivated as houseplants are native to South Africa. *Senecio macroglossus* is a liana with twining stems bearing triangular, lobed leaves, similar to ivy; it produces yellow flowers in summer. There is also a form with variegated foliage. *S. mikanoides* also has twining stems, with thick, dark green leaves divided into three to seven pointed lobes with radiating veins. Native to the Himalayas, *S. cephalophorus* is a branching shrub; its fleshy branches carry thick, bluish-green leaves and orange inflorescences.

Ease of cultivation

These plants require very good light and a period of winter rest in the cool.

Propagation: seed can be sown in spring, in a propagator at 66° to 75° F (19° to 24° C). It is also possible to root some groundsels in water.

Senecio cephalophorus ▼

▼ *Senecio macroglossus* "Variegata"

Siderasis

S. fuscata   Siderasis, brown spiderwort, bear's ears
synonym: *Tradescantia fuscata*

Decorative interest

The genus *Siderasis* contains only one species, *S. fuscata*, which is native to Brazil. This small, tropical plant forms a rosette that grows to no more than 3 inches (8 cm) high. The leaves emerge directly from a short, underground stem. They are elliptical, pale green on the upper surface with a median silvery band, and purple on the underside. They can grow to 8 to 10 inches (20 to 25 cm) in length. At the end of summer, the plant produces flowers with three petals, the color of which varies from violet to pinkish-purple.

Ease of cultivation

This is a demanding plant and is difficult to cultivate anywhere but in a terrarium.

Propagation: mature plants put out offsets that can be removed, taking care not to damage the roots. Pot these up individually and put them in a heated propagator.

Siderasis fuscata ▼

▲ *Siderasis fuscata*

Sinningia

Gloxinia

Decorative interest

The plants sold commercially are in fact hybrids of *Sinningia speciosa* and are sometimes called "florists' gloxinias" to distinguish them from the species belonging to the genus *Gloxinia*. These beautiful plants grow from a tuber, forming a rosette of large, bright green, velvety, oval leaves. The flower stems, about 5 inches (12 cm) long, appear in summer from between the leaves, each bearing a large, long, bell-shaped bloom in shades of red, violet-blue, or white. The edges of the corolla are usually very wavy or fringed. Some hybrids have bicolor or speckled blooms.

Ease of cultivation

Gloxinias can be tricky to keep from one season to the next. They require quite a high level of humidity and a bright position. Their leaves are susceptible to rotting.

Propagation: gloxinias are increased by leaf cuttings or seed but these are complicated techniques for amateurs.

Tip

When the leaves begin to dry, stop watering and keep the tuber dry for the whole winter.

Sinningia speciosa ▼

Sinningia speciosa ▼

Sinningia speciosa ▶

CARING FOR YOUR PLANT

Watering and humidity: water moderately in summer, using soft water at room temperature, but take care not to wet the leaves. Increase the ambient humidity by standing the pot on damp gravel. Gradually reduce watering in the fall when the plant goes into vegetative rest.

Light: requires bright conditions, but make sure you keep it out of direct sunlight.

Feeding: feed every two to three weeks in spring and summer with food for flowering plants.

Repotting and growing medium: repot at the end of February; plant the tuber in a pot filled with ordinary compost with added peat. The top of the tuber should be level with the surface of the compost.

Cultivation tip: in winter, keep the tuber dry and in the cool at about 59° F (15° C). You can treat gloxinias as seasonal plants and discard them after flowering.

Sinningia speciosa ▼▲   *Sinningia speciosa* ▶

Soleirolia

S. soleirolii   Helxine, baby tears
synonym: *Helxine soleirolii*

Decorative interest
This dwarf, carpeting plant produces branching stems which are sometimes tinged with pink. Its small, rounded leaves are less than ¼ inch (2 to 6 mm) long, and fine and silky. Native to Corsica, it is a useful plant for covering the surface of a pot or planter: its stems put out roots as they grow. It is a plant that will grow well in a terrarium.

Ease of cultivation
Easy to cultivate, providing it is given a period of winter rest in a cool place.
Propagation: very easy to propagate. In spring, simply remove and plant up sections of stem with roots.

● RELATED SPECIES AND VARIETIES
Soleirolia soleirolii "Argentea" has leaves with silvery-white variegation.
S. soleirolii "Aurea" has golden-yellow leaves.

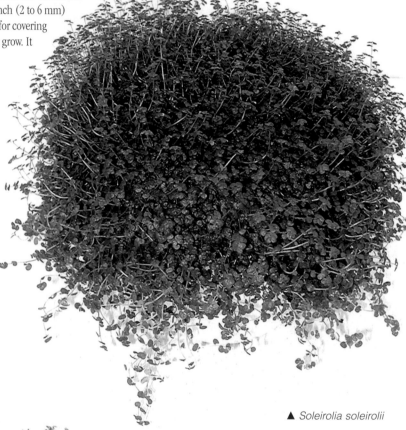

▲ *Soleirolia soleirolii*

Soleirolia soleirolii ▼

CARING FOR YOUR PLANT

Watering and humidity: water your plant freely during the growing period, but don't leave water standing in the saucer. In winter, reduce watering according to the temperature. Maintain a good level of ambient humidity.
Light: medium to bright conditions, with light shade in summer.
Feeding: feed every three to four weeks in spring and summer with half strength food for foliage plants.
Repotting and growing medium: repot in spring, in ordinary compost enriched with good yard soil.
Cultivation tip: in winter, keep your plant in a conservatory or greenhouse at 41° to 50° F (5° to 10° C).

Sparrmannia

S. africana — — — — — — — — — African linden

Decorative interest

This South African native can grow to over 6½ feet (2 meters) when grown as a houseplant. It produces vigorous, hairy stems bearing large, pale green, heart-shaped, dentate leaves which are also slightly hairy. The African linden can flower at the end of winter or in early spring, producing umbels of small, white flowers with orange stamens. Flowering is more frequent in the dwarf variety "Nana."

Ease of cultivation

The African linden needs to spend the winter in a cool, bright position, such as a cool conservatory.

Propagation: in spring, take 6 inch (15 cm) terminal cuttings and root them in a moist mixture of equal parts peat and sand at 64° F (18° C).

Tip

Cut back the stems of your plant in spring to restrict growth and encourage branching.

● RELATED SPECIES AND VARIETIES

Sparrmannia africana "Nana" is a dwarf form.
S. africana "Flore Pleno" produces double blooms.

TROUBLE SHOOTING

◆ The leaves become pale and dry: red spider mites thrive in warm, dry conditions. Increase the ambient humidity and spray the foliage more often. If necessary, treat the plant with an acaricide.

CARING FOR YOUR PLANT

Watering and humidity: during the growing period, water your plant moderately but very regularly so that the compost remains quite moist. During the rest period, water less often but don't allow the compost to dry out completely. During periods of warm weather, spray the foliage from time to time.

Light: full but filtered sunlight.

Feeding: feed every two weeks in spring and summer with food for foliage plants.

Repotting and growing medium: repot every year at first, then every two or three years, in a mixture of equal parts ordinary compost and peat. Use terracotta pots, as they are more stable.

Cultivation tip: give your plant plenty of space to grow and a temperature of around 61° F (16° C).

Sparrmannia africana ▼

Sparrmannia africana ▼

Sparrmannia "Flore Pleno" ▼

Spathiphyllum

Spatiphyllum, peace lily

Decorative interest

This genus, a member of the arum family, includes around thirty species of evergreen, rhizomatous perennials that grow in the tropical rainforests of Asia and America. The plants available commercially are hybrids of *Spatiphyllum wallisii*. This species produces long-stemmed, elliptical, tapering leaves, 6 to 10 inches (15 to 25 cm) long; they are a beautiful, glossy, dark green color. The inflorescences appear in spring and summer, and sometimes at other times of year. As is typical of arums, they consist of a fine, quite short, creamy-white or greenish spadix, surrounded by a tapering spath which is white at first and gradually turns green. The hybrid forms are more compact with wide or narrow spaths. *Spatiphyllum* "Mauna Loa" is a hybrid that is more difficult to cultivate. It can grow to over 24 inches (60 cm) in height and has large leaves, 8 to 10 inches (20 to 25 cm) long and 6 inches (15 cm) across, borne on stems 10 to 12 inches (25 to 30 cm) long; it produces large inflorescences.

Ease of cultivation

Spatiphyllums are robust plants and are easy to cultivate, but will be more attractive if provided with good ambient humidity.

Propagation: divide the clump in spring and immediately pot up the divisions in a suitable compost.

Worth remembering

Spatiphyllums contain toxic substances. Contact with the sap can cause irritation to sensitive skin.

Spathiphyllum "Chopin" ▶

CARING FOR YOUR PLANT

Watering and humidity: water your plant moderately but regularly, allowing the compost to become slightly dry between waterings. Water less frequently in winter when the temperature is unusually low. In a warm room, increase the ambient humidity by standing the pot on a bed of damp gravel.

Light: spatiphyllums prefer bright but filtered light; however, they can also cope with a relatively poor level of light.

Feeding: feed every two weeks in spring and summer with food for flowering plants.

Repotting and growing medium: repot young plants in spring, in ordinary compost with added peat or perlite.

Cultivation tip: ideally, you should maintain a temperature of between 64° and 72° F (18° and 22° C) for your plant throughout the year, and a good level of humidity. Avoid cold drafts and irregular watering.

TROUBLE SHOOTING

◆ The leaves become pale and dry: red spider mites thrive in warm, dry conditions. Increase the ambient humidity and spray the foliage more often with soft water at room temperature. If necessary, treat the plant with an acaricide.

Spatiphyllum wallisii ▶

Spathiphyllum Aqua Magic® ▼   *Spathiphyllum* ▼

Stephanotis

S. floribunda   Madagascar jasmine

Decorative interest

This climbing shrub that grows in the forest interiors of Madagascar produces stems that can grow many feet (several meters) long. Its dark green, thick, oval, glossy leaves measure 3 to 6 inches (8 to 15 cm) in length. Its pure white, tubular, waxy, perfumed flowers bloom in spring and summer in clusters at the leaf axils. Plants sold commercially are usually trained over a hoop.

Ease of cultivation

Madagascar jasmine requires a period of winter rest in order to form flower buds. Once the buds have formed, the pot should not be moved or there is a risk of them dropping.

Propagation: in spring, take 4 inch (10 cm) cuttings from non-flowering side branches. Pot them up in a mixture of sand and peat, and grow on, under cover, at between 64° and 70° F (18° and 21° C).

Tip

In early spring, remove the weaker side shoots. A bamboo support can be used to help the plant climb freely.

CARING FOR YOUR PLANT

Watering and humidity: water generously during the growing period, but avoid waterlogging as this will make the flower buds drop. Stand the pot on damp gravel and spray the foliage (but not the flowers) in warm weather. In the fall, gradually reduce watering; water only sparingly in winter during the period of rest.

Light: bright but filtered conditions.

Feeding: feed every two weeks in spring and summer with food for flowering plants.

Repotting and growing medium: repot every year in spring, in a mixture of ordinary compost with added peat.

Cultivation tip: be sure to give your plant a period of winter rest in a cool spot at temperatures of approximately 55° to 59° F (13° to 15° C).

TROUBLE SHOOTING

◆ Small brown lumps appear under the leaves, which become sticky: these are scale bugs. Remove them with a Q-tip dipped in alcohol, or treat the plant with a systemic insecticide.

Stephanotis floribunda ▲▼

Stephanotis floribunda ▼

Streptocarpus

Cape primrose

Streptocarpus ▼

Decorative interest

The Cape primrose is a small plant that is a member of the saintpaulia family; the cultivated forms are mainly hybrids. The leaves are bright green, oblong to oval, with finely dentate edges and prominent veins; they are usually arranged in a basal rosette. The flowers, carried on quite short stems—4 to 6 inches (10 to 15 cm) long—are gathered in clusters and available in a wide range of colors including white, blue, pink, mauve, and purple. The throat is often striped or in a contrasting color. Flowering continues from spring right through to the fall.

Streptocarpus saxorum ▼

Purple *Streptocarpus* ▶

Blue *Streptocarpus* ▶

➤ *Strobilanthes* see *Pseuderanthemum*

Ease of cultivation

Growing Cape primroses requires a certain amount of experience. Watering is not always easy to regulate correctly.

Propagation: can be grown from seed at the end of winter at 64° F (18° C), or from leaf cuttings in spring, in a mixture of peat and sand.

Worth remembering

Handle this plant carefully as its leaves can be broken or damaged very easily. The Cape primrose will not tolerate smoky atmospheres.

TROUBLE SHOOTING

◆ Gray, cottony marks appear on the leaves: mildew is a fungus that thrives in damp conditions. Treat your plant with a fungicide and move it to a better ventilated position to prevent further problems (but ensure it is sheltered from cold drafts).

CARING FOR YOUR PLANT

Watering and humidity: water moderately, just enough to keep the compost slightly moist, but not wet. Don't wet the leaves as they are susceptible to rotting. If your plant is in a warm room in winter, stand it on damp gravel.

Light: bright conditions, but keep it out of direct sunlight.

Feeding: feed every two to three weeks in spring and summer with half strength food for flowering plants.

Repotting and growing medium: repot every year in spring, in a mixture of equal parts ordinary compost and peat.

Cultivation tip: give your plant growing conditions that are as constant as possible, and always water with moderation. Cut the flower stems off at the base once the flowers have faded.

Streptocarpus wendlandii ▼

Streptocarpus saxorum ▼

Streptocarpus wendlandii ▶

Stromanthe

S. sanguinea   Stromanthe

Decorative interest

This plant, which is related to the calathea, produces a creeping rhizome from which emerge branching stems bearing large, oval leaves, 12 to 20 inches (30 to 50 cm) long; they are dark green with paler green stripes on the upper surface and purple on the underside. The young leaves are rolled up and appear from inside the leaf stalk of the old ones. The inflorescences, composed of small, white flowers surrounded by red sepals and bracts, rarely appear on pot-grown plants. There are variegated varieties such as "Multicolor," which has leaves speckled with pink and cream, and "Stripestar," which has leaves with creamy-white veins that are purple-pink on the underside.

Ease of cultivation

This is a tropical plant and requires a high level of humidity and a high temperature.
Propagation: divide the clump in spring, making sure that each section has a few leaves and well-developed roots.

CARING FOR YOUR PLANT

Watering and humidity: water regularly throughout the year with water at room temperature, so that the compost remains moist but not wet. Stand the pot on a bed of damp gravel and spray the foliage daily when the weather is warm and dry.
Light: medium light conditions.
Feeding: feed every two weeks in spring and summer with food for foliage plants.
Repotting and growing medium: repot in spring if the roots have filled the pot. Use a mixture of peat, ericaceous compost, and sand.
Cultivation tip: maintain a temperature of 64° to 75° F (18° to 24° C) throughout the year, and make sure you keep your plant away from cold drafts.

TROUBLE SHOOTING

◆ Small brown lumps appear on the leaves, which become sticky: these are scale bugs. Remove them with a Q-tip dipped in alcohol, or treat the plant with a systemic insecticide.
◆ The leaves become pale and dry: red spider mites thrive in warm, dry conditions. Increase the ambient humidity and spray the foliage more often. If necessary, treat the plant with an acaricide.

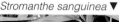

Stromanthe sanguinea ▼

◄ *Stromanthe sanguinea* "Stripestar"

Syngonanthus

S. chrysanthus "Mikado"   Syngonanthus

Decorative interest
This small, tropical plant, which has only recently become commercially available, has a highly original appearance with inflorescences in the form of small, golden pompoms. It forms a basal rosette of leaves, similar to those of grasses, from which emerge a dozen or so straight flower stems, 6 to 8 inches (15 to 20 cm) tall, topped by compact, rounded inflorescences; the small flower buds are button shaped and golden yellow, revealing creamy-white petals as they open. The species is native to Brazil.

Ease of cultivation
The syngonanthus enjoys warm, humid but well ventilated conditions.
Propagation: grown from seed by professionals.

◀ *Syngonanthus chrysanthus* "Mikado"

CARING FOR YOUR PLANT

Watering and humidity: water regularly with soft water at room temperature so that the compost remains moist at all times. Stand the pot on a bed of damp gravel.
Light: bright conditions, but keep it out of direct sunlight.
Feeding: feed once a month in spring and summer with half strength food for foliage plants.
Repotting and growing medium: repot in spring, if necessary, in a mixture of ericaceous compost, peat, and lime-free sand. Don't plant the root ball too deep as the growing point is susceptible to fungal disease.
Cultivation tip: maintain as constant a temperature as possible—between 65° and 72° F (19° and 22° C)—with a minimum temperature of 58° F (14° C).

➤➤ **Succulent** see *Adenium, Aeonium, Agave, Aglaonema, Aloe, Ananas, Beaucarnea, Callisia, Ceropegia, Crassula, Echeveria, Echinocactus, Euphorbia, Gymnocalycium, Hoya, Kalanchoe, Lithops, Opuntia, Pachypodium, Peperomia, Portulacaria, Rhipsalidopsis, Rhipsalis, Sansevieria, Schlumbergera, Sedum, Senecio*

Syngonium

S. podophyllum   Syngonium, goose foot plant

Decorative interest

The long stems—up to 6½ feet (2 meters)—of this plant, native to tropical America, can climb or trail depending on whether they are provided with support. The foliage is variable: the leaves of young plants are entire and shaped like arrow heads, while those of more mature specimens are usually divided into five to eleven leaflets, the terminal one being most developed. They are dark green, with pale green markings on top and a paler underside. There are several varieties with leaves divided or lobed to varying degrees and often with attractive, creamy-white to silver variegation.

Associates well with... syngoniums are sociable plants which lend themselves to foliage plant arrangements with, for example, philodendrons or ivies.

Ease of cultivation

This is a robust plant that is easy to grow indoors.
Propagation: in spring or summer, take 3 to 4 inch (8 to 10 cm) terminal cuttings and root them under cover in a slightly moist mixture of equal parts peat and sand at 68° to 70° F (20° to 21° C).

Worth remembering

Use a moss pole to train your syngonium, keeping it damp by frequent spraying.

CARING FOR YOUR PLANT

Watering and humidity: during the growing period, water moderately to keep the compost slightly moist at all times. In winter, water less often, depending on the temperature. In warm, dry weather, increase the ambient humidity around the plant.
Light: enjoys bright conditions, but make sure you keep it out of direct sunlight. Forms of syngonium that have plain green leaves can tolerate light shade.
Feeding: feed every two weeks in spring and summer with food for foliage plants.
Repotting and growing medium: repot every two to three years in spring, in ordinary compost with some added peat.
Cultivation tip: syngoniums react badly to sudden drops in temperature and dry, warm atmospheres. The minimum suitable temperature for this plant is 59° F (15° C).

TROUBLE SHOOTING

◆ Small brown lumps appear on the leaves, which become sticky: these are scale bugs. Remove them with a Q-tip dipped in alcohol, or treat the plant with a systemic insecticide.
◆ The leaves become pale and dry: red spider mites thrive in warm, dry conditions. Increase the ambient humidity and spray the foliage more often. If necessary, treat the plant with an acaricide.

Syngonium podophyllum "White Butterfly" ▼
Syngonium "Pixie" ▼
Syngonium "Infra Red" ▼
Syngonium hybrid (with tricolor foliage) ▼
Syngonium "Andrea" ▼

Tacca

T. chantrieri   Bat plant

Decorative interest

This perennial native to south-east Asia produces an upright rhizome from which emerges a clump of large, bright green, lanceolate leaves that can grow to 24 inches (60 cm) in length. However, the plant's main attraction lies in its flowers, which are unusual both in form and color. The flower stems, which appear in summer, have at their tip umbel inflorescences composed of green flowers with five petals, and violet, reddish-brown bracts with blackish-brown, filiform appendages 6 to 10 inches (15 to 25 cm) long.

Ease of cultivation

This is a very difficult plant to grow indoors; it is best cultivated in a warm greenhouse with good ventilation.
Propagation: can be grown from fresh seed at 75° to 82° F (24° to 28° C) in a propagator with bottom heat; germination can be very slow. You can also divide the rhizomes in spring when repotting.

◄ *Tacca chantrieri*

CARING FOR YOUR PLANT

Watering and humidity: during the growing period, water regularly to keep the compost slightly moist. Water less often in winter. Maintain a high level of humidity and spray the foliage daily in hot weather.
Light: bright conditions, but keep it out of direct sunlight.
Feeding: feed every two weeks in spring and summer with food for flowering plants.
Repotting and growing medium: repot every two to three years in early spring, in a free-draining mixture of compost and fine bark chippings or fibrous peat.
Cultivation tip: keep this plant away from cold drafts. During the growing period, the temperature must be high—between 75° and 86° F (24° and 30° C)—with a good level of humidity; in winter, you can keep your plant in cooler conditions, but don't allow the temperature to drop below 59° to 61° F (15° to 16° C).

TROUBLE SHOOTING

◆ The leaves become pale and dry: red spider mites thrive in warm, dry conditions. Increase the ambient humidity and spray the foliage more often. If necessary, treat the plant with an acaricide.

Tacca chantrieri ▼

➤ **Tetrastigma** see *Cissus*

Thunbergia

T. alata
Black-eyed Susan

Decorative interest

Native to South Africa, this climber has stems that twine around supports unassisted. It is usually cultivated as an annual and discarded after flowering. However, it can be overwintered in a pot in a greenhouse with a minimum temperature of 50° F (10° C). Its slender, twining stems are very vigorous, reaching a height of 5 to 6½ feet (1.5 to 2 meters) over the course of the summer. It has mid-green, oval, angular, dentate leaves. Solitary flowers, 1¼ to 2 inches (3 to 5 cm) in diameter, appear from summer through to fall. They consist of a dark brown, almost black, velvety tube which forms the central eye, and an open orangey-yellow corolla. There are also varieties in white and in different shades of yellow.

Ease of cultivation

Black-eyed Susan is easy to grow in a bright room, close to a well-lit window.
Propagation: growing from seed is easy and should be done in March. Sow several seeds in a pot and put it in a warm room under filtered light. When the plantlets have grown to 6 inches (15 cm) tall, pot them up individually.

CARING FOR YOUR PLANT

Watering and humidity: water young plants moderately, but increase watering when the flower buds appear and during the flowering period.
Light: bright conditions, with a few hours of sunlight each day. Place near a well-lit window.
Feeding: feed every ten to fifteen days during the flowering period with food for flowering plants.
Repotting and growing medium: repot young plants in geranium compost with added peat.
Cultivation tip: deadhead black-eyed Susan regularly in order to prolong flowering.

Thunbergia alata (white) ▼

◄ *Thunbergia alata* (cream)

Worth remembering

A vigorous climber, this plant needs a support to cling to, either a stake or some trellising. You can also grow it in a large hanging basket as a trailing plant.

● RELATED SPECIES AND VARIETIES

Thunbergia grandiflora is another vigorous species, with large, sky-blue flowers with bright yellow throats; the flowers can be either solitary or in pendant clusters and can grow to 4 inches (10 cm) across.

T. erecta is a bushy shrub with slender stems, producing flowers that are creamy-white on the outside, with a yellow heart and purple-violet lobes.

T. battiscombei has violet-blue flowers with yellow hearts.

T. mysorensis is a very vigorous, climbing perennial; its funnel-shaped, yellow and reddish-brown flowers grow in pendant clusters.

Thunbergia mysorensis ▲

Thunbergia alata (yellow) ▼

Thunbergia erecta ▶

Thunbergia grandiflora ▼

Thunbergia battiscombei ▼

Thunbergia erecta ▼

Tillandsia

T. cyanea   Tillandsia

Decorative interest

This small, epiphyte bromeliad, native to Ecuador, forms a rosette of linear leaves, 6 to 12 inches (15 to 30 cm) long; these are slender, pointed, and gray-green with red markings at the base. The oval, flattened inflorescence, which is 2 inches (5 cm) wide and 4 to 6 inches (10 to 15 cm) long, is composed of overlapping, symmetrical, pink bracts, from which emerges a succession of violet-blue, three-petalled flowers. After flowering, the main rosette dies and is replaced by its offsets.

Ease of cultivation

Tillandsias require a high level of humidity.

Propagation: remove the offsets once the leaves are 3 inches (8 cm) long and plant them in pots filled with a mixture of equal parts peat and sand. Place under cover at 64° to 72° F (18° to 22° C), until growth begins.

CARING FOR YOUR PLANT

Watering and humidity: this epiphytic plant does not require watering. Spray the foliage two or three times a week, and more often in warm, dry weather, with soft water at room temperature.

Light: enjoys bright but filtered light, but be sure to keep it out of direct sunlight.

Feeding: feed once a month in spring and summer by spraying with a foliar feed if the plant is being grown on bark, or half strength liquid plant food if in a pot.

Repotting and growing medium: repot young plants in a light, free-draining, lime-free compost that is peat- or bog moss-based, or special compost for epiphyte bromeliads.

Cultivation tip: grow your tillandsia in a terrarium on a trunk suitable for epiphytes. This will provide it with all the moisture it needs. The minimum temperature should be 55° F (13° C).

Tillandsia cyanea ▼

Tillandsia dyeriana ▼

Tip

During the summer, you can hang your plant on a tree in the shade. Wrap the roots in a little peat and keep the plant moist.

● RELATED SPECIES AND VARIETIES

Tillandsia lindenii is a related species, but its flower stem can grow to 12 inches (30 cm) and its flowers are purple-blue with a white eye.

▼ *Tillandsia argentea*

▼ *Tillandsia* (in flower)

Tillandsia disticha ▼

▲ *Tillandsia juncea*

Tillandsia flabellata ▼

Tillandsia plumosa ▼

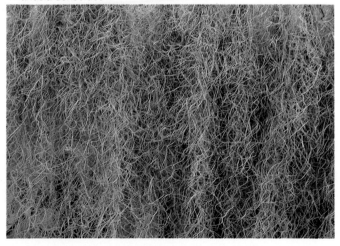

Tillandsia cyanea ▼

Tillandsia usneoides ▼

Tolmiea

T. menziesii   Piggyback plant, hen and her chicks

Decorative interest

This charming little plant, native to North America, owes its common name to a curious feature: it produces young plantlets at the base of the leaves, at the point where the stalk and limb join. The short-stemmed rhizome produces numerous, mid-green leaves that are more or less heart-shaped, lobed, and dentate. The leaves become trailing because of the weight of the plantlets. The small, greenish-white flowers are not often seen on plants grown indoors. This plant can grow to between 4 and 12 inches (10 and 30 cm) high, with a spread of over 16 inches (40 cm).

Ease of cultivation

Tolmieas make easy houseplants providing they are given a cool position—50° to 59° F (10° to 15° C)—with plenty of light in winter.

Propagation: in spring or summer, cut off a leaf with a plantlet attached and about an inch (2 to 3 cm) of stalk. Plant it in a moist mixture of equal parts peat and sand, with the plantlet resting on the surface of the growing medium. Grow on at 64° to 68° F (18° to 20° C).

● RELATED SPECIES AND VARIETIES

Tolmiea menziesii "Taff's Gold" has paler leaves speckled with cream and pale yellow.

Tolmiea menziesii "Variegata" ▶

CARING FOR YOUR PLANT

Watering and humidity: water quite generously during the growing period so that the compost remains moist, but not wet. Reduce watering in winter, particularly at cool temperatures. Spray the leaves from time to time with warm water.

Light: medium to bright conditions, but protect from hot sunlight.

Feeding: feed every two to three weeks in spring and summer with food for foliage plants.

Repotting and growing medium: repot in spring, if necessary, in ordinary compost.

Cultivation tip: when the plant becomes less attractive, replace it using the plantlets that have formed on the leaves.

TROUBLE SHOOTING

◆ The leaves become pale and dry: red spider mites thrive in warm, dry conditions. Increase the ambient humidity and spray the foliage more often. If necessary, treat the plant with an acaricide.

Tradescantia (and other spiderworts)

T. fluminensis

Wandering Jew, spiderwort

Decorative interest

Very common houseplants, tradescantias produce prostrate or trailing stems with oval, pointed leaves that are about 2 inches (5 cm) long; they are pale green with purple on the underside. In spring and summer, terminal clusters of white flowers appear. It is the variegated forms of the plant that are most commonly seen.

Associates well with... spiderworts are very accommodating and can be combined with many other plants.

Ease of cultivation

Spiderworts are particularly easy to grow.

Propagation: you can take stem cuttings about 3 inches (8 cm) long at any time of year and root them in cutting compost or in water.

Worth remembering

Pinch out the tips of the shoots to encourage branching.

CARING FOR YOUR PLANT

Watering and humidity: water moderately during the growing period so that the compost remains slightly moist. Reduce watering in winter, according to the temperature.

Light: spiderworts with plain green foliage are happy in a room with poor light. However, the variegated forms need bright conditions and some sunlight.

Feeding: feed every two to three weeks in spring and summer with food for foliage plants.

Repotting and growing medium: repot in spring, if necessary, in ordinary compost.

Cultivation tip: as spiderworts mature they tend to become leggy toward the base; it is best to renew them regularly by taking cuttings.

TROUBLE SHOOTING

◆ Deformed, sticky leaves reveal the presence of aphids: treat your plant with a suitable insecticide.

Tradescantia fluminensis ▶

● RELATED SPECIES AND VARIETIES

Tradescantia fluminensis "Variegata" is probably the most common variety; it has leaves with green and white stripes on the upper surface and violet on the underside.

T. fluminensis "Quicksilver" has larger leaves (3 inches/8 cm), with green and white stripes, and is a vigorous grower.

T. albiflora "Albo-vittata" produces creeping stems covered in green, oval leaves with white stripes.

T. blossfeldiana "Variegata" produces plain green leaves, cream leaves, sometimes tinged with pink, and variegated leaves.

T. pallida (synonym: *Setcreasea pallida*) produces creeping stems with upright tips and large, purple-violet leaves and small, pink flowers.

● OTHER SPIDERWORTS

Botanists have changed the classification of these plants on a number of occasions, which explains the large number of synonyms.

Zebrina pendula (synonym: *Tradescantia pendula*) produces creeping stems with oval, pointed leaves, between 1¼ and 2¾ inches (3 and 7 cm) long; they are green with large, silvery-white stripes on the upper surface and reddish-purple on the underside. Small, purple-pink, insignificant flowers appear in spring and summer. This spiderwort is a good plant for hanging baskets. *Z. pendula* "Quadricolor" has leaves with green, purple, cream, and silver stripes; it is more difficult to cultivate. *Z. pendula* "Purpusii" is a variety with purple foliage.

Callisia repens produces creeping stems which put out roots at the nodes and it is therefore carpet-forming. It has broad, bright green, oval to lanceolate leaves, between ½ and 1½ inches (1 and 4 cm) long. In the fall, white flowers about ½ inch (1 cm) in diameter appear. It grows no taller than 4 inches (10 cm) but can spread to over 3 feet (1 meter).

Callisia elegans (synonym: *Setcreasea striata*) is a plant with trailing stems. Its oval, pointed leaves are tinged with purple and have white, longitudinal stripes on the underside.

Callisia fragrans (synonyms: *Spironema fragrans*, *Tradescantia dracaenoides*) is a stoloniferous plant with elliptical leaves 6 to 10 inches (15 to 25 cm) long which are a pale, bright green on the upper surface and purple on the underside.

Gibasis geniculata (sometimes sold under the name *Tradescantia multiflora* or *Tripogandra multiflora*) produces spindly stems with lots of leaves—dark green on top and purple on the undersides—and tiny white flowers.

◀ Tradescantia
zebrina

▲ Callisia
repens

Tradescantia pallida ▼

Gibasis
geniculata ▶

Tradescantia

T. spathacea   Rhoeo
synonyms: *Rhoeo discolor, Rhoeo spathacea*

Decorative interest
This plant forms a regularly shaped, compact clump. It is related to spiderworts although the rosette arrangement of the leaves recalls that of bromeliads. The narrowly lanceolate leaves are 8 to 12 inches (20 to 30 cm) long and emerge from a short, fleshy stem. They are dark green on top and dark purple on the underside. Short-lived, small, white flowers surrounded by purple-green bracts appear in the leaf axils.

Associates well with... you can grow rhoeos with other spiderworts with trailing habits, such as *Tradescantia albiflora* "Albo-vittata," which has leaves with white stripes.

Ease of cultivation
Rhoeos are easy to cultivate as houseplants.
Propagation: remove the offsets that form at the base of the plant when they are between 3 and 6 inches (8 and 10 cm) high and pot them up.

CARING FOR YOUR PLANT

Watering and humidity: during the growing period, water generously so that the compost remains moist but not wet. Water less often in winter, allowing the compost to dry out to a depth of an inch or more (a few centimeters) before watering again. In warm weather, spray the foliage from time to time with soft water.
Light: enjoys bright conditions, but filter out sunlight.
Feeding: feed every two weeks in spring and summer with food for foliage plants.
Repotting and growing medium: repot in spring if the roots are spilling out of the pot. Use ordinary compost with some added perlite and a wide, shallow pot.
Cultivation tip: keep your plant in a bright room but not too hot in winter: between 61° and 64° F (16° and 18° C).

TROUBLE SHOOTING

◆ The leaves become pale and dry: red spider mites thrive in warm, dry conditions. Increase the ambient humidity and spray the foliage more often. If necessary, treat the plant with an acaricide.

● **RELATED SPECIES AND VARIETIES**
Tradescantia spathacea "Vittata" is a vigorous variety with green leaves which have yellow stripes on the upper surface and are purple on the underside.

Tradescantia sillamontana ▼

Tradescantia sillamontana ▼

Tradescantia spathacea "Vittata" ▼

Tradescantia spathacea "Vittata" ▶

➤ *Tulipa* see *Hyacinthus*

Utricularia

Bladderwort

Decorative interest

This genus includes around 200 species of insectivorous plants, annuals, perennials, terrestrials, epiphytes, and aquatics in a wide range of sizes—from just a fraction of an inch to several feet (a few millimeters to several dozen centimeters). Their geographical distribution is vast. These herbaceous, rootless plants have developed a very special system for catching their prey: the suction trap. The stems bear two types of leaves: the first are aerial and green, and vary according to the species; the second are translucent, hollow, and bladder-shaped, and grow in water or a moist growing medium. It is the latter that serve to catch their prey—minuscule organisms living in the soil or the water. The pressure inside each utricule (or bladder) is lower than that outside the trap, so that when a prey stimulates the plant's sensitive hairs, a valve opens and the animal is sucked into the bladder and digested.

The bladderworts cultivated as houseplants are terrestrial forms, like *Utricularia sandersonii*, which is native to South Africa; this is a stoloniferous species which produces numerous, small, spatulate leaves about ⅕ inch (5 mm) long, and delicate white and blue flowers during most of the year; it reaches 2½ inches (6 cm) high when in flower. *U. livida* and *U. bisquamata* also come from South Africa. *U. calycifida*, native to South America, is taller and has lavender flowers. *U. dichotoma* comes from Australia and reaches 12 inches (30 cm) when in flower.

TROUBLE SHOOTING

◆ Aphids sometimes attack the flower stems: treat your plant with a suitable insecticide.

Ease of cultivation

These carnivorous plants have very particular growing requirements. *U. sandersonii* is one of the easiest to cultivate.
Propagation: grow from seed in the fall or by clump division in spring.

CARING FOR YOUR PLANT

Watering and humidity: during the growing period, water your plant regularly with soft water so that the compost remains moist; leave the base of the pot standing in a little water. During the winter months, keep the compost moist but don't leave water in the saucer. A high level of humidity is required (from 60% to 80%), particularly for the tropical species.
Light: requires full sunlight. Bright but filtered light conditions are preferable for *U. calycifida*.
Feeding: not applicable.
Repotting and growing medium: repot in spring, if necessary, in a mixture of 70% blond peat and 30% lime-free sand.
Cultivation tip: in summer, utricularias are happy at temperatures of between 68° and 95° F (20° and 35° C). The minimum winter temperature depends on the plant's native habitat: between 41° and 59° F (5° and 15° C) for most species; 61° F (16° C) and over for tropical utricularias such as *U. calycifida*.

Utricularia sandersonii ▶

Vanda

Vanda

Decorative interest

This genus contains around thirty species of epiphyte orchids with evergreen leaves, which grow in the forests of various regions of Asia. Vandas are the source of a vast number of intergeneric hybrids involving other genera such as *Ascocentrum*, *Rhynchostylis* and *Renanthera*. They are monopodial plants without pseudo-bulbs: the leaves form at the tip of the rhizome, which goes on growing longer. The oldest leaves eventually drop, leaving the lower part of the stem bare. These plants also produce strong, aerial roots from the lower part of the stem. The flower stems appear from the leaf axils at any time of year. The large, highly decorative flowers have sepals in a variety of colors and a small labellum. Vandas are often grown in hanging containers with bare roots. They are also sold in glass containers without compost.

Ease of cultivation

These orchids are very delicate plants and difficult to cultivate.
Propagation: in good conditions, the plant puts out adventitious shoots with aerial roots that can be used for propagation.

CARING FOR YOUR PLANT

Watering and humidity: water your plant regularly and often with soft, tepid water. Spray the underside of the leaves and the aerial roots every day.
Light: very bright conditions, but protect it from the direct rays of the sun in summer.
Feeding: feed every two weeks throughout the year with a foliar feed.
Repotting and growing medium: repot every two years, when the plant puts out a new crown of roots, in a free-draining mixture of pine bark, clay balls, and polystyrene.
Cultivation tip: hybrids with blue flowers tolerate cooler conditions. Cultivation in a temperate greenhouse at 53° to 55° F (12° to 13° C) is ideal. A temperature difference of 9° to 18° F (5° to 10° C) between day and night will encourage flowering.

◀ *Vanda* x Rothschildiana

Vanda "Mikassa Pink" ▼

Vanda "Suksamran" ▼

◀ *Euanthe sanderiana*

● RELATED GENERA

The genus **Euanthe** has only one species, *Euanthe sanderiana*, which is very similar to vandas and is sometimes known as *Vanda sanderiana*. Native to the Philippines, where it grows by the sea, this orchid produces tough, strap-like, arching leaves that are 8 to 12 inches (20 to 30 cm) long with a marked central groove. The upright inflorescence is composed of eight to twelve flat flowers, 3 to 5 inches (8 to 12 cm) in diameter, with a dorsal sepal and pinkish-white petals with brown at the base, yellow lateral sepals with carmine-red veins and a small, greenish-yellow labellum with purple-red stripes. Crossing this species with *Vanda coelurea* produced the very popular hybrid, *Vanda* x *Rothschildiana*. Its flower stems bear violet-blue flowers with dark blue veins which are 1½ to 4 inches (4 to 10 cm) in diameter.

Ascocendas (*Vanda* x *Ascocentrum*) are heavily flowering, brightly colored, intergeneric hybrids, often with small flowers. They are especially valued for their elegant appearance and upright flower stems crowned with beautiful, symmetrical flowers in shades of pink, violet, red, orange, and yellow.

▲ *Ascocenda* "Su Fun Beauty"

Ascocenda "Suksamran" ▶

Vriesea

V. splendens   Vriesea

Decorative interest

This bromeliad forms a compact rosette of long, tough, strap-like, arching leaves; they are bluish-green with horizontal, dark green, purple, or brown-red bands. The flattened, lanceolate flower stem carries a spike of red bracts from which emerge short-lived, yellow, tubular flowers. Flowering can occur at any time of year and the flower spike lasts for several months. When pot-grown, vrieseas reach a maximum of 20 to 24 inches (50 to 60 cm) in height with a spread of 12 inches (30 cm). There are numerous hybrids and varieties, some with branching inflorescences, and they are always very colorful.

Associates well with... vrieseas can be grown in conjunction with other bromeliads.

Ease of cultivation

Vrieseas are easy to grow but it may take four or five years before offsets will flower. Propagation: remove the offsets that form at the foot of the plant when they have reached about a third of its height. Pot them up in a bromeliad compost and grow them under cover at 68° to 75° F (20° to 24° C).

TROUBLE SHOOTING

◆ White, cottony clusters appear under the leaves: mealy bugs can be difficult to eradicate. Remove them with a Q-tip dipped in alcohol, or treat the plant with a systemic insecticide.

CARING FOR YOUR PLANT

Watering and humidity: during the growing period, regularly fill the rosette with rainwater at room temperature and keep the growing medium slightly moist. In winter, water less often and empty the rosette of water when temperatures are cool. During periods of warm weather, spray the foliage frequently.

Light: bright conditions with a little direct sunlight, but protect from the hot rays of the midday sun.

Feeding: feed every three to four weeks in spring and summer with half strength food for foliage plants.

Repotting and growing medium: repot young plants in a bromeliad compost.

Cultivation tip: choose a bright spot for your plant and be careful not to overwater it, particularly when temperatures are cool. A normally heated room is suitable, with a minimum temperature of 61° F (16° C) in winter.

Vriesea splendens ▼

Vriesea "Christiane" ▶

Vriesea "Enjoy" ▶

▲ *Vriesea* "Charlotte"

Vriesea "Tiffany" ▼

Vriesea "Poelmanii" ▲

Vriesea "Splenriet" ▶

Vriesea "Margot" ▼

◀ *Vriesea* "Elan"

Yucca

Y. elephantipes   Yucca

Decorative interest

This plant, native to central America, is valued for its striking, structural appearance. Plants available commercially are usually sold with an upright, woody stem, crowned by one or more rosettes of bright green, sword-like leaves, 12 to 32 inches (30 to 80 cm) long, with quite sharp edges. As pot plants, yuccas can grow to between 3 and 8 feet (1 and 2.5 meters) tall.

Associates well with... as the trunks of yuccas tend to be bare toward the base, they are ideal for inclusion in various plant arrangements.

Ease of cultivation

Yuccas are easy to grow and very tolerant, but it is important to avoid overwatering and waterlogging the roots.

Propagation: you can take 4 to 8 inch (10 to 20 cm) stem cuttings and grow them on, under cover, with heat; you can also remove offsets when they are about 8 inches (20 cm) tall and insert them in a mixture of slightly moist sand and peat at 70° F (21° C).

TROUBLE SHOOTING

◆ White, cottony clusters appear on the leaves: mealy bugs can be difficult to eradicate. Remove them with a Q tip dipped in alcohol, or treat the plant with a systemic insecticide.

CARING FOR YOUR PLANT

Watering and humidity: during the growing period, water your yucca moderately, allowing the compost to dry out to the depth of an inch or so (a few centimeters) between waterings. During the winter months, water less often, depending on the temperature. Yuccas adapt well to dry indoor conditions.

Light: bright conditions with as much sunlight as possible.

Feeding: feed every two to three weeks in spring and summer with food for foliage plants.

Repotting and growing medium: repot young plants every year in spring, then every three or four years, using ordinary compost with added peat and a good layer of drainage material in the bottom of the pot.

Cultivation tip: avoid waterlogging around the roots. In winter, keep your yucca in a cool, bright room at 50° to 59° F (10° to 15° C) and water very sparingly. Your plant will also enjoy spending the summer outside in a sunny position.

Yucca elephantipes ▼

Yucca rostrata ▼

Yucca elephantipes "Puck" ▼

Zamioculcas

Z. zamiifolia   Zamioculcas

Decorative interest

This species has only been available commercially for the last few years. It owes its popularity to the unusual appearance of its leaves and to its robust nature. From the same family as the arum, it produces a short trunk from which emerge large leaves composed of tough, lanceolate, bright green leaflets on fleshy leaf stalks. It grows slowly but can reach a height and spread of over 3 feet (1 meter) in a few years.

Ease of cultivation

This is a tough plant which tolerates most things except overwatering.
Propagation: can be propagated from leaflet cuttings but this is difficult for non-professionals.

Worth remembering

The leaves and roots of this plant are fragile, so handle with care.

CARING FOR YOUR PLANT

Watering and humidity: during the growing period, water moderately, allowing the compost to dry out to a depth of an inch or so (a few centimeters) before watering again. In winter, when temperatures are cool, water very sparingly.
Light: bright conditions, but keep it out of hot sunlight.
Feeding: feed every three to four weeks in spring and summer with food for foliage plants.
Repotting and growing medium: repot in early spring if the plant has outgrown its pot, using a mixture of equal parts ordinary compost and peat, with a good layer of drainage material in the bottom of the pot.
Cultivation tip: avoid waterlogging around the roots. Clean the leaves regularly with a damp sponge.

Zamioculcas zamiifolia ▼

Zamioculcas zamiifolia ▼

Zantedeschia

Z. aethiopica   Arum lily, calla lily

Decorative interest

The arum lily is a rhizomatous perennial which grows naturally in wetland regions of South Africa. The plant produces a clump of dark green, arrow-shaped leaves, 12 to 16 inches (30 to 40 cm) in length, on long, sheathed leaf stalks. The flower stems appear at the end of winter or in early spring and are crowned by a broad, trumpet-shaped, white spath enclosing a yellow spadix. This species can be grown outdoors on the Mediterranean and Atlantic coasts. There are numerous hybrids, some of which have a more compact habit, making them particularly suitable for pot cultivation. Callas are also grown for their cut flowers. By using special growing techniques, horticulturalists are able to stagger the flowering periods of callas.

Ease of cultivation

Arum lilies have special growing requirements (temperature and watering) that are linked to their vegetative cycle. They need a period of rest after flowering if they are to flower again.

Propagation: when repotting, divide the rhizomes or remove offsets that have formed at the foot of the plant. Professionals propagate callas from seed.

● RELATED SPECIES AND VARIETIES

Some species have been used to produce the many different-colored hybrids. They include: *Z. albomaculata*, which has white flowers and leaves with white markings; *Z. elliottiana*, with yellow flowers and leaves speckled with white; and *Z. rehmanii*, with narrower, green leaves and pink flowers.

CARING FOR YOUR PLANT

Watering and humidity: after the plant's rest period, when it has started to put on growth, begin to water sparingly: moisten the compost thoroughly and allow about two-thirds of it to dry out before watering again. Then gradually increase watering. When the plant is in full leaf, water regularly to keep the compost very moist. After flowering, reduce watering until the foliage has withered. Keep the rhizome dry in its pot during the period of dormancy.

Light: bright conditions, with sunlight, particularly during the growing period.

Feeding: feed every two weeks with food for foliage plants while the leaves are developing. Then use food for flowering plants once a week to encourage flowering.

Repotting and growing medium: repot in the fall when the plant is coming back into growth, in a mixture of compost, fibrous peat, and sand.

Cultivation tip: after the period of summer dormancy, when the new shoots begin to appear, move your calla to a cool, bright room at 50° to 55° F (10° to 13° C) for three months, then gradually increase the temperature until flowering occurs; your plant will flower for longer if kept at below 68° F (20° C).

Zantedeschia aethiopica ▼

Zantedeschia albomaculata ▼

Zantedeschia "Mango" ▶

Zantedeschia "Garnet Glow" ▲

Zantedeschia "Garnet Glow" ▲

Zantedeschia assorted hybrids ▼

Zantedeschia "Treasure" ▶

➤➤ **Zebrina** see *Tradescantia*

Zygopetalum

Zygopetalum

Decorative interest

These orchids, which are native to central and South America, are mostly epiphytes, and produce ovoid pseudo-bulbs with narrow, tough leaves at their tips. The flower stems appear at the base of the new shoots at different times of year, depending on the species. The fragrant blooms have petals and sepals of the same length, usually brownish-green or green with brown speckles, and a broad, white labellum which is striped or spotted with pink or purple. Both species and hybrids are used for cultivation.

Ease of cultivation

Zygopetalums are not difficult orchids to grow, but their temperature requirements make them unsuitable for indoor cultivation.

Propagation: divide large clumps when repotting, taking care not to damage the roots.

TROUBLE SHOOTING

◆ The leaves become pale and dry: red spider mites thrive in warm, dry conditions. Increase the ambient humidity by putting the plant inside a transparent plastic bag. In cases of severe attack, treat it with an acaricide.

Zygopetalum mackayi ▶

CARING FOR YOUR PLANT

Watering and humidity: water regularly and abundantly during the period when the pseudo-bulbs are forming, using soft water. Then replace watering with a light spraying of the surface of the growing medium. Maintain a good level of ambient humidity, but avoid spraying the leaves as this will encourage the appearance of stains.

Light: bright conditions, but keep it out of direct sunlight.

Feeding: feed every two weeks during the active growing phase with orchid fertilizer.

Repotting and growing medium: repot every two years in spring, in orchid compost composed of bark, fibrous peat, and expanded clay.

Cultivation tip: zygopetalums are orchids that grow naturally in a cold to temperature environment: keep them at 64° to 82° F (18° to 28° C) during the day and 55° to 61° F (13° to 16° C) at night. They will not continue to flower without a temperature difference of 9° to 14° F (5° to 8° C). In summer, move them outside, but keep them out of direct sunlight.

◀ *Zygopetalum* ▶

INDEX

INDEX of vernacular
and scientific plant names

The figures *in italics* refer to illustrations.

INDEX by topic

PHOTOGRAPHIC CREDITS